From F-4 Phantom to A-10 Warthog

Dedication

For my wife, Elaine. For all these years she's been my lover, my best friend, my strongest supporter and my cherished wingman (despite today's obsession with political correctness, 'winglady' or 'wingperson' just doesn't cut it). Without her patience, strength, understanding and inspiration our lifelong adventure would not have happened and this book simply would not exist. Thank you for being my Elaine and for always coloring my world.

To those I've flown fighters with over the years, I thank you for your friendship and for providing the essence of a unique brotherhood that I could fashion a legend around. Your spirit, courage and dedication define a truly unique vocation. As it's reflected in the 'Tribute to the Fighter Pilot' that follows, 'Yours is a dying breed and when you are gone, the world will be a lesser place.'

From F-4 Phantom to A-10 Warthog

Memoirs of a Cold War Fighter Pilot

Colonel Steve Ladd, USAF (Retired)

AIR WORLD

First published in Great Britain in 2020 by
Air World Books
An imprint of
Pen & Sword Books Ltd
Yorkshire – Philadelphia

ISBN 978 1 52676 124 8

Typeset by Mac Style
Printed and bound in the UK by TJ International Ltd,
Padstow, Cornwall.

Pen & Sword Books Limited incorporates the imprints of Atlas,
Archaeology, Aviation, Discovery, Family History, Fiction, History,
Maritime, Military, Military Classics, Politics, Select, Transport,
True Crime, Air World, Frontline Publishing, Leo Cooper, Remember
When, Seaforth Publishing, The Praetorian Press, Wharncliffe
Local History, Wharncliffe Transport, Wharncliffe True Crime
and White Owl.

For a complete list of Pen & Sword titles please contact

PEN & SWORD BOOKS LIMITED
47 Church Street, Barnsley, South Yorkshire, S70 2AS, England
E-mail: enquiries@pen-and-sword.co.uk
Website: www.pen-and-sword.co.uk

Or

PEN AND SWORD BOOKS
1950 Lawrence Rd, Havertown, PA 19083, USA
E-mail: Uspen-and-sword@casematepublishers.com
Website: www.penandswordbooks.com

Contents

Acknowledgments

As I put the finishing touches to my manuscript, I think about the passage of time. It seems as though I've taken nearly as long to write these memoirs as it took to live them. I've had lots of help along the way.

Initial production has been down to a team of two: my wife Elaine and me. Elaine's all about precision: methodical, meticulous and patient. I'm the antithesis of these: disorderly, imprecise and hasty – a broad brush kind of guy. The blending of these approaches has, I hope, resulted in a work you will find both enlightening and enjoyable.

Throughout the project, Elaine has been my motivator, memory-jogger and, simultaneously, a tireless reviewer and my fiercest critic. Without her, everything on the pages to follow would still be firmly lodged between my ears. I could never thank her enough for all she has meant to me throughout our life together and the role she has played in committing so much of it to this narrative.

Normally, when you're looking for someone to introduce your book you focus on crusty old guys (like me) who influenced you along the way. As has occasionally been my custom, I'm flaunting this convention just a bit. Brigadier General (Retired) Pat Malackowski is a great friend and fighter pilot, years younger than I am. We served together when he was a captain at Bentwaters and I was a full colonel, but we share beliefs, philosophies and membership in a fighter pilot social fraternity that stands for nothing, except our families and a brotherhood commitment. Most importantly, Pat's a long-time Hog driver and just the kind of guy I wanted to exemplify in this book – I'm grateful for his endorsement as author of my Foreword.

Thanks to Kate Chetwynd, daughter of a very good friend, for pointing me in the right direction towards my publisher, Pen & Sword.

Thanks again to my brothers in the fellowship of the cockpit. Some of you have contributed war stories, thoughts and images to stimulate my memory and for this I am particularly grateful. It is those shared experiences that provide the foundation for the book.

Foreword

What do you do when one of your life's heroes asks you to write a foreword to a book he's written? First, let me acknowledge, writing a foreword to a book, any book … let alone "his" book, is not something I ever expected to accomplish. After I read his request, I sat alone for a few minutes and reflected on our shared experiences over the last 30 plus years. There is no doubt Steve Ladd, the author of this memoir, had a significant impact on me professionally and personally. Honored, humbled, and somewhat ill-at-ease, I said of course, and I asked if I could read the book first. We shared a laugh as we joked on how long it might take me to read it … an inside joke that undoubtedly isn't nearly as funny to you as it was to us.

I met Colonel Steve Ladd in 1988. I served for and with him until his retirement from the United States Air Force in 1994. Additionally, we share similar backgrounds. I was an American Airman from 1982 – 2016. I enthusiastically flew the A-10 Warthog for most of those years. I served in the skies over the United States, the United Kingdom, Western and Southern Europe, Saudi Arabia, Kuwait, Iraq, Qatar, the south Pacific, Thailand, Canada, South Korea, and Afghanistan. Steve and I experienced similar duties that you will learn about as you read the book: wingman, flight lead, instructor pilot, weapons school instructor, some "big-gray–desk" time, leadership, and commander. Colonel Ladd and I flew together in formations from bases and locations mentioned in this book: RAF Bentwaters, Norvenich, Sembach, and Nellis Air Force Base.

The author doesn't tell you in this reading, so I will. Steve Ladd was a superior warrior, a leader of leaders, and an extraordinary fighter pilot. His presence, skill, and exuberance were an inspiration. From the moment we met, I tried to emulate his example in the air and on the ground. In addition to being a gifted fighter pilot, Steve Ladd is a flat-out, wonderful person. Incredibly talented, but never a braggart. Courteous, gracious, and funny too. He is that "guy" at the bar you want to enjoy your nightcap with; as it turns out, Steve is a terrific writer as well.

Knowing the author personally, being in the fighter community for 30 plus years, and having shared a similar background, I was naturally excited about this memoir. Reading that his purpose would be to provide an insight into the fighter community's spirit, culture, and psyche enhanced my interest even further. What follows in this book is the terrific account of the backstory of one of my heroes, and a wonderful peek behind the scenes of his adventures in the United States Air Force fighter community. There is a straight-forward, casual style to his writing that pulls the reader into the scenario and experience. I didn't want to stop reading, put it down, or for it to end. I enjoyed this book tremendously. His humor is intricately woven throughout this work and I laughed myself to tears numerous times. Although I know it's difficult to accurately document a community's culture in one written work, Steve captures the spirit, essence, and life-experience of the USAF's fighter community spanning the last four decades as well as anything I've ever read.

In the pages that follow, Steve introduces the question: "are you lucky?" I will leave it to you to find the passages and see Steve's answer for yourself. For me, I know I am extremely lucky … even more so now having the great pleasure of reading this memoir; enjoy!

Pat Malackowski
Brigadier General (USAF Ret.)

Nickel on the Grass: A Prologue

Within the US military's fighter pilot community, the adage 'throw a nickel on the grass, save a fighter pilot's ass' embodies an expression of respect from one warrior to another. The phrase is most often invoked when a fellow fighter pilot has met his Maker, in one way or another. In an appropriate irony, it is allegedly an adaptation of an old drinking song called *Salvation Army* as in 'Salvation Army, throw a nickel on the drum, save another drunken bum'.

Tribute to the Fighter Pilot[1]

Say what you will about him: arrogant, cocky, boisterous, and a fun-loving fool to boot. He has earned his place in the sun. Across the span of 95+ years he has given his country some of its proudest moments and most cherished military traditions…but fame is short-lived and little the world remembers.

Almost forgotten are the 1,400 fighter pilots who stood alone against the might of Hitler's Germany during the dark summer of 1940 and gave England, in the words of Winston Churchill, 'its finest hour'. Gone from the hardstands at Duxford are the P51 Mustangs with their checkerboard noses that terrorized the finest fighters the Luftwaffe had.

Dimly remembered; the Fourth Fighter Group that gave Americans some of their few proud moments in the skies over Korea. How fresh in recall are the Air Commandos who valiantly struck the Vietcong with their aging A1 'Skyraiders' in the rain and blood-soaked valley called A-Shau?

And how long will be remembered the 'Phantoms' and 'Thuds' over Route Pack Six and the flak-filled skies over Hanoi, Barrel Roll, Steel Tiger, and Tally Ho.

So, here's a 'Nickel on the Grass' to you, my friend and your spirit, enthusiasm, sacrifice, and courage, but most of all, to your friendship. Yours is a dying breed and when you are gone, the world will be a lesser place!

(Often attributed to) Friar Tuck

Introduction

Now I don't know who this 'Friar Tuck' might have been, but I'd bet my last dollar he was a fighter pilot. He's captured the essence of the profession here, and used some excellent examples to illustrate the achievements of men who strap on large metal tubes with wings and take to the sky to do battle. Volumes have been written about the Richthofens, Bishops and Rickenbackers in the First World War; Erich Hartmann, Dick Bong, Johnnie Johnson and Robert Stanford-Tuck in the Second World War, Joe McConnell, James Jabara and, yes, Nikolai V. Sutyagin and Yevgeni G. Pepelyayev in the Korean conflict and Steve Ritchie, Duke Cunningham, Robin Olds and Nguyễn Văn Cốc in my own fracas, the Vietnam War. Their skill, cunning and bravery, along with thousands of others, are well and deservedly documented, but there are other dimensions of the fighter pilot that have not been given the prominence they deserve. Friar Tuck has mentioned these traits incidentally in his opening line: '…arrogant, cocky, boisterous, and a fun-loving fool to boot.' The psyche and indomitable spirit of the fighter jock are worthy of far more attention and I hope to provide you with an insight into those traits in the pages to come.

I'll start with a brief introduction – but don't expect fireworks or stirring tales of derring-do – there weren't any (well, there weren't *many*) but I couldn't call myself a fighter pilot without first having been endowed with a man-sized ego and a surplus of self-confidence. I had my moments in the air, but they aren't in the same league as those of the gentlemen mentioned previously. Rather than subjecting you to my relatively mundane aeronautical achievements I hope to introduce you to the much more fascinating world of fighter pilots and their unique outlook and culture.

I *was* fortunate enough to spend more than twenty-five years of a twenty-eight-year Air Force career strapping a fighter aircraft to my posterior on a regular basis and my 'job for life' was, in my mind, better than any other on the face of the planet. Was this because of the speed, power and versatility of the aircraft I piloted? Was it the challenge and complexity of employing such a beast (and multiples thereof) in an almost incredibly fast-paced environment, fraught with danger and requiring lightning fast reflexes and razor-sharp decisions? Or was it the unremitting thrill of competition? In the land of the fighter pilot, virtually every action, reaction, success or disappointment is scrutinized, compared and contrasted with those of your comrades and your adversaries, by them, by you and by everyone within the brotherhood.

The answer isn't simple, but I suspect it would be echoed to some extent by every REAL fighter pilot you might come across: we found our immense motivation and gratification in 'all the above' plus one very important extra. In my experience, all these intangible rewards of an exciting career were linked together by the small group of like-minded people who shared the triumphs and exertions, the good, the bad and the downright abhorrent with me daily. These were the aviators I flew with and what you're about to read is a collection of small fragments gleaned from my memories of serving with them.

The vast majority of anecdotes to follow are presented in a flexible chronological sequence; however, in some cases certain topics are more logically portrayed outside this sequence. I've taken the liberty of doing so, and I'll alert you when I wander off-piste.

Chapter One

Flight Training:
Bug Smasher to Combat-Ready

Although this dissertation focuses on fighter pilots, I cannot begin it by suggesting that I was commissioned as a second lieutenant in the USAF at the University of South Carolina and climbed immediately into an F–4 Phantom to strike fear into the hearts of Communists worldwide. The road to flying a fighter is long and demanding and although I can't hope to do it justice as part of a bigger effort, I will have a crack at the high points here.

I entered the Air Force in March 1967, as the Vietnam War was accelerating. The Air Force, having been limited to producing 1,889 pilots in 1966 saw the light bulb come on and frantically lobbied the Department of Defense for more training capacity to support the war effort. Pilot production in 1967 was accelerated to 3,500, saturating the nine Undergraduate Pilot Training (UPT) bases in Texas, Oklahoma, Arizona, Alabama and Georgia and the fodder assembly line went into high gear.[1]

My road to an F–4 cockpit began in 1966, my final year at USC where, as a student enrolled in the Air Force Reserve Officer Training Corps (AFROTC), I was subjected to the tortuous Air Force Officer Qualifying Test (AFOQT).[2] This unpleasant little detour from drinking beer and chasing sorority girls contained 526 test items divided into the following 13 subtests:

- **Quantitative Aptitude** consists of items involving general mathematics, arithmetic reasoning, and interpretation of data presented in tables and graphs
- **Verbal Aptitude** consists of items involving verbal analogies, vocabulary, reading comprehension, and understanding of the background of current events

- **Officer Biographical Inventory** consists of items pertaining to experiences, preferences, and personality characteristics related to measures of officer effectiveness
- **Scale Reading** consists of items in which readings are to be taken of various scales and gauges, many of them calling for very fine discriminations
- **Aerial Landmarks** consists of pairs of photographs showing terrain as seen from different positions of an aircraft in flight. Landmarks indicated on one photograph are to be located on the other
- **General Science** consists of items pertaining to the basic principles of the physical sciences, with emphasis on physics
- **Mechanical Information** consists of items related to understanding of mechanics and knowledge of the function or operation of mechanical devices
- **Mechanical Principles** consists of drawings of complex apparatus and requires ability to determine the effects of prescribed operations of the apparatus
- **Pilot Biographical Inventory** consists of items pertaining to background experiences and interests related to measures of success in pilot training
- **Aviation Information** consists of semi-technical items concerned with types of aircraft, components of aircraft and operation of aircraft
- **Visualization of maneuvers** consists of pictorial items calling for identification of the attitude of an aircraft in flight after executing a verbally specified maneuver
- **Instalment Comprehension** consists of items similar to Visualization of Maneuvers except that the maneuvers are specified by readings of a compass and artificial horizon
- **Stick and Rudder Orientation** consists of sets of photographs of terrain as seen from an aircraft executing a maneuver. The proper movements of the control stick and rudder bar to accomplish this maneuver are to be indicated.

Say what? Hell. I just wanted to climb into a cockpit and do my impression of John Wayne in *Flying Leathernecks*. I couldn't imagine how all this terrifying trivia could possibly contribute to that goal. Nevertheless, filled with much trepidation, I found my seat and leapt into the abyss.

After five hours of scratching my head, picking my nose and selecting multiple choice answers with my eyes closed, I walked out of the room secure in the knowledge that my future as a Whale Faeces Researcher or a Roadkill Collector was assured and reluctantly (or perhaps not) went back to the beer and the sorority girls.

Some months later, a dozen of us were assembled in our AFROTC classroom and the results read out for all to hear. The results were given in the following five specific areas:

1. Pilot
2. Navigator
3. Academic Aptitude
4. Verbal
5. Quantitative (Math)

The last three generic areas weren't particularly challenging and had to be passed in order to be commissioned; of the other two, I was only interested in one and it began with a 'P'. Much to my astonishment (and that of my instructor, judging by the expression on his face), I had somehow successfully stumbled through all five subject areas and instantly became a potential candidate for pilot training and a chance, someday, to wear the coveted silver wings.

The euphoria resulting from this unexpected achievement was short-lived when I was 'invited' to travel to nearby Shaw Air Force Base (AFB) in Sumter, South Carolina to take a preflight physical examination. During this mini–ordeal, I was poked, prodded, scrutinized from every angle and through every conceivable orifice, tested for visual acuity, color blindness and the ability to hear inaudible tones through big, clunky earphones. Blood was drawn, its pressure, viscosity and genetic make-up was analyzed and I had a nice little chat with an Air Force psychologist whose obvious intention was to catch me out in some way, judge me unfit for flight and send me back to spend my career as an administrative officer. My Dad, bless him, was an Air Force Navigator and had tipped me off to the historic show-stopping question. When it came, I was ready: 'Have you ever been unconscious?' asked the Quack. 'No, Sir!' I lied instantly (and apparently, convincingly). I must digress briefly at this point to provide a brief explanation. Losing consciousness (or even having *admitted* to losing consciousness) is an instant career killer for an Air Force aviator. I had a fraternity brother who took the same medical exam some months before mine. A football player, he had had his chimes rung more than once on the gridiron but, never having spoken to my Dad, answered honestly when asked the killer question. Although he was the healthiest of us all, his feet never touched the ground as they eliminated him from the pilot training pool and he spent a very brief Air Force career shuffling papers somewhere unpleasant. Consequently, if not surprisingly, he resigned his commission as quickly as he could and went into the exhilarating world of real estate.

Unlike some natural deterioration in vision or hearing, this prohibition of even the briefest voyage to oblivion was in force as long as you flew USAF aircraft. One more brief vignette and I'll get back on track. Some years later, a number of my colleagues and I were clinging precariously to a bar in our Officers' Club in Thailand. One of those present was our Squadron Flight Surgeon, a doctor with specialized training in aviation medicine. More importantly, he was part of our flying fraternity and flew combat missions in the rear cockpit of the F-4 to observe and experience the psychological stresses and physical demands of fighter aviation. On this occasion, we had all returned safely from combat missions over Laos in the middle of the night and, at 25 cents a shot, the drinks were flowing copiously. After a number of hours of this my few remaining brain cells decided enough was enough and I slid inelegantly off the stool, instantly, unmistakably and deeply in the Land of Nod.

The next morning, I was completely back on form after a good night's rest, and one of the guys filled me in on the previous nocturnal events. As I hurtled into self-induced nothingness, one of my cohorts, unthinking, exclaimed 'Ladd's passed out!' Our Flight Quack took one look at the comatose heap on the floor, gathered the band of drinkers around him, looked them all in the eye and said: 'No, he fell down, and don't any of you <u>ever</u> suggest anything different.' Thanks to his intervention, my lifelong history of *never* having been unconscious remained intact. The Doc and a couple of others hauled me off to my palatial windowless corrugated iron Quonset hut, threw me on the bed and *Voila!* I survived to fly and fight another day. Doc, I am forever grateful.

The First Step

Having, through monumental good fortune rather than any discernible skill or cunning, triumphed over both the AFOQT and the medical assessment/inquisition, I found myself on the way to what I secretly hoped would be a rewarding career. This would be marked by fame, some moderate measure of fortune and a vast number of red stars, each denoting a MiG kill, stenciled on the side of my airplane. Three months after university graduation (and in the midst of my prestigious, albeit temporary interim management position as a bellhop at the Happy Dolphin Inn in St Petersburg, Florida), I received orders to Moody AFB, near the bustling metropolis of Valdosta, Georgia. Not being completely *au fait* with the various pilot training bases available, I was somewhat disappointed with this location, fearing it would not be conducive to the debauchery and uninterrupted hell-raising I had programmed as a significant part of my pilot training experience. In later years, having visited other UPT installations sited in garden spots like Big Spring and Lubbock, Texas, Selma, Alabama, and Altus, Oklahoma, I realized that I'd actually been quite fortunate to end up at 'Moody Air Patch' as we had christened her. I also became conscious much quicker (within twenty-four hours or so of reporting for duty) that debauchery and uninterrupted hell-raising weren't going to be part of the UPT syllabus. Indeed, first impressions were that my new colleagues and I were in for a menu of relentless trials and tribulations if we were going to be successful in having Mom, Dad or the girlfriend pin a pair of silver wings on our swelling chests fifty-three weeks hence.

Having received my passport to eventual greatness, I rewarded myself by purchasing a shiny new British racing green Austin Healey 3000, which I could ill afford, resigned from the Happy Dolphin, and set sail for Moody Patch, where the road to aviation fame and glory started in a pleasant but uninspiring classroom. In these lackluster surroundings, about seventy-five of us were introduced to the delights of flight theory, aircraft systems (although we hadn't gone anywhere near an aircraft), basic instruments (ditto), flight planning, aviation weather, aerospace physiology and aviation medicine. Occasionally, we managed to venture outside and crane our necks to see other, more advanced students burning up the sky overhead in jet (yes, jet!) aircraft. This occasional experience set off a reaction not unlike that of Pavlov's dogs and motivated us sufficiently to plod back into class knowing that soon, we too would be providing incentive to a new class of desk-bound aspiring aviators.

Our heads filled with technical information we would quickly forget, we began our journey to the silver wings in earnest, but not in a jet, quite yet. First the Air Force had a little treat in store for us in the form of a single-engine light aircraft, the Cessna 172 (painted Air Force gray and re-designated the T-41 by the Air Force, it had no official name, but was informally referred to as the Bug Smasher). Six weeks' training in this aircraft, we were told by our instructors, would give us a foundation in flying 'the Air Force way'. This was directed primarily at those of us who had obtained private pilots' licenses prior to entering USAF flight training. It served clear notice that all the sloppy, dangerous habits and laid-back, cavalier attitudes (debauchery and uninterrupted hell-raising springs to mind) we had brought with us from whatever shoddy training establishment we had previously attended were about to be exorcised. What was omitted from the message was the fact that the T-41 provided a peerless attrition machine which would quickly and cheaply weed out those who weren't attuned to 'the Air Force way'. There were numerous reasons a student could fall afoul here. Although some of us had flown before and now had the opportunity to mend our slapdash ways, others had never taken the controls of an aircraft and there were even one or two, believe it or not, who had not so much as flown as a passenger. Add to that the unusual physiological demands of flying: there were a few students who lost their lunch on each and every sortie. Most got over it, a couple threw in the towel and one guy I remember was sick every time he flew, in three different training aircraft types for more than a year. To his great credit, he eventually slayed this personal dragon and went on to happily fly transports for many years.

Finally, 'the Air Force way' clearly wasn't to everyone's taste and we lost a number of students who simply couldn't abide the constant pressure to fly within meticulous parameters in a small single-engine aircraft or tolerate some practices that could easily be portrayed as 'Mickey Mouse'. One of my favorites was the requirement to announce calmly over the radio prior to each landing that the wheels were down. This was a mandatory call despite the fact that the T-41 wheels were welded in place and indisputably down at all times. This folly, of course, was designed to build a habit pattern that would become practical in days to come, but a couple of my colleagues became obsessed with the absurdity of it and similar follies and one of them ultimately resigned to pursue a life of accountancy, or something equally riveting.

I should spare a moment to explain a phenomenon that took place throughout my flying career: exposure to aircrew (or in this case aspiring aircrew) joining us for short stints from other lands. These folks were known as exchange pilots and during my twenty-eight-year tenure, I met a number of them. Some were truly outstanding in every way. Good pilots, enthusiastic members of the tribe; in short, the kind of guy you would enjoy going to the bar (or going to war) with. On the other hand, we were occasionally exposed to someone who never should have pitched up in the first place. At the risk of revealing my recently increasing intolerance and tendency to racially profile, most of the latter emanated from the Middle East. Some of this was blatantly political: a pair of USAF silver wings for a fourth-level Saudi prince could be parlayed into everlasting (maybe) international goodwill, but this wasn't the case for our Iranian exchange pilot, Nader Afsar. Indeed, none of us ever figured out why he was there, but he was a thoroughly pleasant individual and none of us bore him any malice. Nevertheless, it became abundantly clear within the first week or so that Afsar wasn't going to be in the running for any of the prestigious flying awards. This was driven home by a single incident in the T-41 (and reinforced many times as we proceeded through the program).

As we neared the end of our T-41 adventure, the time came for those of us who had progressed to take the Bug Smasher out on our own for an hour or so of solo flying. Afsar had somehow made the cut, so he was duly launched, alone and unafraid, to meander about our tiny training area. Under no circumstances would any of us have been expected to roam beyond 15 or 20 miles of the airport, so when Afsar failed to make an appearance back in the landing pattern within forty-five minutes alarm bells began to ring. After an hour, instructor pilots launched in an attempt to locate him and the Big Boys flying more advanced trainers – T-37s and T-38s – were alerted to look out for the wayward T-41. Radio calls were made on 'Guard', the emergency aviation frequency but, for some considerable time, these went unanswered. Urgent calculations were done on the available fuel he might have remaining and how far he might have progressed. As all was looking very bleak, a weak radio call was received: 'Sluggo Operations, it is Afsar here.' He had obviously forgotten his formal call sign, but never mind, he remembered he had a radio and was back in contact at least. The supervisor of flying, an IP with thousands of flying hours under his belt, began the process of a) locating him and b) bringing him home. A minute or so of questioning revealed (not surprisingly) that he didn't have the faintest idea where he might be, so the IP went back to basics: 'What can you see, Afsar?'

'I see big water,' came the response and the enormity of his escapade began to dawn. Some 120 miles to the east of Moody lies the only 'big water' anywhere in South Georgia. It is known to the locals as the Atlantic Ocean and is fully 90 miles beyond the limits of the designated T-41 training area surrounding the Valdosta Regional Airport. To bring a lengthy tale to an end, once located, the instructors talked Afsar down at a tiny airport near Brunswick, Georgia. After he had safely landed, they told him to shut down the engine and sit quietly in the cockpit without touching anything, awaiting the arrival of adult supervision. When two instructors turned up a couple of hours later, they found he had about twelve minutes' fuel left in the tanks and, after replenishing that crucial commodity, one of them climbed aboard and brought him home. We never determined just how he had managed to stray quite so dramatically (because he couldn't provide even a shred of useful information about his adventure). Consequently, he was watched very closely during the remainder of his training experience (washing him out was apparently not a politically correct option) and somehow, he survived to wear the silver wings. Although we were always cordial to him (and vice versa), those of us who aspired to flying fighters occasionally experienced stimulating daydreams which revolved around Afsar piloting a Russian-built MiG on the opposing side in some future aerial combat scenario and the clear-cut likelihood of chalking him up as a kill.

At the conclusion of six weeks and fourteen or so hours' flying time in the T-41 (plus a few more for our friend Afsar), our class was around 15 per cent lighter than it had been when we walked in the door and those of us who remained girded our loins for turbine-powered aviation and moved up a giant step to our first jet trainer. The aircraft, like the T-41, was built by the light aircraft manufacturer Cessna – this in itself prompted more than a few jokes – and it was officially designated the T-37. Not wishing to allow our tender young egos to grow at a disproportional rate, the Air Force shunned heroic monikers for the aircraft and we ventured forth to learn bigger and better things in a vehicle known colloquially as 'The Tweet'. The origins of this nickname could, of course, be traced to the cute, bright yellow cartoon nemesis of Sylvester the Cat. Ashamed of this in our own special way, we swiftly adopted an alternative appellation, previously bestowed by generations of student pilots and based on the aircraft's light weight and, shall we say, unique engine sound. Yes, we were about to take to the skies over southern Georgia in the 6,000 Pound Dog Whistle.

The 6,000 Pound Dog Whistle

The Dog Whistle was a jewel of a basic jet trainer: side-by-side seating, two turbine engines (but no afterburners), fully aerobatic and spinnable, it had all the right credentials to turn a newly Air Force-indoctrinated Bug Smasher pilot into a fledgling jet jockey, albeit of the lower and slower variety. At the same time we improved our social standing, we 60+ were split into equal groups, assigned to two training squadrons, the 3552nd and 3553rd, and began the indoctrination into the tribal entity that would become our culture in the future. We worked, flew and studied together, drank together, went to Valdosta State University hangouts and chased the coeds together and immediately relegated 'those guys in the 3552nd' to second-rate status. The die was cast. As new guys in the T-41, we had wandered around in nondescript flight suits with no identifying markings other than the single gold bars that most of us wore on our shoulders as second lieutenants (earning, by the way, appreciably less than I had – in tips – as a bellhop at the Happy Dolphin Inn in St Petersburg, Florida). Having now successfully conquered the T-41 and achieved subsequent allocation to the 3553rd Training Squadron, we set out to create an identity. Within weeks we had designed and acquired colorful patches that identified us as members of the class: a stylized T-38 aircraft superimposed on a gold spider's web on a black background. I have no idea what it symbolized but it sure as hell looked good, and we had nametags with squadron colors as well. After a thoroughly inauspicious start, we were now well on the road to being Some…body!

We'd worked hard to survive in the T-41 program. Now we were working harder to come to grips with jet-propelled aviation. We sat through a whole new set of academic courses on jet engine propulsion, T-37 aircraft systems and performance plus a refresher basic instrument course, which obviously we had all forgotten since there was no serious instrument flying in the T-41. We went through fundamental ejection-seat training (slammed up a 25-foot rail in a seat propelled by an explosive charge not unlike that in the aircraft) and parasailing (hauled about 500ft into the sky on a tether by a pickup truck, then cut loose to descend under an inflated parachute). Fortunately we had learned to hit the ground by performing a parachute landing fall (PLF) from a platform 6ft or so above the ground. The standard here was described by the instructor who demonstrated the PLF flawlessly as:

> 'Jumper's feet strike the ground first and, immediately, he throws himself sideways to distribute the landing shock sequentially along five points of body contact with the ground':

1. the balls of the feet
2. the side of the calf
3. the side of the thigh
4. the side of the hip, or buttocks, and….
5. the side of the back (*latissimus dorsi* muscle)

We all watched and listened intently, then lined up to conduct the parasail. I was first in the queue and my PLF was performed as follows:

1. the balls of the feet
2. the shins
3. the leading edge of the knees and thighs
4. The stomach, chest, and…
5. The chin, nose and forehead in very quick succession.

Oh, how my squadron mates laughed, but I was subsequently able to do the same (through the congealing blood on my chin, nose and forehead) as many of them followed suit in ways I could not now even begin to describe.

At about the same time, we also entered the much less painful world of the Link Trainer. In 1967, this was a state-of-the-art simulator which admittedly couldn't hold a candle to today's computer-based flight Sims. There was no visual presentation of the outside world or sexy hydraulic motion systems, just the aircraft instruments in a dark, menacing cockpit that was never going to budge, let alone break ground. Nevertheless, it was the closest we had come to the jet at this point so it was fascinating and exciting; for about an hour, at which time we realized that we were going to be unsympathetically scrutinized at every turn and critiqued unmercifully for our performance. Jet pilots have notoriously short attention spans and Mr Link's pride and joy rapidly became the bane of our existence. This utterly unreasonable attitude towards a device designed to enhance training and make me a better pilot persisted throughout my career; nevertheless, shallow and unappreciative bastard that I was, I always approached a sim mission as something slightly distasteful, an unsatisfying parody of the real thing.

Today's simulators are magical pieces of equipment, comprising graphic suites Hollywood would envy and as accurately as some very clever designers can replicate it, high speed, high 'G', 360-degree fighter performance in the form of hydraulic motion, inflating 'G'-suits, and a hundred other special experience enhancers.

Having said that, I've spoken with a number of current fighter pilots and to a man they approach a sim mission as something slightly distasteful, an unsatisfying parody of the real thing. Shallow, unappreciative bastards; some things never change.

Trudging over to the simulator building notwithstanding, these were exhilarating times for fledglings. We were about to experience the jet age first-hand and nothing was going to dampen our enthusiasm; well, almost nothing. Let's try to remember that UPT was conducted 'the Air Force way' so, far from being the congenial flying circus we'd all fantasized about, T-37 training promised to be pretty grueling. We were separated into twos and threes and assigned to a primary instructor, whose job it was to shepherd us through the program, encouraging where appropriate but more likely kicking our butts when we screwed it up. My assigned Tweet instructor was a captain named Tony Chace and he quickly became one of my all-time Air Force heroes. Unlike some of the other IPs, Tony was seriously laid-back and infinitely patient with his three rookie jet pilots. On our first meeting, around a small table which became our office, he leaned back, plopped a scruffy flying boot on an opposite chair and said with great solemnity: 'I'm very picky about boots, as you can see I take excellent care of my boots.' We three looked at each other, at first apprehensively, then bemused, because Tony's boots were a long, long way from some of the spit-shined glistening black footwear adorning some of the other more fashion-conscious IPs. He continued: 'I never let my boots go completely brown, and as long as your boots look at least as good as mine, we're going to get along just fine.' From that moment, we all <u>knew</u> we were going to get along just fine and in what promised to be a very high-pressure environment, this was of great consequence.

Despite Tony's abundant good nature, the tempo and complexity of learning everything about the Dog Whistle pushed us all to the limit. As student pilots, we were fair game for any instructor who wanted to savage us with no-notice quizzes on operating limits, maneuver parameters, immediate action (rote memory **Boldface**) Emergency Procedures or any of a thousand other Q&A topics we needed to be intimately familiar with. The morning brief at 0500 hours (that's 5.00 am for you 12-hour clock aficionados) began with a twenty-five-question quiz covering all the above and IPs would toss ad hoc questions at you all day long. This approach was exasperating but very effective. At the end of each week, the quiz results would be tallied and the student table with the lowest score overall (or the individual student making the most glaring blunder during the week) became the recipient of the Bonehead Trophy in a formal ceremony (actually a femur mounted on a wooden base, as I recall). This tribute to incompetence would sit prominently on the table and publicly highlight the occupant's shame until another table or student plumbed the depths and stole it away.

Flying the Tweet was, all at the same time, a delight and an ordeal. My class moved into the T-37 program in late May 1967. May, June, July and August in Valdosta, Georgia are characterized by high temperatures, even higher humidity and regular, violent afternoon thunderstorms. To best exploit these weather phenomena for training purposes, our Tweets were equipped with feeble, ineffective air conditioning systems. Consequently, for most of the day, we resembled a small colony of drowning rats, with green flight suits soaked through and through with sweat providing a dazzling array of salt stains when they dried out. Our combined aroma would have felled an ox. Nevertheless, the sheer jubilation of controlling a jet aircraft won out over this discomfort on every level.

Strapping into a jet for an inexperienced student is a fairly complex undertaking: connecting inertial reel parachute shoulder harness, an automatic opening lap belt, and a seat separator (butt snapper), oxygen and communications leads, all in a specific sequence using a thick yellow checklist. As a rule of thumb, the more sophisticated the jet, the more intricate the strap-in process, so the Tweet was comparatively simple. Nevertheless, it took a rookie methodically using a checklist considerable time to complete. Our first flights were always with IPs and the syllabus was thoughtfully designed to maximize our manpower. While student 'A' fumbled through the strap-in sequence, his table mate Student 'B' would run through the external aircraft pre-flight sequence, also using the thick yellow checklist. The instructor divided his time between ensuring Student 'A' wouldn't be emasculated by a poorly situated parachute harness strap if he had to eject and guaranteeing he wouldn't have to eject in the first place because Student 'B' failed to notice a hydraulic leak or a control lock that hadn't been removed. At the end of this well-choreographed division of labor, the instructor would saunter around to the right side of the aircraft, vault lightly into the right seat and conduct the same strap-in sequence Student 'A' had just struggled through, but in fifteen seconds flat. We students would look on in undisguised awe. Student 'B' would then trudge back to the Squadron Ops building, soaked in salty Georgia sunshine and smelling for all the world like O'Leary's goat while his buddy and the IP cranked up the Dog Whistle and went out to do loops and barrel rolls for the Air Force. Life's not fair, but there was no ill will as he knew later that day or, at worst tomorrow, the roles would be reversed.

Transitioning from the T-41 to the Tweet was akin to locking up your bicycle and climbing into a Porsche. While still a long way from the performance of a Phantom or an F–105 'Thud', it was a quantum leap for us. A squat little airframe, it was capable of 380 knots and could withstand a 'G' loading of 6.6, all of which attributes enabled it to roll, loop, spin and *feel* like a jet. We reveled in the upgrade, learning to fly tight racetrack 360-degree fighter-style overhead landing patterns, perform aerobatics and enjoy a forward view not obstructed by a spinning propeller. Regrettably the aircraft configuration lent itself to some slightly traumatic situations. I didn't always get to fly with the imperturbable Tony Chace, and unfortunately there were a couple of aerospace sadists in the instructor corps. Since seating in the aircraft was side-by-side, we, the students, were within easy range. From time to time we had the opportunity to survive with the IP whose unique approach to motivation was crimping your oxygen hose so breathing was not an option and delivering corrective commentary at a decibel level that rivaled the Dog Whistle's. Not surprisingly, most of us didn't respond well to this kind of instruction, and luckily it was the exception, not the rule.

Most students soloed after about fifteen hours of flying with an IP and at that point, an even greater euphoria ensued: swaggering out to the flight line to take to the skies in your own personal jet! Not only did we have an opportunity to exist for very short periods upside-down and view the earth 2 plus miles below at over 300 miles per hour, but we also started to learn the rudiments of navigation and some (very) basic instrument flying techniques. If that wasn't enough, we actually flew some formation with other aircraft (or to be more accurate we *rode* in formation). As I recall, in the Tweet, formation was primarily flown by our instructors while we sat patiently and watched it happen, anticipating our own chance to shine in the near future. Finally, in recognition of our growing hankering for fame and recognition, we were allowed to take our Tweets (two at a time, with instructors) cross-country. This meant we could spend the weekend at a location of our choice (within reason), landing at an unfamiliar airfield. Since many of us opted to return to our roots, we headed for familiar pastures and spent the weekend strutting around home towns, our old university campuses and local bars, trying desperately to convince adoring family and envious friends that we were pilots and really knew what we were doing.

We spent about four months driving the Tweet (and polishing our egos). As we became more comfortable in the bird, we began stealing occasional furtive glances at the adjacent parallel runway where the next object of our envy operated. Whereas the Whistle was low–slung, stubby and only just aerodynamic in appearance, the next step up the aviation ladder for us was pure white, sleek beyond belief and closely resembled an arrow in flight, even when it was standing still. It was built by Northrop, bore the Air Force designation T-38 and was officially named the Talon, but generations of students referred to it most reverently as the White Rocket.

The White Rocket

This most elegant bird first came off the assembly line in 1961 and marked its golden anniversary as the world's first supersonic trainer in 2012. As I write this, it's still serving as the USAF's advanced pilot trainer and well over 72,000 student pilots have delighted in its agility, power, speed and undeniable sex appeal. I could write a book about this beauty, but because my focal point is fighter pilots, I won't. What I will do is try to briefly convey how perfect the airplane is for making that transition into the world of the front-line fighter. The Rocket was conceived by a combined team of civilian engineers and selected Air Force officers, most of whom were pilots. Now you would be correct in thinking that combination of skills would be perfect for the task, but you would probably be amazed to learn that it was a unique concept. All too often, aircraft have been designed with little or no input from those who might fly them. Many pilots are convinced that, as in the legend of all the great books, most aircraft cockpits are designed by an infinite number of monkeys. This is because, more often than should be the case, instruments, controls and other elements of 'human engineering' are situated illogically in the cockpit by otherwise brilliant engineers who will never wrap their fingers around a stick or throttle in anger. The objective of the collaborative approach to designing the T-38 was to produce an aircraft that closely replicated the performance of a supersonic fighter, but without the sometimes insidious idiosyncrasies that make such aircraft difficult to fly. The result was better than anyone had dared to hope: an aerodynamic dream propelled by two afterburning engines capable of sliding effortlessly through the speed of sound. Its performance was destined to be impressive as it was developed originally as the F-5 Freedom Fighter, a lightweight, low-cost tactical interceptor.

In addition to its success as an advanced trainer, the Rocket established additional street cred by being the taxi of choice for NASA's astronaut corps, who paraded all over the country in these sleek white aerospace sports cars. The aircraft even made an appearance with the USAF Demonstration Team, the Thunderbirds, as a cost-saving measure due to the global fuel crisis in the mid-70s. While the Rocket was a terrific performer, it lacked the intimidating size, presence and **NOISE** that made for a great formation demonstration. Although the Thunderbirds would never say so publicly, they were all a bit miffed at not performing in a front-line fighter. Those of us flying F-4s at their home base, Nellis AFB, Nevada, were always more than happy to sidle up to one of them in the bar and remind him that he and the rest of the Air Force's poster boys were prancing around the skies not in combat jets (like us), but in trainers.

I digress, again. The transition from Dog Whistle to White Rocket was challenging, but more than that, it was exhilarating. Arrogant 'almost-pilots' that we were, we began to look back at the T-37 days as being a little bit like masturbation: it was fun while you were doing it, but just a little bit embarrassing afterward. This is certainly not casting aspersion towards the venerable Dog Whistle: it was perfect for its task, but human nature being what it is, we were ready to trade the relatively tedious T-37 take-off roll for the smooth and glorious kick in the butt and breathtaking acceleration provided by the Rocket's two General Electric J85-5A afterburning turbojets. The Porsche had morphed backwards into the bicycle and we were now firmly in Maserati mode. We were now halfway through the year-long program and had six months of what the Air Force referred to as Advanced Jet Training ahead of us. We thought of it as an introduction to the most fun we could have with our clothes on by far (albeit involving far more hard work than we'd ever experienced in that alternative scenario).

The first flight in the White Rocket is an orientation ride; we called it our 'Dollar ride' as the tradition is to hand your IP a buck after he's impressed you for sixty minutes. The student is relegated to the back seat on this trip (T-38 seating is tandem; no more oxygen hose strangulation) while the IP does most of the flying, demonstrating to a thoroughly awestruck apprentice just what this beast is capable of. It begins with that kick in the butt I mentioned earlier: 5,800 pounds of thrust boosting a very swift transition from world's fastest tricycle to airborne at 160 knots. Gear and flaps are raised (quickly as there's a very real danger of exceeding the aerodynamic limiting speeds for both) and at the end of the runway (and .9 Mach, very nearly the speed of sound) the IP rotates the airplane to a 45-degree climb and casually 'suggests' you check the twin rear-view mirrors. This glance provides a surreal presentation of the airfield below falling away at a breathtaking rate. The T-38 once held the world time to climb record for a few heady months in 1962 until the F-4 reclaimed it for fighter aviation. This sensation is truly overwhelming. Passing through 20,000ft, he rolls the airplane inverted, brings the nose down to the horizon and rolls upright. 'Check your clock,' he says and I peek at the dash-mounted clock that I 'hacked' or started as the take-off roll began. This entire mind-boggling dash for altitude has taken less than a minute and I am about as impressed as a man can be.

The rest of the 'Dollar ride' can't compete with this curtain-raising event; nevertheless, I remain amazed throughout, anticipating the sheer indulgence of mastering such a machine. A tour of the training area is followed by a demonstration of the Rocket's 720-degree-per-second roll rate. This is suitably memorable as my IP, no doubt in time-honored tradition, slaps the stick full right without warning, banging my helmet against the left side of the canopy as the airplane snaps to the right and laughs at my anticipated involuntary vocal reflex: 'Shit!' He follows this nifty little surprise with some stall demos and aerobatics and then he says (queue the drum roll): 'Let's go supersonic!'

If the T-38 take-off roll was historic, going supersonic for the first time can only be described as underwhelming. I suppose I was expecting bells, whistles and some kind of dazzling physical sensation, but when my IP pushed the throttles forward and advised me to look at the Mach meter, the only indication was a fleeting wobble of the needle as it went through Mach 1.0. Trying not to sound too much like Peggy Lee, I said 'Is that all there is?' and he laughed again. Nevertheless, I'm only slightly ashamed to admit that I called home that night to gloat to Dad and Mom, 'I went supersonic today.'

Having whetted our appetite for the speed, power and maneuverability of the White Rocket, the Air Force deftly sucked the wind out of our burgeoning sails by moving us into the phase of training known as Instruments. Instrument flying is undeniably one of the most challenging and essential aspects of modern aviation but it's not, by any stretch of the imagination, exhilarating. It consists of flying and navigating exclusively through use of the many gauges and electrical systems in the aircraft without reference to the world outside. This enables safe flight in clouds and at night and relies on a number of admittedly sophisticated devices: attitude indicator(s), Horizontal Situation Indicator (a rotating compass with many magical electronic navigational features), turn and bank and vertical velocity indicators, to name just a few. These operated both on internal systems – gyroscopes, for example – and external navigational aids such as radio beacons and had but one purpose: to take you safely where you want to go without being able to see ground, horizon, or stars and planets. Using them successfully relied on developing an efficient crosscheck of the many instruments on the panel, so the pilot was constantly aware of speed, altitude and relative position as well as aircraft engine and system performance.

To this end, the T-38 was fitted with what could only be described as a trainee's torture chamber: a back seat canopy hood which, pulled forward and fastened, completely obscured any vision outside the aircraft. In essence, they temporarily converted this gleaming, responsive speed and power machine into a glorified simulator, and you know what I think of *them*.

I should interject that there was a similar initiative in the T-37 for the much shorter and less demanding Instrument phase, but like the aircraft itself, it was much less sophisticated. This consisted of a large reinforced fabric visor that was mounted on the helmet and jutted out from the forehead (think oversized baseball cap bill) to restrict vision outside the aircraft. As student and instructor sat side-by-side in the Tweet in theory the IP, in the right seat, could ensure the student wasn't stealing a glance at the horizon by lifting his head. In fact, this was one of few occasions when we were able to circumvent the system. Careful ironing of the thick cloth visor resulted in the right-hand edge drooping towards the IP while the left and center remained elevated just enough for the furtive glance outside and reassurance that we were, after all, not inverted. This practice gave rise to two principles which have served generations of pilots very well indeed:

1. One peek's worth a thousand crosschecks…and…
2. If you ain't cheatin' you ain't tryin' hard enough.

Despite the spirit-dampening effect the T-38 instrument phase had on most of us, we managed to struggle through it and became if not accomplished, at least competent basic instrument pilots, ready to move on to contact (or visual) flying. This was far cooler than driving around in the back seat under a hood and, along with proficiency, we began to rebuild our slightly dented self-esteem. Contact flying involved aerobatics, low-level navigation, formation and combinations of these. We also had occasional opportunities to go cross-country, mainly to other pilot training bases, and some of these were strategically situated just across the frontier from Mexican border towns: Nuevo Laredo, Ciudad Acuña and Ciudad Juarez. In those pre-drug cartel days, Mexican border festivities consisted of energetic visits to 'Boys' Towns', centers of flourishing bars and dance halls and boasting a plethora of nubile Mexican maidens (well, 'maidens' may not be technically accurate, but you'll be getting my drift). These were a real treat for the growing boys that we were and we took full advantage of the opportunity to investigate this fascinating culture. Thanks to the White Rocket and all that she gave us, we began to feel more like pilots and whenever we had the chance, to act like we thought pilots should.

As we became more comfortable in our environment, we began to seek other social distractions to afford some respite from the long hours and hard work involved in learning to pilot Uncle Sam's jets. The most memorable of these events was provided compliments of the United States Navy and took place just 146 miles south-east of Moody at the Jacksonville Naval Air Station.

A word about the Navy: those of you who've seen *Top Gun* will already have formed an image of naval aviators, and the image they would like to portray is embodied in Maverick. Both the nickname and the Tom Cruise character depict the poised, devil-may-care fighter pilot every self-respecting naval or Marine aviator would like to be. I won't rain on their parade – I've met some outstanding Navy and Marine pilots – but they're no more special or talented than the Air Force variety, just a little different. To be honest, I thought Val Kilmer played the more believable fighter pilot in *Top Gun* (and he had a far better call sign, 'Iceman').

The Stars and Bars (named for the familiar Confederate flag configuration; this would no doubt be banned today) at the Navy Jax Officers' Club drew Navy and Air Force aircrew by the dozen. This was true despite the fact that these festivities took place on Sunday afternoons, traditionally the day you recovered from Saturday night and got psyched up for Monday's flying schedule. The Stars and Bars' popularity resulted from an ingenious format which, in today's wonderful world of political correctness would not make it past the Entertainment Committee's weekly meeting. Stars and Bars was predicated on one simple concept: that of successful social interaction or sudden and humiliating banishment. It revolved around the arrival, at around 2.00 pm, of large numbers of local girls looking for a good time. They were welcomed by the club, provided with cut-price drinks and good quality entertainment. There was only one catch: unless these southern belles were able to round up an escort of their very own by 6.00 pm, they were unceremoniously asked to leave. This scenario turned the traditional hunter into the hunted and fending off the advances of girls on the prowl became an unaccustomed (but far from unpleasant) chore as traditional roles were, at least for the afternoon, reversed. The successful ladies were assured of a pleasant evening with a dashing man in (or possibly out of) uniform, a good meal, fine wine and perhaps even more, while those less fortunate had to find other entertainment elsewhere. Our only dilemma, should some fetching young thing sweep us off our feet at Stars and Bars, was getting back to our place of work to serve our country on Monday morning. More than once, the Austin Healey tore up the I-75 towards Moody Patch at 0500, but I was very young then and could comfortably hack the tempo.

The occasional opportunity for enjoyment was heavily overshadowed by the workload. Flying the Rocket was serious business, and a harbinger of things to come. Events happened far quicker in the fast lane than I had ever experienced before and I'm not ashamed to say that on many, many occasions I found myself thinking 'How am I ever going to learn this or keep up with that?' Learn and keep up I did, and after nearly six months of breakneck pacing in both academics and flying, there was a faint light at the end of the tunnel. This light dawned as we were turned loose (sometimes solo) in the formation phase, flying a scant few feet away from another aircraft (or in some cases, *three* other aircraft) at 450 knots or so. It was at this time, six weeks or so before scheduled graduation that we realized, barring genuine disaster, we had hacked the program and we were – really – going to wear those silver wings.

Reaping What We'd Sown

This was also time to start appreciating the culture of competition we were going to participate in from this moment on. Indeed, the competition had commenced the minute we walked through the gate at Moody Patch, but we had all simply been too busy surviving the syllabus to become openly embroiled in the politics of rivalry. Now, as graduation grew near we realized that, although it was far too late to further influence the outcome, our destiny would be governed by our performance.

The pilot graduate assignment process in the '60s was a relatively uncomplicated affair. We had, of course, been graded on every single deed we had done throughout the fifty-three-week program. Every test, flight, oral quiz and extra-curricular activity we participated in (except the likes of Stars and Bars) had a grade attached to it. Although flying had the priority weighting, these factors were all combined to arrive at a class standing. More than seventy of us had pitched up on Day One and there were fifty-four left when it came time to parcel out the goodies.

The aircraft assignments came down from the Military Personnel Center as a 'block' of aircraft-one flying machine for each graduating pilot, and each pilot training base had a unique, if very similar block to the others. I honestly don't remember the total make-up of Class 68-F at Moody AFB, but I do recall a couple of examples that were, to me, of paramount importance. Our block of fifty-four aircraft included a grand total of fifteen fighters. There was one F-105 Thunderchief (or 'Thud' or 'Lead Sled' should you wish to use more ubiquitous nicknames) and fourteen F-4 Phantoms. The other thirty-nine aircraft assignments were in trainers (remaining in the T-38 or returning to the Tweet as 'First Assignment Instructor Pilots (FAIPs)') or the 'Many Motor' category, multi-engine aircraft that fulfilled a number of roles. There were ten or so each of C-141, C-130, C-123 and C-7 cargo aircraft, commonly referred to as 'trash haulers', a few KC-135 tankers, 'gas passers', and a similar number of the great behemoths known as the B-52, known universally to aviators as the BUF (Big Ugly Fucker) until the budding Politically Correct Enforcement Corps got wind of it and decreed the nickname was no longer tolerated. Naturally, we continued to call it a BUF, but started to pay more attention to who was in the vicinity whenever we used the term.

The selection process was reasonably straightforward. Nearing graduation, we were all asked to fill out a 'Dream Sheet'. Each type of aircraft that was potentially on the auction block was placed in our own order of preference and we all held our breaths for a couple of weeks waiting for the actual block of aircraft to appear.

When it did, the culmination of a long, long year was swift and unambiguous. That class standing I mentioned before was the final arbitrator. Sid Wise, the guy who finished *numero uno*, was summoned into the commander's office where he was introduced to a wall-sized blackboard containing each and every aircraft allocated to Moody Class 68-F and invited to take his pick. He chose the only single-seat fighter, the F-105, and it was removed from the availability list. So it went, for most of the day. There were a couple curves thrown into the mix. For example, instructors were polled throughout the course and there were a few graduates-to-be that would not be considered for fighter slots because these aircraft required reflexes and decision-making skills that weren't necessarily universal. Unless you were among this group you never knew who or how many were in the non-fighter category, because there was no intent to attach a stigma to these guys. They would undoubtedly succeed as pilots; just not as fighter pilots.

I was tapped as number 5 in the roll-call and was absolutely delighted to see a few F-4 Phantoms remaining. I grabbed one and the next twelve years or so of my life was from that moment ordained. The parade of hopefuls continued, each man in order of descending merit having less choice than those who had preceded him. As a general rule of thumb, the fighters went first, followed by the jet trainers and 'trash haulers' C-141s, gateway to an airline job, C-130s – a versatile bird with many roles – cargo, intelligence-gathering, and the awesome firepower of the AC-130 Spectre Gunship. Then came the tankers and finally (I suspect this repeated itself at most of the pilot training bases on selection day) our tail-end Charlie walked away with the only remaining choice on the board, not surprisingly a BUF.

I was elated; I had my fighter and I would soon be going to war in her. There was only one downside: the Air Force Personnel gurus, in their infinite wisdom, had determined that there was a danger of running out of pilots and this risk could best be mitigated by ensuring pilots were produced in large numbers, but where can we put them all while we're waiting for this attrition to occur? I know; we can put all the new fighter pilots in the back seat of the F-4 to 'learn the trade' and, over time, they will gravitate 6ft forward to the front seat and become aircraft commanders. The co-pilot concept works fine for the airlines and many-motors in the military, but it never took the rapidly-inflating ego of the brand-new fighter pilot into account. After all, we had just taken on the toughest flying training course in the world and emerged victorious (and pretty high in the class standing to boot), so why shouldn't we climb into the pointy end, fire up the bird and go kill Commies for Uncle Sam with, perhaps, a bit of help from a compliant navigator established 6ft in trail? Indeed, the F-4 was the only front-line fighter with two seats (please don't send irate messages reminding me of the F-111; not a fighter, never a fighter) and we saw no reason why we should not climb into the one up front.

As in so many cases, what we thought was of no consequence at all, but within eighteen months of my class graduation, the AF came to its senses and started moving new pilots into the aircraft commander role. Nevertheless, it was too late for me and an awful lot of other guys, so I began my fighter career as a lowly, much-maligned GIB (Guy in the Back), enduring taunts and catcalls such as 'Once a GIB, always a GIB' and being able to fire back only feeble retorts like 'GIBs is people, too.'

Replacement Training Unit (RTU)

Having successfully negotiated the rigors of undergraduate pilot training, the next step on the way to armed combat was the RTU, or upgrading to your battle steed. If the year-long journey at UPT could be categorized as earning a 'degree' in aviation, the RTU equated to an airborne Master's course. My first up-close-and-personal viewing of the 'Phabulous Phantom' was on the ramp at MacDill AFB in Tampa, Florida (not a million miles away from the Happy Dolphin Inn in St Petersburg). MacDill had long been in the F-4 training business and had once been known for generating 'One a Day in Tampa Bay', a reference to the less than stellar safety performance of the unit in the early days. These teething problems had been overcome and the three participating squadrons were safe, efficient and competent to churn out fighter crews at an adequate rate to do battle with the Asian hordes across the Pacific.

RTU took us from the realm of basic flying trainee and introduced us to the art of war, fighter aircraft style. We began to employ the basics of contact flying to position a 20-ton behemoth in order to accurately deliver weapons of many different types or outmaneuver an airborne adversary who wants to stencil an icon of *you* on the side of his aircraft. Our instructors at MacDill had virtually all been there, done that during the first few years of the South-East Asia war and we hung onto their every word. We realized that their experience could make the difference between coming home after 100 missions with a colorful warrior's patch on our sleeve or slowly descending into a North Vietnamese or Laotian rice paddy underneath a parachute to face terrifying consequences.

In the relatively benign environment of Central Florida, we saddled up daily to lay waste to constructed targets at the Avon Park Gunnery Range near scenic Lake Kissimmee. (Not so) heavily laden with 25lb practice bombs fitted with smoke charges so our bombing accuracy could be plotted, we learned how to meet the demanding airspeed, altitude, 'G' and dive angle parameters that in the days before smart bombs and computerized deliveries would result in accuracy we would not be too ashamed of. We explored the realm of level and low-angle releases, replicating delivery of that most spectacular and effective of munitions, napalm. Then we climbed to medium altitude to hurl our bodies at the ground in 30-, 45- or even 60-degree dive angles, replicating dive-bombing with general-purpose weapons against harder targets or those that were heavily defended. As we progressed, we graduated from box circuits, concentrating on accuracy alone, to multi-ship tactical approaches and roll-ins which optimized our electronic countermeasures against simulated surface-to-air missile threats.

When we weren't learning the gentle art of 'mud moving', the techniques of air-to-ground conventional and nuclear weapons employment, we headed out over the Gulf of Mexico, dipping our wings into the fabled Bermuda Triangle to do mock battle with our colleagues in an air-to-air environment. Many of the basic maneuvers governing air combat have not changed substantially since the Red Baron and Billy Bishop were going at it. Given the size and performance of modern aircraft, the geometry of these maneuvers takes up far more airspace to achieve. Suffice to say a couple of 20-ton+ Phantoms pushing the speed of sound will dominate an enormous chunk of sky and the variety of weapons available results in an hour's worth of aviating that taxes the participants in a thousand different ways. Tactical flying is, to a far greater degree than basic aviation training, demanding, exhausting, sometimes frightening, but virtually always exhilarating.

After a hard day's aviating in the subtropical Florida sunshine, we retreated to the cool calm of the MacDill Officers' Club. Here drinks were comparatively cheap and the company consisted of like-minded colleagues replicating aircraft flight paths with their outstretched hands and initiating tales of derring-do with variations on a theme: 'There I was at 20,000 feet...'

When you got tired of hangar flying, it rapidly dawned on us that the club was a magnet for comely young ladies in search of bold young flyers; some things never change. 'Flower children' were everywhere in the '60s. I recall one particularly poignant encounter with a fetching young lady in the Officers' Club at Happy Hour on a Friday evening. How (or why) she ended up in a fighter base bar is beyond me (the daughter of a senior officer, perhaps?), but I suspect it was her way of taking us all to task for our outrageous activities in South-East Asia. She was 100 per cent hippy: blonde, tie-dyed little dress and clunky boots, and she homed in on me, my beer and my flight suit, ready to take a scalp. She motored up in front of me, pulled herself up to her full 5ft 3in or so, looked me coldly in the eye and said: 'How can you strafe innocent women and children?' I'd had a few and decided the best response would be honesty and sensitivity. I fixed her with my most earnest gaze, and with a voice absolutely brimming with sincerity, replied: 'Well, in general they don't run as fast as the guys, so you have to learn to lead them a little less.' The blood drained from her face, her mouth repeatedly pouted like a recently hooked fish and she tried (but failed) to frame a blistering retort. Speechless (for the moment), she wheeled and flounced off to try it on with someone else. I swear if she'd been the proud owner of an M61 Vulcan Gatling gun (as was hung on the Phantom in those days), she'd have strafed me.

Chapter Two

Getting There Was Half the Fun

A s a fresh-faced lieutenant and proud recent graduate of both Undergraduate Pilot Training (UPT) and the F-4 Replacement Training Unit (RTU), I was savoring the delights of bachelorhood and anticipating the challenges of taking my Phantom to war. Between me and glory, however, were a couple of less satisfying events in the form of Air Force Survival training courses.

Practice Captivity

The first of these was the USAF Survival, Evasion, Resistance and Escape (SERE) Course at Fairchild AFB in Washington State and was designed to equip the combat aircrew to cope with the most fearsome scenario of all: being shot down over enemy territory and scooped up by angry little people who weren't at all delighted to host someone who had recently been dropping bombs on them. Fate would have it that my completion of F-4 Fighter training in Florida and subsequent reporting date in South Vietnam (more about that later) resulted in a Survival Training date of November 1968. This was poor planning on my part, as winter temperatures in the North-Western US would test the most robust of arctic explorers. I was a mere apprentice fighter pilot, adept at lounging in front of the television set at USC's Phi Kappa Sigma Fraternity House with a cold beer and more recently basking in the balmy breezes of South Florida while learning to fly the 'Phabulous Phantom'.

Nevertheless, I pitched up at Fairchild as directed and joined a class as diverse as the military itself: there were lots of lieutenants like myself and mid-level officers, captains and majors. Since no one was exempt from entering the fray there were a few senior officers, full colonels, on their way to command combat aircraft wings and the like. Finally, there was a handful of civilians, whose role in the conflict was never,

ever discussed, and who very much kept to themselves throughout the delightful experience that was about to follow.

That event kicked off with a couple days of academics designed to put us in the proper mindset for learning how to survive as a prisoner of war. Unfortunately, our knowledge base for this in the context of South-East Asia was severely limited. Although there had been a number of aircrew captured and imprisoned, virtually none had escaped to tell the tale; a tall (or stocky) white (or black) American had precious little chance of blending in with the population and evading capture in South-East Asia for any significant time. Consequently, the Air Force was attempting to give us the best information available, but it was based on a Korean War model which we discovered years later bore little resemblance to the barbaric treatment suffered by those unfortunate enough to fall into enemy hands in Vietnam, Laos or Cambodia.

The academic program was designed to familiarize us with the basic tenets of behavior expected if we should be captured. These principles were enshrined in the Code of the United States Fighting Force:

I am an American fighting in the forces which guard my country and our way of life. I am prepared to give my life in their defense.

I will never surrender of my own free will. If in command, I will never surrender the members of my command while they still have the means to resist.

If I am captured I will continue to resist by all means available. I will make every effort to escape and aid others to escape. I will accept neither parole nor special favors from the enemy.

If I become a prisoner of war, I will keep faith with my fellow prisoners. I will give no information nor take part in any action which might be harmful to my comrades. If I am senior, I will take command. If not I will obey the lawful orders of those appointed over me and will back them up in every way.

When questioned, should I become a prisoner of war, I am required to give name, rank, service number, and date of birth. I will evade answering further questions to the utmost of my ability. I will make no oral or written statements disloyal to my country and its allies or harmful to their cause.

I will never forget that I am an American, fighting for freedom, responsible for my actions, and dedicated to the principles which made my country free. I will trust in my God and in the United States of America.

I can state with confidence that, to a man, we believed in the code and, with that self-assurance that comes from not having all the information, we were convinced we would uphold its doctrine to the letter.

The learning exercise began at dusk, in a driving snow, when we were broken up into teams of three or four, given maps and compasses and told to evade to a geographic point (known to us as the 'safe zone'). Naivety reigned and many of us actually believed if we could avoid capture we'd be back in the Officers' Club bar for a late-night beer within a few hours and would all get gold stars on our records. My little team, led by a major, did a marvelous job of circumventing the bad guys we knew were hunting us down. Within two hours, we were at the appointed 'safe zone' where, in the midst of our brief victory celebration, we were set upon, thrown to the ground and had our hands bound behind us and bags unceremoniously draped over our heads. For us the war was over, we were told and we had become prisoners of the People's Republic of Washington. Indeed, as it transpired, no one was captured during the 'evasion' phase, as the bad guys (or survival school directing staff, DISTAFF) had simply been chatting among themselves, drinking coffee and waiting for us to turn up at the 'safe zone', where the entire class, in threes and fours, was 'captured' and spirited off to places unknown.

My unseen escort from the ludicrously-named 'safe zone' was not a gentleman. He butted, pulled and otherwise manhandled me, while bringing the legitimacy of my parentage into question and producing an amazing lexicon of Anglo Saxonisms in what I believe was intended to be a Russian accent. As my vision was obscured by burlap at the time, I had no idea what he might look like, but I could tell from the relative bearing of the tirade's source that he was considerably shorter than I.

We stumbled along together for some substantial distance, after which I heard the sound of a large metal door being unlocked and opened and I was unceremoniously dumped onto a cold concrete floor. Except for the sounds of other unfortunates being tossed into cells, there was no noise and, of course, inside my burlap bag, total darkness. Lesson one: sense deprivation makes one feel very, very vulnerable. After the first half hour or so, the concept of time became extremely vague and I began to twitch slightly about my situation. I decided, as I had learned in class, to have a shot at contacting my fellow captives: 'Steve Ladd, Lieutenant USAF, here; who's with me?' I shouted courageously (but very unwisely).

No sooner had the words left my mouth than the metal door was thrown open and someone wrestled me to the floor. This was accompanied by sounds of a terrible beating and blood-curdling screams of pain (as I was to learn later, a very vivid taped recording for the benefit of my buddies in cells up and down the corridor). We all knew they weren't supposed to be kicking our butts for real, but when you're in a cold, dark place with a bag over your head, your mind plays tricks on you.

The Rules of Engagement (ROE) were briefed during the academic session: there was to be no actual brutality administered, but a reasonable level of physical contact was fair game. Oh, where were today's flaming liberals eager to fight our corner and demand our civil rights be honored? We could feign serious injury, weep, wail and ask for medical attention to our hearts' delight and that was considered a part of the game. Having been trained at great expense by the American taxpayer, we were clearly briefed that if we specifically asked to see 'The Doctor', the fun and games would cease. Medical attention would immediately be provided, bringing with it a very real risk that the complainant would not be finishing the course and would have an opportunity to start all over again. There were one or two of these requests generated by stress during our few days in captivity and the individuals involved were treated to what, in today's parlance, amounted to counseling, removed from the program and rescheduled for the next class, much to their annoyance.

After an indeterminate period of time in solitary, we were debagged but left in the cell with only our thoughts. We were then treated to a constant cacophony of oriental music (catchy little combinations of a Tiny Tim concert and the strangling cat aria of a connecting dial-up modem). There was also anti-American propaganda, supplemented with alternating blinding floodlighting and flashing strobes. These were all designed to fray the nerves (and were reasonably successful in doing so). Surreptitious communication had begun between us, cloaked with coughs, belches and anything else that might provide a cover and this raised the spirits to some extent, but our tormentors weren't stupid and we were often apprehended in mid-belch. This was punishable under the ROE by being subjected to 'stress positions' which weren't immediately painful or likely to cause lasting injury, but after a period of time became difficult to bear. Although I hesitate to elaborate in a book my wife is likely to read, here are a couple that I found particularly entertaining:

1. Forced to stand with feet something like 18 inches apart and 3 feet away from a wall, leaning in with hands pressed against the wall high above head height. This may sound like a piece of cake to you, but give it a try for an hour or two in the comfort of your own home; you might be surprised.
2. Kneeling upright (not resting my butt on my heels) with hands clasped on the head, and forced to look down, with my chin on my chest, restricts breathing somewhat, and will eventually become quite painful. A couple of the more fun-loving guards reintroduced the hood to this position, which increases the restriction on your airflow.

The stress position was also an integral part of what was to follow. For no apparent reason, we were herded out of the cell block into a compound fenced with barbed wire and ringed with manned guard towers. It reminded me of the great William Holden PoW film *Stalag 17*. Indeed, as mentioned earlier, the camp set-up was probably based on the best information available from the Second World War and/or Korea, which didn't turn out to be particularly accurate for the North Vietnamese environment. The dramatic importance of the change of venue was the fact that we were now together and could coexist, communicate and commiserate with others in the same boat, so to speak. This placed us firmly in the realm of articles 3 and 4 of the Code of Conduct so we began to organize accordingly: the senior officers taking command and the rest of us eager to do whatever we could to make things difficult for the People's Republic of Washington. It was many years later, chatting with my high school friend and PoW Tom Hanton, I discovered that our resistance *did* mirror reality in that our PoWs in North Vietnam established a very credible organization, the 4th Allied PoW Wing, while in captivity. At the direction of our senior officers, we were as obstinate and uncooperative as dozens of aviators could be. We took great delight in disrupting prisoner formations and plotting mayhem wherever possible. Despite the heavy odds against being able to impersonate a 5ft tall, 130lb Oriental long enough to trek the length of Vietnam to safety, we conspired to escape with plans we considered quite credible. Fights were staged as distractions while one, two or ten of us slid under the wires and bolted for freedom and similar ploys. Strangely, we never even reached the wire before a crowd of Washingtonians appeared out of nowhere and scooped us up. The hoods went on and the would-be escapees were bundled off for another session or two of enthusiastic abuse and stress positions.

There was little interrogation conducted while we were in solitary. This changed abruptly when we moved to the compound. I don't recall exact numbers, but there were probably sixty or seventy of us in total and guards were constantly hauling one or two of us off to be grilled. Interrogation was probably the least effective element of the training experience. There were a number of reasons for this, but the most influential was the fact that we all knew we weren't in this situation for the long haul and we also knew that there was a very stringent limit to what the DISTAFF could do to extract information. While the North Vietnamese could (and often did) rope a prisoner's elbows together behind him and hang him in agony from a hook on the ceiling, the DISTAFF was constrained to smacking us around and applying stress positions. Woe betide the guard who actually injured a very expensive pilot through over-exuberant application of force in a training scenario. Nevertheless, they were enthusiastic and used some fairly subtle tactics to make an impression on us. I remember being brought, hooded, into an interrogation room, subjected to the usual tirade and told to assume a position of attention. The hood was whipped off, I was ordered to look down and there I stood, firmly on the Stars and Stripes which they had bunched around my boots. Flashbulbs popped and they gleefully told me just how patriotic I would look in my hometown newspaper, dancing on the flag. For some reason, I had not been my usual jovial self for a few days, so this subterfuge did not amuse me.

It was at this stage of the proceedings that we got our first real introduction to the DISTAFF. Like us, they varied from very young to advancing middle age. Dressed in black uniforms (naturally), all were military and, as we discovered during the course out brief, they ranged from junior airman to lieutenant colonel. We also learned that they switched roles regularly, so the junior cell guard or interrogator who was so enjoying our discomfiture during stress positions might well be the camp commandant for the next class and vice versa.

There was one particularly loathsome interrogator who apparently took an instant dislike to me and clearly set out to make my life miserable. He was my age (24) or younger and constantly in my face. His arsenal of expletives was impressive and once when I innocently asked him 'Do you kiss your mama with that mouth?' I learned a few new ones and had an opportunity to crawl around the cell under my hood with the occasional well-aimed kick as a bonus. I swore if I ever had the opportunity, I would happily rip his throat out and leave his carcass out in the sun so everyone could see.

That opportunity came only a day after the PoW course ended when I strolled over to the Base Exchange to buy some cigarettes (this was the '60s, remember; most fighter pilots smoked and those who didn't knew better than to question the habit). As I headed for the cash registers, I saw my arch enemy at the magazine rack. He was in uniform, with two small stripes on his sleeve and now appeared very much younger and more fragile than he had while tormenting me. Now, I would have put him at 19 or 20 at most. As he caught sight of me marching purposefully in his direction there was a clear but fleeting glimpse of apprehension in his eyes and he pulled his pretty wife and 2 or 3-year-old daughter in a frilly pink dress a little bit closer to him. I steamed up directly in front of him and fixed him with a steely gaze. My seething vengeance went something like this: 'Son, I'm sure you've heard this before, but you're very, very good at what you do. Thanks for the excellent training and good luck wherever you go.' In a quiet voice I'd never heard before (devoid of venom and vile oaths), he replied 'You're welcome, Sir, it was my pleasure' and I chuckled as I walked away because I knew he meant it, particularly the last bit.

This was the same day I learned a lesson in trust. We met for an overall debriefing of the course and our performance as a class. We were about average: doing our best to uphold the tenets of the Code of Conduct, organizing as best we could and providing a reasonable level of resistance. The 'real' commandant of the Survival School, a lieutenant colonel, led the debriefing and as he summed it all up, he called one of our fellow captives to the podium. 'Colonel Chuck' was also a lieutenant colonel who had gravitated to a position near the top of our leadership ladder. He was active in the Escape Committee, well liked and respected by one and all and, indeed, was a role model for those of us much younger. The Survival School Commandant introduced 'Col Chuck' (as if we didn't all know him) and then said 'Did any of you wonder why your escape attempts failed abysmally time after time?' We all looked at each other, slightly perplexed, and then he continued:

> 'Col Chuck, here, was recruited on Day One to help us provide a bit of a learning outcome over the length of your captivity. You'll be interested to know that every escape plan, every plot and every attempt to disrupt proceedings was passed to us immediately by our 'turncoat' here. Under real circumstances, he would have received special treatment from us and no doubt would have contributed to very tough times for some of you. I think you'll agree he played the role very well and if you've learned something from his act, I think you'll also agree he deserves a round of applause.'

He got it and, although there may have been a couple of more senior types who felt seriously aggrieved (and probably even more embarrassed) about being caught out to lunch, we filed the episode away and, as was the custom in those days, vowed never again to trust anyone over 30.

The SERE course at Fairchild AFB provided us with some very useful tips on how to cope in captivity, but the lack of accurate intelligence on actual conditions in North Vietnamese prisons left some very significant gaps. We departed a bit more knowledgeable, but significantly more apprehensive about that most intimidating scenario: capture by the enemy.

There was one more stop prior to combat operations, and this was designed to bring us up to speed on escape and evasion in a hot, steamy and clearly hostile environment.

Specialized Jungle Survival Tuition: Snake School

During the Vietnam War, Angeles City, the Philippines, was renowned for three separate but tenuously linked activities.

Firstly, Clark Air Base, hub of the US logistic effort to support the war. Arguably the busiest airport in the world during certain periods, Clark hosted vast numbers of cargo aircraft transporting all manner of weaponry and equipment to bases in Vietnam and Thailand. It was also a stopping-off point for troop-carrying airliners, both MAC (Military Airlift Command) and numerous commercial charters, many of which are now long defunct (World Airways, Flying Tiger, Seaboard, Continental, Braniff, etc., etc., etc.).

While most of the passengers enjoyed a short travel break before proceeding to South-East Asia, many of these flights disgorged aviators and other combatants at Clark to attend jungle survival training en route to combat tours in South-East Asia.

Never a nation to ignore marketable opportunities, the Filipinos cultivated a thriving sex trade in Angeles City, adjacent to Clark. This industry was not limited to hundreds of girls who populated dozens of bars in the city to offer various essential services to soldiers and airmen on their way to and from the war. These activities were immensely popular and relatively safe (remember, in the '60s and '70s, even in the Philippines, there was no AIDS), but Angeles City will always be remembered by many of those who passed through Clark as the home of the live sex show. I'm not going to dwell on this, but for comparatively straight-laced Westerners, establishments like the Fire Empire and the Nipa Hut provided an open-air, on-stage demonstration of doing what comes naturally (and sometimes *not* so naturally). This was a unique and trendy form of entertainment during a one- or two-day en route stop-off and richly supplemented a few days of learning all about the jungle.

I mentioned a tenuous link between these activities. For the fighter pilot (and to be fair, all the other guys) on the way to combat the Clark Air Base hub afforded an opportunity to pursue any of a myriad of stewardesses from the Charter Airlines ('stewardesses' on MAC military flights wore sweaty olive drab T-shirts and had 5 o'clock stubble and hairy armpits). The REAL stewardesses could often be found at the Clark Airbase Officers' Open Mess (CABOOM) bar, and were often approachable. It was a golden opportunity indeed to run into one or a group of them enthusiastically attending the Friday night live sex show in Angeles City! Well, I did say the link was tenuous.

Ah, again I stray. My focus here is jungle survival training and our personal health and safety objectives for combat flying were, in order, don't get shot down. If objective number one was breached, don't die or be captured. Consequently, we approached jungle survival training with a healthy respect. 'Snake School', as this course was informally christened, was held in the jungles adjacent to Clark AFB in the Philippines. Unlike the Fairchild experience, Snake School was based on centuries-old principles of survival in a lush, steamy, utterly horrible environment populated by insects the size of small birds and reptiles capable of dispatching an unwary human in a very few seconds. No one was particularly enthusiastic about spending a few days in the humid tropical rainforest, but to a man, we wanted to soak up the knowledge that might keep us going if indeed we were forced to jettison the airplane that provided us sanctuary over some very unfriendly territory.

The Snake School instructors were Air Force specialists well versed in the characteristics of the bush, its flora and inhabitants and they presented a credible academic introduction to the real experts, the Negritos. These aboriginal tribes of Philippine pygmies had mastered jungle living over a period of thousands of years and were linked to the US military through their exemplary service hindering the Japanese on our behalf during the Second World War.

Armed with the academic presentations we had absorbed, we sallied forth into the jungle with three or four Negritos who gave us a superb introduction to the environment. They demonstrated how to construct shelter, hammocks and other creature comforts from the raw materials we would find in great profusion and pointed out flora and fauna we'd never imagined. One of them captured a small green snake and, in pidgin English, cheerfully explained how we would, if bitten by this delightful creature, experience about two minutes of inconceivable pain and suffering prior to expiring. We began to pay far more attention to where we stepped from this point on, but our guide quickly transitioned to what the hungry evader might find to eat in the jungle. After describing numerous plants and berries that would have a similar effect to that of the green snake, he took a length of bamboo, blocked one end, filled it with all sorts of fruits, leaves and other strange flora. He then started a small fire in about thirty seconds flat (again using bamboo without a perceptible ignition source) and cooked up a meal that this dedicated carnivore found to be utterly delicious. I ignored the fact that it would probably take me weeks to accomplish the same thing – poorly – and was comforted by the fact that starvation was probably not my biggest challenge should I be forced to depart my comfortable jet via an ejection seat in the months to come.

Having now been introduced to the basics of staying alive in Tarzan's neighborhood, the Air Force graciously provided an occasion to put all this knowledge into action. We were briefed by the Snake School staff and looked forward (?) to the exercise which would commence immediately. The rules of engagement were relatively straightforward. Each of us was paired with another apprehensive aviator, given five aluminum discs, and would be airlifted by helicopter into the jungle and deposited unceremoniously into the lush greenery. Once on the ground, our mission was to evade capture for three long, hot, sweaty days. We would be pursued by Negritos. Remember? Those little guys who knew the jungle like the inside of their loincloths. If discovered we would give our successful pursuer one of the aluminum discs, which he would subsequently exchange for 5lb of rice and everyone (with the possible exception of ourselves) would be happy. The Negrito would then melt into the jungle in search of other evaders and (we were told with a straight face) wouldn't divulge our location to his family and friends. At the end of our ordeal we would be picked up by helicopter and returned to civilization. We could hardly wait to begin (and I write this with a straight face).

The chopper trip out was one of the most unsettling rides I've ever taken. Below us was green, nothing but green, and you could tell it was thick and steamy and full of unspeakable terrors. My assigned companion was Tony, another F-4 pilot who had gone to Clemson University, where a fierce interstate rivalry with my own alma mater South Carolina had existed since the early nineteenth century. We both resolutely undertook not to be a pussy in the company of our collegiate rival and I'm sure this improved our performance on the exercise. Our chauffeur found a small clearing, dropped deftly into it and his colleague motioned us out the side door, politely reminding us to duck our heads lest the rotor blades separate them from our bodies. We half-heartedly climbed out, looking back at a half-dozen other apprehensive adventurers who would soon be similarly jettisoned at other, equally abhorrent locations.

Tony and I managed to avoid decapitation in exiting the helicopter and, as it powered up and departed, we looked at each other, both contemplating just what the hell we were doing here. Professionals both, we soon agreed that the name of the game was evasion and we needed to find cover. As we'd been dropped off late in the afternoon, the priority was shelter and a safe place to sleep. We didn't exactly melt into the jungle – it was more like lurching – but we did locate a small stand of trees. As we'd been allowed the luxury of a hammock each in addition to a small bag of survival items of our choosing, we set out to construct our hidden hideaway. Because of the configuration of my chosen tree, my hammock was only a few feet off the ground, but I was convinced this would keep me clear of any loathsome beasties we had been warned about. Tony's was quite a bit higher and although it was likely to hurt more when he fell out (which we both did on more than one occasion), this increased elevation had advantages which will be covered shortly.

Luxurious accommodation constructed, we resigned ourselves to the fact that we weren't going to find a friendly bar or steakhouse and decided to apply our new-found knowledge to preparing dinner. We foraged for an hour or so, came up with a number of vegetarian delights that didn't appear to be lethal and set out to transform these leaves, vines and berries into *haute cuisine*. The small fire our Negrito mentor had torched in less than a minute took us about an hour due to the fact that everything we tried to light was damp and slimy. Once it was ignited we replicated the bamboo 'pot' and then watched helplessly as our culinary masterpiece began to smoke, then spontaneously combusted. Tony and I looked at each other and broke into uncontrollable fits of laughter, despite the realization that it was going to be a hungry few days.

As night fell (quite early as the setting sun couldn't penetrate the jungle canopy), we settled down. We'd decided not to talk as we knew the Negritos heard everything in the jungle, and we really wanted to remain 'uncaptured'. Night-time in the jungle is not a nice situation: hot, humid and characterized by a plethora of strange noises, all of which, in your mind, are made by something that would happily eat you. As I stopped moving and achieved tenuous equilibrium in my hammock I became more aware of insects. I had a small aerosol can of repellent in my survival bag and had coated face, arms and anything else that wasn't covered so most of the insect activity was aural rather than actual contact. It was annoying having them buzzing around, but somehow I managed to doze. I was awakened by relentless activity around my feet. I had kept my boots on, but half asleep, it took a few seconds to register the revolting source: my boots were being chewed enthusiastically by a rat.

The USAF had been conducting survival training in the Philippine jungle since the early days of the war, years earlier. Most evaders brought some morsels of food along to the party and as the area we'd been dropped in was fairly compact, there were the usual food wrappers and associated detritus left around inhabited areas and where there are people, and food, there are rats.

The bad boy who had developed a taste for my boot leather wasn't quite cat-sized, but although I couldn't see him (it's seriously dark in the jungle at night), I could tell by the gusto of the nibbling and the effect it was having on my hammock's stability that he was a sizable creature. I kicked once, and amid some pretty horrendous squealing and high-pitched shrieking, he disappeared (down the opposite tree trunk I must assume). A few minutes later, however, he was back with a vengeance. I don't know what I had stepped in during the day but he apparently found it irresistible. Another kick, another noisy departure...and then he was back. I was beginning to get a bit spooked by his tenacity, wondering when he was going to transition from boot leather to ankle leather, so I decided to escalate.

After the next sequence of nibble/kick/withdrawal I located my aerosol insect repellent, felt around for the nozzle and, when I'd located it, gingerly sat up in the hammock, stabilized the can at toe level and pointed the spray nozzle directly at the space between my feet. I waited silently for what seemed like a considerable time, not wanting to fall out of the hammock prior to the moment of truth. Finally, I heard movement on the tree trunk and felt a tentative footfall on the hammock. Patiently, I waited for the gnawing to commence. When it did I delayed until he seemed to be in between boots and gave him a three-second burst which, from the din that erupted, must have caught him full in the face. This time, the squealing and shrieking didn't cease when he was out of boot range and he didn't come back. Result: fighter pilot 1, loathsome rodent 0.

I related this momentous skirmish quietly to Tony the next morning. He'd slept through it but wasn't particularly impressed. 'Sling your hammock further up the tree, Dumbshit,' he said. I couldn't argue with him.

We went deeper into the jungle during the day and remained quiet; it became extremely boring, but we weren't apprehended on day two. That night, having learned my lesson, I elevated the hammock and had a reasonable sleep.

Day three was a repeat. We didn't see or hear anything and silently gloated over the fact that the native jungle-dwellers had failed to bring us to bay. We settled down for the night and I slept as soundly as you can in a jungle full of strange noises, potentially lethal wild life and human-induced rats. I woke to the sound of distant rotor blades and the elation of knowing we were going to be extracted very soon. It was still quite dark, but I had an uncanny feeling that Tony and I weren't alone. He was about 10 yards from me and as the light began to filter through the canopy, I sensed more than saw a half-dozen forms in between us, keeping an eye on us both. When I could finally focus, the only appropriate reaction was to laugh, long and hearty. Sat on the ground between us, barefoot and in loincloths, were seven or eight Negrito children ranging between 5 or 6 and about 12 years old. It was obvious that our delusions of our triumphant 'evasion' had been totally unfounded. These kids had obviously known where we were from Day One and had probably been watching us like hawks throughout our little ordeal. Tony woke to the same sight, had a similar belly laugh and the kids beamed at us both. They had tiny homemade bows and arrows to 'sell' us and, of course, when the chopper arrived to take us back to Clark, they waved goodbye and went home proudly to present ten shiny aluminum discs to their families.

Tony and I had enjoyed this conclusion to our evasion exercise immensely and, when reunited with our colleagues we related what we believed to be a unique experience. Not so, we discovered, as other 'evaders' came back at us with virtually the same story and the same outcome. We had been spread all over the Philippine jungles surrounding Clark AB and in virtually every instance, it was obvious the adult Negritos we believed to be tirelessly stalking us went about their daily business and left the village kids to hunt us down. They did this with ease and deservedly took home the spoils. Damn clever, these aboriginals.

The Hitchhiker's Guide to South-East Asia

The Snake School experience was completed with an enormous steak, many drinks and the telling of stories in the CABOOM. While nursing the hangover from these festivities I had a day or so to contemplate the mortal combat that awaited me in Vietnam. The obvious venue for such musing was in the CABOOM bar where I joined other cannon fodder-to-be. There weren't any nurses or Charter Airline stews in attendance so I found myself holding up the bar with a tall, lanky major. Just below the left shoulder seam of his flight suit was a simple red and blue patch similar to an interstate highway sign. It read: North Vietnam//100 Missions F-105. Five short words that conveyed the unmistakable message: 'I've been there and done that.'

I glanced sideways at him while sipping my scotch. He bore an uncanny resemblance to James Coburn, the knife-throwing gunslinger in *The Magnificent Seven*, and this image of casual cool, combined with the patch, gave him credibility beyond words. He noticed I'd been checking him out and in a drawl that could have been North Texas or possibly Oklahoma, he said 'Where are you headed, L/T?' In a reverent voice that could have come from an 8-year-old introduced to Babe Ruth, I said 'Danang, Sir.' He fixed me with a baleful gaze, slowly shook his head and came back with 'You don't want to go to Danang, son. Those guys get rocketed every other night and you can't even go downtown and chase the girlies.'

It is safe to say my world crumbled upon hearing those words and I looked at him in utter desolation. He grinned, bought me another scotch, and said 'Let's talk about this.' For the next two hours, he regaled me with stories from the combat zone. He was returning from leave in the States for a second tour in '105s and indeed, had 'been there and done that'. I hung on his every word and he got the adrenaline flowing with tales of missions to Hanoi and Haiphong, SAM launches, MiG engagements and hauling downed pilots out of the jungle. He also spent a fair amount of time contrasting Danang with his own base, Takhli in Thailand; mission quality, lifestyle issues (which included going downtown and chasing the girlies). When he had finished I was even more depressed, realizing what I would miss by serving my tour in purgatory (known as Danang). He read me like a book, put that infectious grin on me and said: 'Here's what you need to do, L/T.' He laid out a plan, amazing in its simplicity, but in my mind, it was full of holes. 'It can't work, can it?' I asked. 'Trust me,' he said. Trust him? Hell, I would have bought the Brooklyn Bridge from him and so I went away to convert his words into action.

I've mentioned the operational tempo at Clark during the war. Busy airport doesn't do it justice and the folks who were responsible for moving people in and out of the Philippines struggled to maintain a semblance of organization in the face of a quite overwhelming maelstrom of mobilizing humanity. Often they failed to do so and this was the foundation upon which my benefactor's plan was based.

My flight to Danang was scheduled for Tuesday, two days from my mini master's course at the bar. On Monday morning, I checked out of my quarters, grabbed my duffle bag full of not much more than my helmet, 'G'-suit and basic clothing and toiletries and headed for the passenger terminal. Picture, if you will, a factory farm populated with people; probably 1,000 sweating souls milling around a building far too small to accommodate them all. Occasionally, an unintelligible message came across on an antiquated public address system and thirty or forty of the human herd would break away to one of three exits at the far end of the building to be ushered through with great haste. The good major's plan seemed more and more viable.

I watched this turmoil for a couple of hours until I heard the words I was waiting for: '*blftsfx, woqrsiweg, kjerkud Don Muang xvgtryts*', Don Muang being the primary military hub air terminal just outside Bangkok in Thailand. I watched as some of the gyrating crowd headed for the middle exit, took a deep breath and positioned myself right in the middle of the small stampede. Remember, 1969 was decades prior to Jihadis flying airplanes into buildings and the resulting paranoia that now renders the prelude to commercial air travel one of life's great aggravations. As I approached the exit, duffle slung over my shoulder, I saw one lone, tired, fed up airman obviously processing the entire rabble. I emulated my colleagues who waved pieces of paper at him as we swept past; mine looked just like theirs except it said 'Danang' on it instead of 'Ubon', 'Udorn', 'Korat' or 'Takhli'. In retrospect, this kid wouldn't have cared if it had been written in crayon and hieroglyphics and I emerged from the scrum one step closer to victory, facing a venerable C-130 Hercules which already had two of its four engines running. I clambered aboard, unhindered by probing questions about my orders (or anything else) and prepared for the four-hour ordeal that would spirit me to Thailand. On a modern airliner, I could have faced a bit of a problem; sixty seats for sixty-one passengers, for example. In a C-130 there is good news and bad news. The good news is that seating is on a series of linked web seats not unlike mini hammocks all the way down both sides and the centerline of the aircraft. Thus there was always space somewhere. The bad news is that seating is on a series of linked web seats not unlike mini hammocks all the way down both sides and the centerline of the aircraft. This is arguably the most uncomfortable aircraft seating configuration on earth and enduring it for four hours plus is not an experience one looks forward to. Nevertheless, under the circumstances, I was absolutely delighted, thank you.

The trip to Don Muang (1,105 nautical miles) was almost as uneventful as it was uncomfortable and we arrived as night fell. We gathered in another passenger terminal, this one made of corrugated metal and heated all day by the unrelenting Thai sunshine. The factory farm wasn't quite as hectic; fewer cattle but in a much smaller area, so the milling around was less chaotic and it was even possible to decipher the tannoy announcements. There were far fewer of them and I was waiting to hear either of two magic words: Ubon or Udorn, the two Thai bases that supported F-4 operations. The Don Muang operational tempo was significantly slower than the madhouse at Clark, so I settled down on a rickety metal chair with a paperback book and waited almost patiently. I was somewhat apprehensive at the comparative calm of the environment; more opportunity for someone to scrutinize my dodgy documentation and send me back from whence I had come to eventual banishment to Danang.

About three hours later, I heard the call I'd been waiting for: 'MAC Flight XYZ will now be departing for Ubon.' I got up from my delicate perch and silently rehearsed my line of patter for anyone who might question my paperwork. I needn't have worried: as I approached the exit gate I was delighted to note there was no one even faintly interested in checking the tickets. I bounded into the darkness and then up the tiny stairs which extended from the small side door forward of the C-130 engines, onto my horrible webbed seat and then quietly ticked off another small step on the road to the Promised Land.

Forty-five minutes later, the 130's wheels kissed the tarmac at Ubon and we taxied past a huge sign reading 'Welcome to the 8th Tactical Fighter Wing – Home of the Wolfpack' painted on the back side of a number of aircraft revetments in 8ft tall letters. The Wolfpack was renowned; recently commanded by Colonel Robin Olds, a triple fighter ace with sixteen kills in the Second World War and Vietnam and just the kind of charismatic leader I'm hoping to do justice to in this book. The 8th was now home to four fighter squadrons, the 25th, 433rd, 435th and 497th comprising nearly 100 F-4 aircraft and, with just a bit more luck, I was going to be a very small part of it.

The 130 rolled to a stop and the loadmaster dropped the steps. I joined the throng of thirty or so passengers and descended into the pre-dawn sultry warmth of Ubon Ratchathani. I took a very deep breath, keenly aware that if my adventure was going to unravel, it would do so spectacularly right here. Slipping past semi-comatose airmen onto a C-130 was child's play compared with trying to explain to someone in authority who I was, what I was doing here and why I didn't comprehend my now rather sweaty and wrinkled orders which clearly read: 'Unit of Assignment: 366th Tactical Fighter Wing, Danang RVN.'

I was wearing a flight suit: a shapeless green bag, similar to a boiler suit with a single zipper which extended from crotch to throat, an embroidered silver bar on each shoulder and a patch with embroidered pilot wings, plus my name and '1/Lt USAF' above my left zippered breast pocket. I was also carrying a fairly distinctive helmet bag which identified me as a guy with a helmet, a fighter pilot. There were three of us who fitted this description on the flight and we were met by a similarly attired officer with the gold oak leaves of a major on his shoulder. He was carrying a clipboard which I stared at with trepidation. This guy could, in a heartbeat, not only banish me to Danang, but also shred my very brief career by branding me a charlatan, thoroughly dishonest, devious and a horrible role model for America's youth.

I hung back while he approached my travelling companions (I had studiously avoided speaking with them en route). He took their names, glanced at their orders, which undoubtedly read 'Ubon', and ticked them off his sheet, directing them towards a small open pickup truck with wooden seats where further instructions would follow. There's only one course of action when you're clearly in the shit: I took a deep breath, sauntered up to him, fixed him with my steely blue eyes and, as nonchalantly as I could, said 'Mornin' Major, nice day to get to the War Zone' or something equally absurd. He nodded at me, took my orders, looked at them for some time and then back at me with an expression that unmistakably demanded an explanation. Right now. I was instantly conscious of the fact that my mentor, the wise and persuasive F-105 driver at the CABOOM Bar, hadn't covered this particular chapter in the story and I was well and truly on my own.

My synthetic cool evaporated instantly. I instantaneously developed a small tic over my right eye and I could feel my lip trembling as the bravado melted away and I began to grovel: 'You're not going to send me to Danang, are you, Sir?' He stared at me for a long, long time, evaluating the level and sincerity of my remorse. He looked back at my orders, winked at me, crumpled them up and said quietly: 'Welcome to the Wolfpack, son. I can't very well cull someone who got here the same way I did.'

Some weeks later, the major (my new best friend) sidled up to me to say they'd received a tracer message from 7th Air Force Headquarters in Saigon seeking Lieutenant Ladd (and numerous other 'misplaced' personnel). The chaotic nature of South-East Asia assignment and mass transit was apparently more widespread than I had envisaged. The Wolfpack administration had replied, stating that the said Lieutenant Ladd was present, accounted for, and performing a reasonably positive function in the 435th Tac Fighter Squadron and the major didn't anticipate any repercussions. That's the last I ever heard of the issue, but to this day, every now and then, I get a conspicuous feeling that someone's about to tap me on the shoulder and say 'Weren't you supposed to go to Danang?'

Chapter Three

My Personal War: An Anti-Climax

D ozens of books have been written about the Air War in South-East Asia, most of them cataloguing harrowing missions over Hanoi, Haiphong, Laos and other highly-defended hotspots. There are some very good ones: *Thud Ridge* by Colonel Jack Broughton comes to mind. As I stated upfront, it is not my intention to compete with these accounts for a couple of reasons. First, my own individual wartime exploits can't equal some of the experiences of other authors. The combat tour at Ubon was exhilarating for me in a thousand different ways but, by comparison, it was no more or less perilous or heroic than that of hundreds of other fighter pilots during that period.

Although I flew 204 missions, demolished a number of Uncle Ho's moving vans, bridges and other infrastructure, soaked up a number of bullet holes and dodged the occasional surface-to-air missile (SAM), most of my individual exploits were relatively underwhelming. Secondly, I'm much more interested in providing an insight into behaviors and experiences which make this noble profession unique, rather than providing an autobiographical portrayal of my own year in the combat zone.

There are a couple of combat tour anecdotes worthy of note. Neither of these refers to my conspicuous heroism or skillful airmanship, but both left a lasting impression on me for very different reasons.

The Father and Son Reunion

I mentioned my father in a previous section of this book. He was a quiet man, intelligent and athletic with a dry wit that didn't surface often, but very, very modest. He was always my hero. Dad had served in the South Pacific during the Second World War as a navigator on B-24 Liberators (I didn't hold that against him, but we never missed an opportunity for a round of good-natured fighter pilot vs. bomber navigator insults). It was during this tour that Dad and his fellow crewmembers in the B-24 ironically named 'Round Trip' were shot down by a Japanese Zero fighter and spent a few idyllic days feasting on coconuts on a tiny uninhabited island until the good guys arrived to rescue them. Not many years later, when the Korean War came along, he was there as well, flying night interdiction missions in A-26 Intruders.

He was out of the flying club when the Vietnam era dawned, but still wearing the uniform of a lieutenant colonel in the Accounting and Finance Directorate. Even those guys went to war, and 1969 saw him stationed at the 7th Air Force Headquarters in Saigon. Yeah, Dad was now a shoe clerk, but I never had the heart to bait him on that one.

As it happened, Dad arrived in Saigon a few short months after I had scammed my way into the Wolfpack at Ubon, so there we were: father and eldest son participating in the same Southeast Asia war games. I'm sure this wasn't totally unique, but it wasn't commonplace either.

My mother, bless her, was not the least bit pleased with this arrangement, but being an Air Force wife of the old school, she put up with the challenge and the double-barreled worry with great dignity and patience.

I tried on a number of occasions to get Dad to visit. Air shuttle transport from Saigon to the Thai combat units was readily available, but he always seemed to be too busy. Looking back, I suspect he would have preferred not to be in the vicinity while I was flying combat missions, but after a certain amount of nagging/cajoling he agreed to spend a couple of days with me.

I was on the night mission schedule when Dad pitched up, so he and I went into town on the afternoon of his arrival. We did NOT chase the girlies, and I avoided taking him to SbaiThong, the fighter pilots' favorite massage parlor. I just didn't think he'd understand. Instead we checked out the sights, surveyed a massive assortment of Seiko watches, sampled char-grilled frogs on sticks and other Thai delights.

We returned to Ubon in plenty of time for me to throw on my flight suit and we went across to the Ops Center for the early evening intelligence brief. Dad's security clearances allowed him in, just. There he learned all about the significant anti-aircraft artillery threat surrounding our general target area and the search and rescue effort that was in progress to attempt to extract a Cam Ranh Bay F-4 crew who had just been shot down in Southern Laos. I assumed this would all roll off his back as he'd been a party to many similar briefings during his own combat tours. As I was only 24, incredibly naïve and a bachelor without children of my own, it just never occurred to me he would be apprehensive and he didn't let it show. I've always felt guilty for subjecting him to it.

We headed over to the Squadron Ops building and I suggested he should join some of the day shift boys at the Officers' Club for a good steak, a couple of beers and a bit of live entertainment, which normally consisted of a scantily-clad all-girl Thai band which played the hits of the day (in a manner of speaking). At the time, I recall, the favorites were *Yellow River* by Christie, which in Thailand always came out sounding like 'Jerro Leaver' and was often followed by the Creedence Clearwater classic 'Big wheel keeps on turnin', Ploud Melly keeps on burnin'.'

I left Dad with a couple of my buddies, grabbed my helmet, donned my 'G'-suit, parachute harness, survival vest and Smith & Wesson .38 caliber Combat Special pistol and headed off to do my thing.

Three and a half hours (two air refuelings and a successful jousting contest with a 37mm anti-aircraft gun) later, I completed our flight intelligence debrief and headed back to drop off my flight gear, expecting then to join my Dad at the club. I walked into the squadron and there he was, pacing back and forth like (dare I say it?) an expectant father. It was only then that the light bulb came on and I realized that tonight's mission had been a lot harder on Dad than it had been on me. We never spoke of it, but we both learned something about each other that night.

We did finally make it to the club that never closed and, despite the fact that it was 2.00 am enjoyed chilling out. The girls were gone, but there was still entertainment. Most if not all South-East Asia Fighter Base bars were equipped with a long brass rail, similar to a footrest, but installed with sturdy brackets on the ceiling *above* the bar. This was to facilitate one of the more bizarre fighter pilot pastimes: Bat Hanging.

How? Why? Damned if I know, but in the wee small hours a visitor to the Ubon Club was likely to encounter a half-dozen or more fighter pilots – somewhat the worse for wear – dangling by their toes from the aforementioned hanging rail and attempting to imbibe their 25 cent beer or shot from an inverted configuration. This spectacle was most effective when early flyers arrived for breakfast and the jeers and catcalls flew back and forth between walkers and hangers. On one occasion, a US senator visiting the War Zone happened upon a large group of 'bats' and nearly broke his neck when he foolishly attempted to join them. My Dad may not have been impressed with these shenanigans, but most certainly he was amused. He caught the following afternoon shuttle back to Saigon and didn't visit again, but we often talked about his 'trip to the combat zone'. Only in later years did it dawn on me that his combat zones had certainly been far more challenging than mine.

Fun-Loving Fools

This would appear to be an opportune time to further astonish those of you who are now shaking your heads at the thought of allegedly intelligent adults hanging upside down in a bar. Fighter pilots have, over the years, developed a number of pastimes designed to blow off steam, foster camaraderie and establish a level of exclusivity that others would not even wish to achieve. Most of these amusements fall into certain categories: mindless, irresponsible, uncouth and immature. I wouldn't expect anyone outside our band of brothers to fully understand, but these diversions are the bonds that hold us together (and set us apart). I'll elaborate on just a few.

Dead Bug: this activity has, to my knowledge, no discernible origin and certainly no tangible benefits or redeeming features. Nor does it require any equipment to participate. The 'rules' are simple. In any gathering of fighter pilots, the game is initiated simply by someone shouting the magic words 'Dead Bug!!' The last man flat on the floor with his arms and legs wigwagging in mid-air is the loser and theoretically must buy drinks for all the others. In practice, no one ever admits to being the last on his back, so free beverages are rarely delivered.

My first Dead Bug encounter was very special. As lowly student pilots at Moody AFB, we were visited by a genuine hero: Navy Commander Alan Shepard, former fighter pilot and Mercury astronaut. He talked to about 200 of us in the 'O' Club bar on a Friday afternoon and had us all awestruck with his experiences. As he concluded his motivational talk, he became very intense: 'No matter what aircraft you fly and where you go in your military career, don't ever forget...DEAD BUG!!' America's first man in space and 200 or so second lieutenants hit the deck near simultaneously, arms and legs flailed, and I was inexplicably but undeniably hooked.

By the way, when discussing this phenomenon, it is possible to avoid the mayhem simply by substituting the words 'Lifeless insect' for the trigger phrase. No responsive action is required.

Crud and Sockey: these are team pursuits and, normally, full contact sports. Crud was invented by Royal Canadian Air Force fighter pilots. It is played on a pool or billiard table and governed by a set of rules often misunderstood and/or ignored. The game involves two balls, a shooter and an object ball. The shooter is launched across the table by hand. The basic objective involves moving around the table and other players trying to grab the shooter ball and either strike the object ball before it stops moving or sink it. Pushing, blocking and general havoc are an integral part of the game, but actual bloodshed is relatively rare.

Sockey (soccer + hockey), on the other hand, is utterly devoid of rules and, as played at Ubon, simply consisted of kicking an empty beer can past your opponents into a 'goal' by any means possible. Teams were formed on the hoof and the concept of refereeing was non-existent. Minor injuries were commonplace and I cannot remember a win/loss result ever emerging from what was essentially an alcohol-fuelled street brawl. During one spirited match, following an interdiction mission over Laos, I had disengaged from the melee to quench my thirst at the bar. I, First Lieutenant Ladd, was accosted by a major (a shoe clerk, naturally) who got right in my face and advised me that all fighter pilots were 'disgusting, a disgrace to the Air Force' and as sub-humans shouldn't be allowed to inhabit a civilized earth. Lost for words after absorbing this tirade, I bestowed a single right jab to his nose and he became, without anyone shouting the trigger word, a solo dead bug. He leapt to his feet, shouting that he would have me court-martialed and drawn and quartered with my head mounted on a stake. My boss, a lieutenant colonel (and Sockey teammate that night), reached over my shoulder, poked the shoe clerk in the chest and said quietly: 'He didn't hit you, Buddy, I did.' Exit humbled shoe clerk, stage left and thanks, Boss.

Sadly, the passage of time has not made the pursuit of happiness easy for the fighter pilot. Political correctness, Health and Safety, and deglamorization of alcohol have combined to drive the brethren from their historic lair, the Officers' Club Bar (and for those who remember, the Stag Bar). Most of these former shrines have been downgraded to all ranks clubs where officers and NCOs/airmen are encouraged to fraternize together when off-duty. This arrangement pleases no one, since the fighter pilots and NCOs are terminally inhibited by forced social proximity to each other. Consequently, separate, once-thriving officers' and NCOs' clubs have now become dreary, under-patronized mausoleums with little soul and even less activity.

Yet again, I have digressed. Back to Ubon Ratchathani.

Tumbling Gyros

Amid the excitement and adrenaline rushes available in abundance in a combat environment (including those recreations described above), there are other experiences equally dramatic which could occur anywhere above the planet. I'll relate one of those to you before I move on from the Southeast Asia scenario.

During pilot training, we were all exposed to various physiological phenomena we needed to be aware of as aviators. These ranged from the insidious effects of hypoxia, resulting from oxygen starvation at altitude. Given a short period of time, hypoxia could deceptively rob a pilot of awareness, leading to total unconsciousness and all the bad things that result from snoozing while you're piloting an aircraft. This training was applied in an altitude chamber which very effectively replicated high-altitude flight. Half of us at a time were 'invited' to drop our oxygen masks and perform some very simple tasks (writing our signature or counting backwards from 100, for example) while deprived of oxygen. The other half of the class observed. The effects were stealthy but dramatic; over the space of a couple of minutes, the signatures gradually became unrecognizable scrawls and the countdown from 100 evolved into an incoherent babble. When the mask was reapplied by one of the medical technicians who took the ride with us, recovery was immediate and complete. Those who had observed were treated to an entertaining tableau of cognitive deterioration that left an indelible mark on their memory and portrayed a valuable lesson in the importance of monitoring your oxygen status in the air.

This lesson learned, I never faced a problem with hypoxia. I can't say the same for another physiological demonstration we experienced: vertigo. Vertigo can be at least as deceptive as hypoxia and while a lack of oxygen can send you peacefully to the land of dreams until you hit the ground, vertigo generates a particular level of terror which I'll come to shortly.

Vertigo (or spatial disorientation) results from the senses, primarily the balancing mechanisms of the inner ear, going out of kilter for any one of a number of reasons. It is a complex concept and, as I'm just a dumb ex-fighter pilot, I won't attempt to elaborate on the technicalities but I will say that a serious dose of vertigo can ruin your day in a very big way.

From the earliest stages of pilot training and throughout my career, the decree remained constant: no matter what your brain is telling you about your spatial position and orientation, believe your aircraft instruments! Unlike your brain, they will not lie to you. This is far easier said than done and I'll try to convince you with one anecdote from my combat tour.

We departed Ubon as a flight of four in the evening and headed north-east to locate some of Ho Chi Minh's haulage vehicles and convert them to scrap metal. As most of the traffic proceeded down the trail from North Vietnam through Laos and then back into South Vietnam at night, the air war after dark was unrelenting. As we would likely spend some time waiting for targets to appear, our first port of call was a KC-135 tanker aircraft orbiting in one of three racetrack-shaped orbits – designated cherry, peach and orange – over north-eastern Thailand. The tankers were there for us thirsty fighters 24/7, 365 days a year and the normal procedure was to fill up prior to heading into the target area and recycle as required for as long as it took to do the job.

We joined with the tanker and cycled onto the boom while the other three Phantoms flew loose formation awaiting their turn to top up the tanks. I was flying with Major Bob Fickle, and it was my turn to get the gas on this particular evening. Air-to-air refueling can, under certain circumstances (weather, turbulence and so forth) be challenging, but in essence it is an exercise in formation flying. The F-4 refueling receptacle was positioned on the spine of the aircraft directly behind the cockpit by that infinite number of monkeys I mentioned previously. It was impossible to see the point of tanker boom/fighter receptacle connection from the cockpit, so it was necessary to innovate à la Rube Goldberg to keep track of the aircraft position in relation to the boom. This involved setting the rear-view mirror to a position that would afford a view of the boom emerging from its housing directly above your head. Watching relative movement in a mirror can be disorienting at the best of times, but on this particular evening, the gods conspired against me with a number of additional complications which nearly did me in. The night was moonless and very dark and, as north-eastern Thailand was very sparsely populated, the few ground lights 20,000ft below us bore a marked resemblance to the visible stars light years above us. This in itself was not a problem, but as I struggled to maintain position via the mirror set-up, the tanker smoothly rolled into 20 degrees of left bank and simultaneously entered a thin layer of stratocirrus clouds that we slipped in and out of throughout the turn. This combination of visual anomalies and the gentle turn played havoc with the balance sensors of my inner ear and when we emerged from the wispy clouds, the internal gyroscope between my ears had catastrophically tumbled. My brain sent a red alert out to the rest of me warning that we, three other F-4s and a giant KC-135 tanker were all upside down in the dark skies over Thailand. I clearly remembered my pilot training creed: 'No matter what your brain is telling you about your spatial position and orientation, believe your instruments! Unlike your brain, they will not lie to you.'

Unfortunately, despite my fleeting and frantic glances at the attitude indicator, which clearly showed us in a mild 20-degree bank to the left and otherwise safe and stable, my brain wasn't going to be silenced: 'You're upside down, you stupid bastard and you, your wingmen and this tanker are all going to crash and burn; you need to do something drastic and do it fast or you're all going to die!'

I worked very, very hard to ignore this hysterical virtual cacophony and, reverting to my training, I took some immediate and positive steps. I recited the traditional fighter pilot's mantra 'Shit!' and struggled not to follow up the verbalization with a corresponding activity. When my partner up front responded, with some understandable urgency, to this surprise proclamation 'What do you *mean*, shit?' I calmly informed him (and I was calm, I can assure you; one thing a fighter pilot NEVER does is lose it on the radio) that I was experiencing the mother of all vertigos and I was truly, madly, deeply upside down. Like most pilots, he had been there and done that and offered a most reasonable suggestion: 'Do you want me to take the airplane?' 'Nope,' I responded with all the bravado (and sheer senselessness) of a man bent on slaying a windmill and unwilling to accept any direct support, 'Just talk to me.'

To his great credit, he did, reverting to air traffic controller mode to assist me in preserving my sanity: 'Level flight, 20 degrees of bank, now rolling out of the turn, still level...' and I hung onto the tanker boom for dear life, blinked my eyes, glanced at the attitude indicator and waited for my head to screw itself back on straight. After two or three minutes (most of an eternity to me), the brain finally admitted the instruments were reliable and I found myself soaked in sweat and hyperventilating, but thankfully right side up again. Only then was I willing to relinquish control. 'You've got the bird, Bob,' I said, and when he acknowledged and gently shook the stick I took a very deep breath, rested my hands on the canopy frame either side of me and silently thanked the gods for letting me live through the last few minutes.

In twenty-five years of high-performance flying I've had my share of close calls: I've been shot at and hit; run very low on fuel; contemplated stepping over the side more than once and dealt with a number of serious aircraft emergencies. Those moments all got the heart beating very rapidly, but paled in comparison with the sheer, unrelenting terror of not knowing which way is up and the helplessness of being unable to resolve the situation.

A Warrior's Demise

We didn't experience the massive attrition faced by the Allied bomber crews during the Second World War, but the skies over Vietnam, Laos and Cambodia were perilous and losses were not infrequent. Any loss of a friend or colleague is a wrenching experience, but some are more poignant than others.

I often flew with Captain Gray Warren during my combat tour. He was an exceptional pilot and one of the guys with whom you enjoyed a beer after a mission. Gray moved on from the squadron to the Wolf FACs (Forward Air Controllers), a voluntary and exclusive cadre who operated single ship, often at very low level, locating targets and directing other fighters against these targets. Unlike the smaller, slower FACs who flew unarmed, propeller-driven OV-10s or O-2s, the fast FACs had the firepower to mount their own attacks when other airpower wasn't available. This is exactly what Gray and his backseater Lieutenant Neil Bynum were doing on 26 October 1969. They had identified a bulldozer repairing a bombed-out road intersection near the Laotian/North Vietnamese border and Gray elected to take out the bulldozer while waiting for other flights to arrive. He rolled in to strafe and, at some point, took enemy ground fire and impacted the ground. Gray and Neil were originally listed as Missing in Action (MIA) but this was reclassified in 1976 to 'Killed in Action (KIA) on 26 Oct 1969, Body not Recovered.'

In 1970, an organization called VIVA (Voices In Vital America) began distributing brass bracelets commemorating both prisoners of war and those missing in action. I wore a bracelet with Gray Warren's name on it for many years. When his status was changed to KIA, I attempted to locate his family and send the bracelet to his widow. I managed to get an address from a friend of a friend, but sadly I don't know if the bracelet was ever delivered.

Chapter Four

Squadron: The Fighter Jock's Tribe

C ompletion of my combat tour released me into the F-4 pilot pool and I was subsequently assigned to the 353rd Tactical Fighter Squadron at Torrejón AB, just outside Madrid. Before I launch into those specific memories, however, I'd like to lay a foundation with a chat about the squadron environment and leadership issues: the elements that make the organization tick.

Fighter pilots, particularly those who plied their trade during the Cold War, are nomadic creatures, not in most cases by choice, but because of the Air Force's rotation policy. As I write this, in my study which is bedecked with the mementos of my former trade, I count eighteen colorful wooden plaques, each of which was presented on my departure from a fighter squadron after a significant tenure, normally (but not always) one to three years. Reflecting the span of assignments, two of these plaques are from German units and one is Iranian. In the '60s, '70s, '80s and most of the '90s, hundreds of American military installations, large and small, dotted the globe. From the Continental United States, where the Air Force churned out legions of aircrew and thousands of highly-skilled maintainers and support personnel, the fighter community extended as far as Central and Southern Europe (to the Iron Curtain) in the East and Vietnam, Thailand, Japan and South Korea to the West. It's not my intention to snub the rest of the Air Force (not to mention the Army, Navy and Marines), but my focus here is fighter aviation. If you flew, worked on or supported operations in any of a dozen or so single- or two-seat fighter aircraft, you could find yourself in any of these far-flung outposts and each of them comprised smaller groups known as squadrons.

A fighter squadron is a fascinating entity – a sociologist's delight – and it is impossible to grasp the psyche of the fighter pilot without understanding the basic workings of the tribe. There is absolutely no comparison between a fighter squadron and a civilian organization of a similar size. A squadron is the focal point for the job, a ready-made social environment, and in those locations where families can accompany, the wives and girlfriends establish and maintain invaluable built-in support groups to look out for each other while the menfolk are deployed or otherwise away from the nest.

The typical US Air Force fighter squadron consists of 25 to 30 pilots to employ between 18 and 24 aircraft, depending on the mission and location. Add a similar number of weapons system officers if you're thinking two-seat aircraft; the F-4, for instance. At the top of the squadron food chain is a lieutenant colonel commander and an operations officer (lieutenant colonel or major). Authority flows down to the three or four flight commanders, normally senior captains or junior majors, each of whom rides herd on an equal percentage of line pilots (or in the vernacular, 'crew dogs').

On the periphery are attached aircrew who work in wing or higher headquarters staff jobs above the squadron level and come to the trenches occasionally to maintain their flight currency. These guys are either revered by squadron jocks if they are good guys with a reputation for skill in the air, or loathed and detested if they are arrogant, pedantic, temperamental, excessively principled or all of the above. In any event, they are received with a certain amount of skepticism, because they are not 'crew dogs', don't fly as regularly as the line jocks and consequently are by and large stereotyped as potentially hazardous in the air. There are exceptions to this, of course, but the healthy pit-of-the-stomach apprehension that normally builds as you go out to fly is trebled when you're scheduled to aviate with a 'Wing Weenie'.

In addition to the Crew Dog/Wing Weenie gulf, there has always been another subtle division within the fighter pilot tribe. The very real difference between fighter pilots and pilots who just happen to fly fighters is rarely discussed, but always present and clearly recognized, at least by the fighter pilots. This is a difficult concept to explain to a layman, but it personifies the arrogance of the breed (not necessarily a bad trait) in that the former designation (fighter pilots) naturally emerge as the Alpha Male figures in a squadron, while pilots who happen to fly fighters are, through no fault of their own, consigned to follower status. I'm not remotely qualified to dissect this concept clinically, but I was always aware of the differences, as were my contemporaries. My old buddy John Allevato recently articulated this concept in a social media joust better than I could:

> 'There was a huge and important distinction between fighter pilots and guys who flew fighters. In the squadrons I was in, you knew the difference immediately, and it had nothing to do with labels. It had everything to with the ability to fly, fight, and lead. If you never met a fighter pilot, you missed one of life's great experiences.'

The management structure and relationships in a fighter squadron are also completely different from those I've seen in any civilian organization. For starters, the boss doesn't sit in an office and watch the underlings perform; that is, not if he's a quality commander. Unlike the typical civilian executive, he spends a sensible amount of time with his flock, where fighter pilots are happiest and most productive, in the cockpit. He will have achieved the same or probably better aviation qualifications than those who work for him. He is typically a flight lead, who can brief and lead multiple ship flights, and perform capably in the squadron's assigned mission, air-to-air, air-to-ground or all the above. Virtually all the best commanders I ever worked for were, in the vernacular, 'good sticks' – talented aviators – and this is, albeit understated, the most glowing accolade a crew dog can bestow on a boss.

This trait pays dividends in a thousand ways: the troops respect the 'Old Man's' flying abilities and his versatility at juggling the demands of tactical flying with the equally challenging responsibility of riding herd on twenty-five or so free-spirited young bucks. It's his responsibility to ensure they are flying safely, their training is up to speed, alternatively praising and disciplining as required to maintain that *esprit de corps* that characterizes a top-notch unit. Oh, and by the way, the boss and his wife are also, unlike their civilian counterparts, the glue that holds the squadron 'family' together. They are the don and matriarch, agony aunt and uncle, child psychiatrist and pediatrician, social organizer, sage philosopher and independent financial advisor all rolled into one neat package, the feminine half of which the Air Force gets for free. Depending on the organizational make-up of the squadron, this 'additional duty' may only pertain to squadron aircrew and their families. In some organizations, however (and the AF, like the Romans, tends to reorganize every few years, just to keep everyone on their toes), the flock will also include squadron aircraft maintainers and support personnel and *their* families, numbering into the hundreds.

Certainly the boss and his lady will delegate much of the day-to-day family stewardship down to ops officers, flight commanders and their significant others, but the extraordinary bosses are always aware of what's going on within the social sphere of the organization and their wives are working just as hard on it from their side. This may have evolved in current culture as far more ladies are involved in serious careers than they were in my day and, in the '70s, '80s and '90s, 'wife' was the accepted designation. The pursuit of success was never an easy one, but it was a helluva lot tougher for the senior officer who wasn't fortunate enough to have a supportive wife as a co-pilot. As a rule of thumb, the flourishing squadron was run by a commander and wife team who were dedicated, empathetic and skilled in the management of people. My Elaine was masterful in this role, applying equal measures of experience, empathy and authority to keep the organization's better halves relatively contented, supportive of their husband's important mission and, in general, pointed in the right direction. This is a very tough role for a wife. She doesn't (or certainly shouldn't) wear her husband's rank and has to generate her own credibility. She is often confronted by officers' wives (both senior and junior to her in the informal pecking order) who are arrogant, pushy, self-serving and downright rude and she has to handle these issues without direct involvement from her old man. I can only recall one instance when, in the interest of unit morale, it was necessary for me to take the offender's husband aside and 'suggest' that he should, in turn, 'advise' his wife that her only acceptable course of action was to put a sock in it.

Occasionally (read on), a squadron is saddled with leadership that is either incompetent or too wrapped up in their own career progression to take reasonable care of the troops and their families. Unless the second-in-command and his wife took the reins, the unit was invariably mediocre, at best. (I'm not being sexist in this discussion; in my day, there were no female flying unit commanders. If necessary, I'll absorb the charges of chauvinism, but that's the way it was.)

Leadership (or not)

Let's go back to the tribe and a word about commanders, ops officers and flight commanders. As in any other profession, there are good, bad and absolutely dreadful bosses. During my quarter-century in the cockpit, I worked for guys who I would have happily followed anywhere, any time because their leadership was so powerful as to earn unconditional loyalty. I haven't got nearly enough space (or the memory) to name them all, but Gerry Cashman, Duke Terry, Chuck Donnelly, Jack Bennett, Dick Fisher, Mac Staples, John 'Ole' Olson, Tommy Thompson, Dick Swope, Billy McCoy, Jim Jamerson, Skip Harbison and Eddie Pickrel immediately come to mind. Only five of them ever pinned on a general's stars, many of them are no longer with us and I'm embarrassed to say I've lost track of the others, but all had something in common: they were genuine, Grade A fighter pilots. I met them all at different stages in my career and I spent virtually all of that career trying to emulate them in one way or another.

These guys weren't one-trick ponies: their talent ranged from brilliance in the air, as pilots, tacticians and aerial choreographers, to that magic and indefinable 'something' that characterizes a superlative leader of people. These were men who could outfly and outthink you in the air, then stand you up against a wall in a flight debriefing and tear little strips off your ego in the presence of your peers (who enjoyed the performance immensely, until it was *their* turn). An hour later, in the bar, he'd buy you a beer, slap you on the back and, in a matter of moments, reattach all those little strips – again in the presence of your peers – because he knew that without them, you were a lesser young fighter pilot and his tribe would be weakened if that situation wasn't resolved.

Unfortunately, there's always that other side of the coin, and I would be negligent if I didn't address the bitter as well as the sweet. The world abounds with bullies, buffoons and bastards; unfortunately some of them find their way into fighter aviation and some of *those* actually reach levels of authority they should never have achieved. Due to the tight team persona of a fighter squadron, its performance and collective morale will soar if it's led by a charismatic boss; conversely, it can plumb the depths if driven by an egotistical, self-serving glory-seeker or a waffling, incompetent marionette. I've served under both types and neither scenario is a pleasant experience.

In the first instance, I once worked for an operations officer who, in my opinion, was adept at passing the buck, sidestepping responsibility and climbing relentlessly over better men to reach his desired goals. His ambition was shameless and he exploited anyone who could forward his personal causes and, perhaps most importantly, blew great volumes of smoke up the bottoms of his bosses to further his individual ambitions. Far be it from me to say he was unpopular, but most of his peers and underlings enthusiastically simulated spitting on the floor whenever his name was mentioned. If he was woefully inadequate as a human being, he was unrivalled at self-promotion and, if there was a visiting journalist, politician or general officer nearby or a public appearance in the offing, he would move heaven and earth to cozy up accordingly.

In a perfect world, a guy like this would get his just desserts by being devoured by piranha or disemboweled during the Pamplona Bull Run. Sadly, in my humble opinion, he employed Lincoln's postulate, fooling some of the people (mainly those he worked for) all of the time and ended up with a couple of stars on his shoulders. He met his end in an Air Force C-21 (executive jet) accident, but I can say with some degree of confidence that most who knew him professionally were somehow able to contain their grief. He'll be popping up again, so henceforth in this dissertation I'll be referring to him cryptically as 'The Politician'.

Another notable encounter with appalling leadership came about as a result of the untimely death of one of the truly charismatic bosses mentioned above. Lieutenant Colonel Gerry Cashman was a superb squadron commander and he had the unflinching respect and loyalty of everyone who served under him in the 614th Tactical Fighter Squadron at Torrejón AB, Spain. During one of our regular deployments to Incirlik, Turkey, he and Captain Ron Bewley, another of the good guys and one of our flight commanders, took off on a single-ship training mission and simply never came back. We all participated in the Search & Rescue (SAR) effort, combing hundreds of miles of the Mediterranean from the rear end of a slow-moving C-130 search aircraft. Nothing was ever found and their disappearance remains technically unexplained to this day.

The Air Force acts quickly in situations such as these, sometimes too quickly. Within days of the accident, a new commander was identified; we didn't know him, as he had been stationed at another base at the time of the accident. We were a tight, disciplined, motivated and professional squadron. Indeed, we had recently won the commander's trophy as the best fighter squadron in the European Theater under Gerry Cashman's command. Despite our despondency at losing one of the truly great skippers, we set out to welcome the new boss with appropriate professionalism. We were keenly aware that he had been thrown in at the deep end with very little notice and would need all the help that we, as a team, could provide. He responded to this collective outstretching of hands with a display of sycophantic toadying towards his superiors that was seriously demoralizing for those of us who were used to reasonable top cover from the skipper. He almost immediately (and very publicly) threw a couple of our colleagues to the wolves for minor transgressions and, within weeks, had earned the nickname 'Ricochet Rabbit' due to his propensity to waffle and/or heave to and fro in search of an elusive decision or, more likely, a scapegoat. We saw some disturbing similarities between 'The Rabbit' and Captain Queeg of *The Caine Mutiny* fame and planted three or four ball bearings in his desk drawer as a gentle (well, maybe not) hint. He didn't get it. Because we were all professionals and fighter pilots, our personal dedication and pride kept us, as a squadron, from going off the deep end. In contrast to the fierce loyalty we had developed for our previous commander, no one was willing to stick their neck out even a few inches to protect 'The Rabbit's' reputation. Consequently, we lost the competitive edge we'd had under adult leadership and our collective performance and eminence suffered. Most of us younger guys who kept a mental journal filed 'The Rabbit' under 'Do not emulate'.

Baiting 'The Rabbit': The Piano

Working for bosses like 'The Rabbit' has an intriguing effect on fighter pilots. The frustration of knowing you can't rely on the skipper gives rise to an immature desire to turn the tables. This leads to some fairly sophisticated plots designed to cause exasperation, anxiety and, with a bit of luck, nervous twitches and tremors. One such plot was hatched after 'The Rabbit' read us all the riot act over some moderately spirited drinking and singing of crude and blasphemous aviation arias at the Incirlik, Turkey Officers' Club. (A few examples: *The Balls of O'Leary*,

Strafe the Town and Kill the People and *Mary Ann Burns, the Queen of all the Acrobats.* Google them; even if you don't approve, you'll find them fascinating.) We were, he pointed out, acting disgracefully and therefore we were banned from the club on the next Friday night. He'd obviously made the assumption that we'd all go to the Base Library instead, but then again he didn't know us very well.

The scheming began almost immediately and we decided it would be appropriate to have a nice sedate barbecue on the patio outside our quarters (with, perhaps, a twist or two thrown in). Our billeting at Incirlik was a reasonably modern two-story dormitory with two to a room overlooking a large circular courtyard, whose seams, ironically, formed a perfect concrete peace symbol. No one ever spent any time in the courtyard as there were far better recreational facilities available elsewhere; however, on this occasion, 'The Rabbit' had denied them to us. With undisputable innocence, we set out to organize the barbecue: food was sourced, a couple of grills were located and for all practical purposes, we emulated a church social planning group preparing for an evening of light entertainment. In the background, the forces of evil were at work (well, 'evil' may be a bit harsh, but there's no denying the boys were up to no good). One of the guys had noticed an ancient piano being transported to the salvage yard and with a minimum of negotiation, secured it for free. We transported it to a safe area, parked it out of sight and my buddy John Allevato, our resident musician, tickled the ivories until he found a reasonable number that still worked and committed them to memory. The stage, as they say, was set...and significantly, one of the boys offhandedly (but intentionally) informed 'The Rabbit' that we had borrowed a piano from the Officers' Club for a tasteful sing-along to atone for our previous appalling behavior.

As dusk fell on Friday, the squadron gathered at the peace symbol for a convivial evening of camaraderie, good food, a beer or two and uplifting music. Most of the group was there, the notable exception being 'The Rabbit' as his perception of leadership and his role as commander didn't involve socializing with the rest of us. Come to think of it, he may have been in the library wondering where all his underlings were.

Hot dogs and burgers sizzled on the grill and John sat down at the piano to prompt the songfest. As few beers had been consumed (and remember, John had a limited number of functional keys), the first tentative attempts at making melody were relatively clean and inoffensive. As time went on and more beer flowed, the volume began to increase and the renditions began to edge towards *I love my wife* (not nearly as romantic as you might think), and one of John's favorites, *Oh, I want to play piano in a whorehouse*.

By nine o'clock or so, no one particularly cared whether the piano was providing tuneful accompaniment or not and what had begun as a reasonable attempt at harmony a couple of hours earlier had transitioned into a piercing cacophony unfettered by any semblance of rhythm. Only a few of us were aware (spontaneity was key to success here) that imminently it would be…Showtime!

The performance began as the combined voices of a dozen or so somewhat inebriated aviators soared in a stirring rendition of 'Dear Mom your *SON* is dead, he bought the *FARM* today; he crashed his *OV-10* on Ho Chi Minh's highway….' (bellowed to the tune of Edith Piaf's *Milord*, but without a single fragment of the Little Sparrow's renowned grace and style).

Up on the corridor that circumnavigated the dormitory's first floor, a lone figure appeared in his boxer shorts. I'll call him Boudreaux, for indeed, that is his name. Bud looked out on the revelry going on below him and in a clear, commanding voice roared: 'Hey, knock it off down there, I've got an early briefing tomorrow, trying to get some sleep!'

A couple of choir members glanced in his direction, but didn't miss a beat as they continued the serenade: '……He made a *ROCKET* pass and then he *BUSTED* his ass; HMmmmm, HMmmmmm, HMmmmmm!'

Bud went back into his room, emerging a few minutes later with the same demand, slightly louder and much more aggressively. John continued to tickle the operable ivories, the choral group launched into another, even more vigorous cacophony and Bud again retreated.

When, some moments later, he reappeared, he was wielding the fire axe kept on the dormitory passageway for emergencies. Inexplicably, a number of other crew dogs (some clutching similar tools) emerged with him and they all converged on John and his slightly dysfunctional piano. As most of the gathered brethren were not read in, the collective reaction when Bud buried his axe in the piano was at first shock, then bewilderment, followed by what can only be described as bemused fascination. Bud's impulsive band of allies energetically joined in and the piano was systematically reduced to kindling with John smiling broadly and continuing to attempt to play what little was left of it. Kindling being the operative word, the next step involved a number of curiously well-prepared merrymakers who torched the rapidly disappearing piano, causing flames to shoot into the night sky. A few of the brothers had appropriated a quantity of survival devices – pen gun flares which were fired from spring-loaded cylinders – from the squadron's life-support stores. These added a touch of carnival to the proceedings, hurling brightly blazing projectiles a few hundred feet into the darkness. Each pen gun launch was now accompanied by an appreciative 'Whooooaaaaaa!!' from the assembled multitude, and the surreal specter of the blazing piano, howling fighter pilots and arcing pen gun flares is a memory I'll forever treasure.

Within a scant few moments, our revelry was shattered by the arrival of two separate and distinct forces of all that is good and right with the world. First, a sizable Security Police delegation in a phalanx of vehicles, complete with M16 assault rifles and accompanied by snarling German Shepherds struggling to break free of their leashes and savage a few drunks. They were followed in short order by 'The Rabbit', obviously tipped off by the base command post that his flock was wreaking havoc at their home away from home. He pulled up in his commander's pickup truck and screeched to a halt, surveying the pandemonium around him with widening eyes and quivering lip, looking much like the small furry animal whose tag he unsuspectingly bore, when cornered by a hungry fox.

The simultaneous arrival of the *Gendarmes* and our valiant commander had an abrupt calming effect on the proceedings. Pleasantly inebriated and full of high spirits we might be, but we weren't totally mindless. As one of our southern boys was prone to say: 'Momma didn't raise no FOOL!'

Indeed, for many of us, the source of entertainment swiftly shifted from piano conflagration to 'Rabbit's' reaction. We watched surreptitiously as he took in the entire panorama which was unfolding before his eyes: the piano was now little more than a smoldering pile of ashes but 'The

Rabbit's' expression betrayed his belief that it was the *Officers' Club's* smoldering pile of ashes. He was clearly envisaging the remnants of his career wafting into the summer sky along with the wisps of gray smoke it was generating.

This image was reinforced by the base's entire Security Police population, most of whom, accompanied by a canine colleague, were striding resolutely around the scene of the crime, looking for agitators. There weren't any, of course, as the perpetrators had now adopted the persona of a troupe of altar boys out for a stroll on the village green. The cops were losing interest as it was becoming increasingly obvious they wouldn't have an opportunity to bust any heads or release the dogs to maul any criminals.

'The Rabbit', however, decided his last hope was to assert his authority to bring the situation to a conclusion that would establish him as the fearless leader, righter of wrongs. He purposefully strode around the area, confronting one after the other of us, confident someone would betray us all and name the ringleaders, who would then be suitably pilloried and brought, on their knees, to justice.

Instead, what he got from all and sundry was the 'USAFE Salute' and this must now be explained to be appreciated. The United States Air Forces in Europe (USAFE) was our major command staff, overseeing all European operational matters from their headquarters at Ramstein Air Base in Germany. The headquarters was populated by a mixture of higher-level shoe clerks and unfortunate aviators who were either shanghaied against their will or (suspiciously) joined the headquarters voluntarily as a stepping-stone to promotion. In any event, not unlike their even loftier counterparts in the Pentagon (often referred to by aviators as Fort Fumble, the Puzzle Palace or the five-sided wind tunnel), their judgment, decisions and very existence were questioned by those of us who considered ourselves at the pointy end of the spear. Frankly, although the HQ wielded a great deal of power over us all, we believed them to be utterly clueless.

The USAFE salute, then, was the physical gesture that most effectively portrayed our considered assessment of HQ capability: palms upraised and extended slightly forward accompanied by an exaggerated shrug of the shoulders and a facial expression of complete and utter bewilderment.

Occasionally this could be supplemented verbally: 'Ahh, *I* dunno', but 99 per cent of the time a silent salute successfully conveyed the desired message.

It was this defining gesticulation 'The Rabbit' encountered repeatedly as he attempted to unravel the actions, motives and most importantly the identities of the guilty bastards who had committed these heinous acts (and dashed his fantasies of accelerated career progression).

As 'The Rabbit' lurched from one USAFE-saluter to the next, the gathering slowly dissolved, the police took Rin-Tin-Tin and his friends back to the kennels and the altar boys drifted away from the site of Armageddon, finally leaving 'The Rabbit' alone, wondering where it had all gone wrong and how could he salvage the shreds of his deteriorating command.

For the next couple of days, we surreptitiously watched 'The Rabbit' like hawks. When the phone rang he trembled slightly and he'd developed a perceptible facial tic, waiting for the Officers' Club to confront him about returning their piano. To the best of my knowledge, no one ever enlightened him and forty-odd years later, I occasionally have invigorating thoughts that somewhere, he may well be looking over his shoulder for the piano Gestapo at this very minute.

Chapter Five

The 'Lucky Devils'

Serving under 'The Rabbit' aside, probably the most gratifying squadron assignment I ever had was with the 353rd (which in 1971 was redesignated as the 614th Tactical Fighter Squadron, the 'Lucky Devils'). I was initially less than positive about linking up with this crowd only because I had volunteered for but not been granted a second combat tour assignment in South-East Asia and I was having a moderate sulk about this rejection.

At this point, you have no doubt stopped reading, and are shaking your head and thinking 'What kind of an idiot *volunteers* for a second year-long opportunity to be shot down, killed or captured?' Well, I'll provide my rationale and let you form your own conclusions. At the end of my first tour, December 1969, I was a 24-year-old bachelor, flying the hottest airplane in the world in a combat environment that allowed a great deal of flexibility in applying virtually all the skills I had assimilated in my chosen profession, fighter aviation. In short, I was doing exactly what I aspired to when I pointed at that F-4 on the commander's blackboard on judgment day at the culmination of flight training.

So, as briefly as I can put it, barring the aforementioned shoot-down, death or capture, a second tour would give me another twelve months to live the dream. Unfortunately, the slave-traders who dealt out assignments at the Military Personnel Center in San Antonio, Texas had denied me this golden opportunity and I was not best pleased with the peacetime alternative they forced upon me.

Resentful though I was over this flagrant rejection, I gradually became aware of a few mitigating factors. The 614th, one of three squadrons assigned to the 401st Tactical Fighter Wing, was based at Torrejón, just a few miles east of Madrid, a vibrant, stimulating city. In one of our less direct assaults on good taste, wherever we went, we referred to ourselves as 'The Spanish Flyers'.

The US dollar was riding high against European currencies, particularly the Spanish peseta; living a slightly different dream in Madrid was cheap. Also, in contrast to Vietnam, Laos and Cambodia it was exceedingly rare to be shot at while flying over Spain.

Indeed, as I became more immersed in peacetime flying, the more relaxed I became about plying my trade in Europe rather than South-East Asia. A suitable abode would go a long way towards easing the pain of what I initially perceived to be a far less stimulating aviation environment. Two other bachelors, one each from the other two fighter squadrons, and I secured a magnificent ninth-floor penthouse apartment in one of Madrid's trendier areas for the princely sum of just over $350 per month (*in toto*). The fact that each squadron deployed to Turkey for thirty days in a continuous rotation ensured that only two of us would be sharing this palatial accommodation at any one time.

As I had recently completed 204 combat missions over North Vietnam, Laos and occasionally Cambodia, I felt justified in rewarding myself with an appropriate gift for having survived the fracas. This took the form of a shiny new white Porsche 911T and, due to the exchange rate previously mentioned, it set me back all of $6,100.00 (yeah, I know, that was still an awful lot of money in 1970, but hell, this was a Porsche!). One of my roommates already had purchased a 911 (in Day-Glo orange) and the third followed suit quickly with a navy-blue model. We kept them all parked in a nearby garage that serviced our apartment and paid next to nothing to have them cleaned, polished and otherwise pampered in ways that I now consider mildly embarrassing.

We also hired a maid, as befits three young *bon vivants* in Madrid. She was a cheerful, rotund 60-ish Spanish señora named Candi who spoke not a word of English, but bustled about the apartment three or four days a week rectifying the horrible mess we persistently left in our wake, darning and ironing our skivvies, and rendering the place resplendent over and over again. We paid her far more than the going rate, which still wasn't nearly what she was worth to us, but occasionally supplemented those morsels with sweets and other goodies from the base for her grandchildren. Her eyes lit up when one of us passed her a bit of 'Yankee treasure' – a sack of Butterfingers, Baby Ruths and Almond Joys – and she would reciprocate by conjuring up a wondrous tortilla brimming with onions, peppers, and tomatoes; we invariably got the best of the arrangement.

While peacetime aviating in España offered little of the day-to-day raw excitement and tension of South-East Asia, it was still flying fighters for a living and we were a very close-knit outfit. Playing hard was an important part of the equation and we took great advantage of our Spanish environment (and that favorable exchange rate). Wives and families were an integral part of the peacetime squadron composition and they, too, enjoyed the pulsating social life Madrid afforded us. We regularly had squadron parties in town at some of the most upmarket venues, and despite the shenanigans you would expect from a large group of mainly 20- and 30-year-olds, they were stylish events: jackets and ties for the gents and fashionable frocks for their ladies. Our sole departure from reasonably good taste was our small group of Am Dram comedians, the Skit House Players, purveyors of bawdy satire. Our revelries went well into the wee hours – great food, freely flowing drink – and we were truly enjoying the good life.

Olé

One of the genuine delights of being stationed abroad was the opportunity to adopt a bit of the local culture for socializing. My single fondest memory of Spanish festivities revolves around the Finca (Spanish for an 'estate' or 'ranch') party. The Finca we frequented was a sprawling hacienda a few miles outside the city. There was a large central farmhouse with plenty of room for merrymaking, a swimming pool and, as the business of the rancher was breeding and raising fighting bulls for Spain's most popular blood sport, a slightly smaller than regulation size bullring. The significance of this edifice will emerge later. We had a few of these bashes while I plied my trade with the 'Lucky Devils', but one in particular stands out from the rest.

On a beautiful sunny Spanish Sunday in late July 1970, the 'Lucky Devils' headed out of town for the aforementioned Finca. All anticipated a terrific time and none were to be disappointed. A brief sidelight here: in 1970, certainly in Spain, there was no danger whatsoever of being accosted for driving under the influence or similar transgressions. I cannot recall whether these offences simply did not exist or were totally ignored by Franco's paramilitary police force, *la Guardia Civil*. I do remember that no one spent any time at all worrying about it and, to the best of my knowledge, no one was ever apprehended for motoring offenses during my four-year tour. Consequently, when we set sail for the Finca, we did so in convoy.

The festivities were centered on a superb barbecue and copious quantities of that most quaffable of Spanish delights, sangria. This sangria, mixed by our host, the affable rancher, was quality stuff and very, very potent. By mid-afternoon, we were all well fed and watered and more than ready for a hearty dose of *Viva España*. A few languished by the pool, soaking up the Iberian sunshine, but most headed for the bullring and the entertainment that would surely be provided there.

The revelries began in a relatively civil fashion. Wives and girlfriends were 'invited' to enter the arena where our host, in seriously fractured English, announced a unique sporting competition whose triumphant winner would be rewarded with a bottle of (what else) very fine *vino tinto*. As most of the adventurous ladies in the group were already reasonably well-oiled, the motivational aspect of the liquid trophy was secondary and they were well and truly up for the scrimmage to come. Ominously placed in the center of the bullring was a large box. Although none of us not involved was aware of what was to come, our host quietly gathered the ladies and, amid much tittering, gave them their rules of engagement. He then strode to the box and dramatically lifted it to reveal...chickens! Dozens of them. Once abruptly released from their cool dark prison, they acted, well, very much like headless chickens. Clucking and squawking with great vigor, they headed in virtually every direction, hotly pursued by otherwise sophisticated officers' ladies whose focus was now on bagging as many as possible in the quest for a 750ml flagon of Marqués de Riscal Reserva (which none of them really needed by this time). Now, if you've never actually tried it, you probably won't realize just how difficult it is to capture a free-ranging capon intent on evasion. The other thing you may not be aware of is just how hilarious the spectacle of a dozen or more ladies trying to effect such a capture really is. The combination of aggressive pursuit punctuated by squealing indecision whenever a targeted fowl stood its ground can only be fondly remembered, if not accurately described. The whoops and guffaws of those assembled to watch ensured that those previously reclining by the swimming pool quickly joined the rest of us as we delighted in the sight of what could best be described as spirited chaos. The pandemonium continued for some fifteen minutes, after which the squadron womenfolk were clearly breathless, exhausted, but most of all jubilant (unlike the chickens, who appeared decidedly glum in the pen in which they had been deposited by their captors).

How could you follow this spectacle, you may ask, but our *amigo* the rancher had done this before and, with the help of the squadron boss, recruited two teams of eight men each from the four flights comprising the squadron configuration. A long line was drawn in the dust at the center of the ring and teams were arranged, on each side of the line facing each other. The rancher produced a long thick rope and it was obvious that what he had in mind was a classic tug of war.

Ho, hum…not much excitement there, we heckled, but he quietened the unruly onlookers with a wave of his hand, a twinkle in his eye, and a very theatrical wink. Once again, the stakes were defined, and once again the prize was a bottle of the Marqués de Riscal's finest for each member on the winning side.

The teams were instructed, the lines of pure muscular combat established, and battle commenced with a loud whistle. Each team strained mightily against their adversaries and ground was gained and lost, step by step. Ho, hum…

After a minute or so of this less-than-scintillating entertainment, a vertical gate at one end of the ring slid silently upwards and our warriors sensed more than realized that they had company. Bad company. Advancing just inside the ring, alert and obviously fascinated by the spectacle of swearing, perspiring, grunting young men pulling ropes before him was one of our host's prize fighting bulls (to be). Not yet a fully-fledged *Toro Bravo* (who would someday weigh in at 1,400 to 1,600lb), this beefy apprentice was less than a year old and little more than a calf. He weighed somewhere around 300 to 350lb and had small blunt instruments where large curved sharpened horns would someday appear. Nevertheless, this young fellow was being groomed for the big time and he was self-assured, with ears erect and a distinct enthrallment with what was occurring a few yards in front of him. Fighting bulls are selected primarily for a certain combination of aggression, energy, strength and stamina and Junior here undoubtedly had all these traits in abundance. The spectators saw him first and an apprehensive 'Whoooaaaaaaaaaaa!!!' welled up from the sidelines.

Hearing this, our noble contestants hastily looked around for the source of the anxiety and having seen the burly intruder eyeing them from the end of the arena, many of them instinctively uttered the universal fighter pilot expression signifying far-reaching concern: 'Oh, shit!'

Credit given where it is due, despite this new and somewhat astonishing dimension to what only a moment ago was a humdrum tug of war, not one of the participants broke ranks to flee for the safe haven available outside the ring. The competition continued unabated (well, perhaps slightly abated) for the contestants now seemed to be spending a fair amount of time keeping track of the interloper. For his part, the neophyte *Toro* was beginning to take a much keener interest in the strange tableau before him: sixteen fit young men with a long rope in their hands, moving jerkily back and forth. You could almost read his mind: 'These creatures seem to be enjoying themselves and *this* looks like something I want to get involved in…'

Of course, get involved he did. With a toss of his brawny head, he cruised towards the sweating, swearing gladiators in the center of the ring. As he at least appeared to be comparatively small, most of the combatants continued the contest, evading the charge as best they could while maintaining a firm hold on the rope. The bullock glanced off a couple of the warriors, then caught one squarely and effortlessly tossed him aside where he landed in a crumpled heap in the dust. Observing this one-sided scuffle, a number of the lads uttered the magic word for the second time – 'Shit!' – and the complexion of the contest changed abruptly. Torn between not wishing to let the side down and not wanting to join their buddy curled up in a fetal position in the dust, our heroes began what can best be described as a Keystone Cops parody. Tug of war now conveniently marginalized, they forfeited all semblance of synchronization and composure. Much to the delight of the assembled audience, they collided, tripped, stumbled and collapsed, individually and in small intertwined groups, while the marauding baby bull ran amok. The more havoc he wreaked on the now-cowering competitors, the more galvanized he became. One or two at a time, the campaigners surreptitiously abandoned the tournament and hastily found their way to one of the small gates in the ring, accompanied by the hoots, whistles and catcalls of their compatriots, already comfortably ensconced in the safe seats alongside the arena. Thanks to an inventive rancher, elusive chickens and a neophyte *Toro*, the party was proceeding quite nicely, thank you.

Throughout the spectacles of chicken-chasing and veal-assisted tug of war, those not actively participating were taking advantage of a world-class barbecue washed down with copious quantities of potent but very deceptive sangria that slid down smoothly, just like the fruit juices that supplemented its rioja foundation. The assembled multitude was now, in mid-afternoon, reaching delightful levels of jolly inebriation and it was within this congenial setting that the day's main entertainment event was launched.

In Spain, bullfighting was in its heyday in the '60s and early '70s. Matadors were the rock stars of their day in Iberia, and none was more renowned than Manuel Benítez Pérez, more commonly known as El Cordobés (as he had originated in the Andalusian city of Córdoba). Using bold, unconventional physical techniques and sporting a commanding flair in the ring, he had a massive following among Spanish youth. He was young, courageous, handsome, athletic, charismatic and innovative and, Dear Reader, after more glasses of sangria than I care to remember on that hot summer's day... so was I.

Consequently, when the call went out for brave *toreros* to step forward for the amusement of their compatriots and families in the First Annual 'Lucky Devils' *corridas de toros*, yours truly was the first to be upstanding (more or less). From that moment on, in certain circles and situations, I became more commonly known not as *El Michigander* (reflecting my own humble birthplace), but instead as *El bufón* (the buffoon).

There were three of us, as I recall; shades of Larry, Moe and Curly. We were all bachelors, all in the moderate to severe stages of intoxication and, therefore, immortal. As I had stumbled forward first, I was given the honor (?) of being *numero uno* to face *El Toro* in the ring. I was dressed for the occasion, not in the traditionally flamboyant 'Suit of Lights' fashioned in the forerunner of Spandex emblazoned with sequins and other sparkly bits, but in a reasonably conservative pair of slacks and a short-sleeved shirt with a button-down collar. As I strode (well, it felt like striding to me; others advised later it was more of a lurch) into the arena, my new best friend the rancher handed me a *capote de brega* – a bullfighter's red cape – and wished me luck (at least I <u>think</u> that's what he said; his command of English was feeble and, looking back, I can't help thinking I heard the word *bufón*).

I managed to find my way to center arena, visions of thrashing a huge *Toro Bravo* revolving in my head; hell, I could almost hear the stirring bullfight trumpet fanfare. It wasn't long before the small gate opposite slid upward and another muscle-bound miniature *Toro* made his appearance. Slightly smaller than the great disruptor of the tug of war, he still topped 200 pounds of dynamite, jet black with a massive neck and shoulders and two thankfully underdeveloped blunt horns. He was momentarily distracted by the whistles and taunts from the spectators – all directed at me – but soon became aware of the intruder standing nonchalantly in *his* bullring. Harking back to Tyrone Power in *Blood and Sand*, I puffed out my chest, waved my *capote de brega* elegantly and barked '*Hola, Toro!!*' ('Hello, Bull!!' Well, it seemed like a good idea at the time). His response to this friendly greeting was a lowering of his mammoth head, a loud snort, and a narrowing of the eyes which, despite my energetic waving of the cape, appeared to be focused directly on my crotch. Without further ado, he tossed his head, snorted again and accelerated in my direction. Forgetting all about Tyrone Power (and El Cordobés, for that matter) I flung the cape in one direction and pirouetted (well, staggered, actually) in the other. Much to my surprise – and his, I assume – he missed me completely. Confidence flowed back into my veins along with abundant adrenaline and I was now ready to fulfill my destiny as a matador. I turned back to him, waved the cape and tossed my head in triumph. Once again, illustrious. My *Toro* was momentarily thwarted, but again as he turned to confront me, his gaze locked onto the family jewels. He shook his head from side to side, lowered it and once again set sail in my direction. Inebriated tactician that I was, I figured the same maneuver that worked before would succeed again. *Toro* wasn't buying it. As the *capote de brega* fanned to the left and I quick-stepped to the right, I looked into his eyes and saw *bufón* written all over his face. He dropped his head, planted one of his blunted horns in my thigh (thankfully missing the *cojones* by an inch or so) and with a nonchalant upward flick of that great neck, propelled all 190lb of me vertically. I missed the next few seconds, but somewhere out there is a long-lost photo of yours truly, inverted, on the way back to meet *terra firma* head-first. Final score: Toddler Toro 1; well-oiled fighter pilot 0.

Something in my right shoulder went pop when I bit the dust, but it is important to note that at no time did I lose consciousness. Indeed, for the rest of the afternoon, buoyed by my new-found notoriety (and quite a bit more sangria) I paddled happily around in the pool and stoically ignored the pain while draining the last few hours' enjoyment out of a hot Spanish Sunday afternoon.

The significance of my folly wasn't obvious until the following morning, when I awoke to find my right arm was no longer functioning properly and indeed, was hanging at an angle that resulted, appropriately, in my knuckles nearly dragging the floor. Somehow, I managed to get dressed and into the car, but immediately realized that shifting my five-on-the-floor gear lever was going to be today's Mission Impossible. I kneed the lever into first and crept down the road in front of my apartment, keenly aware that Madrid's horn-blowing drivers were going to have a field day berating me. Then....a miracle happened: I spotted a young American airman waiting for a bus to the Air Base. I pulled over, asked him if he'd like a lift and, when I had him trapped in the passenger seat, I tried to diplomatically explain why I would need his services as a gear-shifter. He looked at me as if I had said 'Would you like some candy, young man?' but slowly it dawned on him that I was genuinely in pain rather than perverted. He shifted artfully for the dozen or so miles to the Air Base and its state-of-the-art hospital, no doubt considering what he was going to tell his buddies in the jet propulsion shop about the weird fighter pilot who had accosted him in town.

I struggled into the hospital and, on the strength of the flight suit I was wearing, I managed to jump the queue to see our assigned squadron flight surgeon who took one look at me and said 'Went to the Finca party yesterday, eh?' He continued by telling me I was the third 'Lucky Devil' he'd seen that morning in varying states of suffering and by far the least ambulatory. After an X-ray that highlighted a broken collarbone and some gentle poking and prodding, he announced that my aviating for the next six weeks or so was hereby curtailed; unhappily placed in a category known to us as DNIF (Duty Not Involving Flying). This meant temporary banishment to the land of the shoe clerk: answering phones, shuffling paperwork and generally paying for my stupidity of the previous afternoon with a numbingly mundane existence. Looking back, however, I was, yet again, fortunate. Although forced to absorb the jeers and unbridled mockery of my peers, I was spared the fate of today's fighter pilot, who would undoubtedly face far more severe sanctions – including formal disciplinary actions – in an era of humorless leadership.

Some twenty-four years later, at my retirement party on Mount Charleston just outside Las Vegas, I was surprised and delighted when formally presented with a framed copy of the paperwork that un-grounded me and realizing that I am likely to be the only Air Force pilot possessing an official medical record proclaiming: 'Captain Ladd fractured his right clavicle while fighting a bull.'

Ah, there you have it: my fifteen minutes of fame.

The Spanish Fliers Invade England

I couldn't move on from this discussion without mentioning the dramatic participation of the 'Lucky Devils' in one of life's great experiences, my wedding. I met my bride-to-be Elaine in Madrid. She's English and was teaching in a Spanish school when we met up. It would be misleading of me to claim I swept her off her feet; wooing her was a challenge on a number of levels. She was neither particularly fond of Yanks, nor the least bit awed by my fighter pilot credentials; it took some time and effort to convince her that I was telling her the truth about my profession. Even my shiny new Porsche didn't convince her: she thought it was a SEAT; a misidentification that triggered some mild and temporary friction. Nevertheless, I gradually gained ground and, while we were dating, she validated her 'right stuff' qualifications (it takes a very special lady to tolerate a fighter pilot), putting up with my numerous absences and sophomoric antics with patience and good humor.

I attempted to influence her by mentioning I had often used her home town of Wallasey as a turn point on cross-country flights, guided by TACAN Channel 44, a navigational radio beacon a quarter of a mile from her house. She finally believed me when, just before the wedding, we took a walk and I pointed out what looked like a large traffic cone near the shoreline of the Irish Sea: 'Channel 44,' I said, very much vindicated.

Inevitably, and rather hastily, we set a date in January 1973. There was no ulterior motive in this swiftness; I simply wasn't interested in treading water. I had to settle on a phone call to ask her Mum and Dad for her hand and having gained that approval, set about organizing a very short-notice wedding (by English standards). In the background, some of my buddies were lobbying our commander for approval to attend the ceremony and, since the squadron couldn't spare a substantial number of aircrew away on a boondoggle for a few days, the only option was to convert that boondoggle to a training opportunity. Enter the fighter pilot's favorite off-duty diversion, the cross-country (XC).

A brief explanation: the cross-country consisted of a number of navigational training sorties, often to desirable locations (Copenhagen, Amsterdam, Munich and Taipei ring some very enjoyable bells for me). The only firm destination requirement in my day was the existence of a nearby military air base that could service and refuel the aircraft. The definition of 'nearby' was flexible, depending on the popularity of the selected destination. In the '70s and '80s the cross-country was a genuine treat. There were no requirements for a certain number of sorties or training hours, so the typical XC was an outbound sortie (we could make the Værløse Royal Danish AFB from Torrejón in a single hop, barely). Once we had the aircraft parked, we were free to undertake other maneuvers in Copenhagen, returning a couple days later for the long flight home. As the years have gone by, my sources tell me, the cross-country has become the target of the 'Good Deal Committee', an alleged cabal located in the bowels of the Pentagon whose mission it is to root out potentially pleasurable activities and curtail or if possible eradicate them. These days, that idyllic trip to Copenhagen would involve a mandatory two or three legs each way with a couple more in the intervening day(s) just to keep the aircrew off the streets and out of the bars.

In the case of my impending nuptials, our boss went to bat for us and elevated the XC request to the wing's deputy commander for operations, Colonel Chuck Donnelly, one of the good guys. He agreed to approve the boondoggle navigational training flights, but with a couple of reasonable restrictions. First, the potential for atrocious weather in England in January required some mitigation. Colonel Donnelly approved a seven-aircraft deployment comprising a four- and a three-ship which would need to land at separate bases to avoid all being grounded by regional poor weather. Secondly, the wedding was on a Saturday afternoon. The flights were cleared to depart Torrejón on Friday morning but were required back by mid-day on Monday. Pretty sensible, we all thought.

This was one instance where the definition of 'nearby' was stretched to the limit. Elaine and I were to be married in Wallasey, Wirral, near Liverpool in north-west England, and all the available air bases were in central and eastern counties. The flight leaders planned on RAF Bentwaters in East Anglia (which you'll be reading much more about later) and RAF Upper Heyford in Oxfordshire.

So it came to pass, on 5 January 1973, seven F-4 loads of 'Spanish Flyers' made their way from these RAF bases into London to rendezvous, then travel north together to Wallasey where the inhabitants hadn't set eyes on a Yank since 1945. Because of the likelihood of no-shows due to bad weather and other potential calamities, we hadn't told Elaine's mother that there would be fourteen additional guests (although Elaine had greased all the skids for accommodation and seats at the wedding reception). After the boys had assembled in London, all fourteen tried to wedge into a British telephone box to call for directions to Wallasey; we then broke the happy news to Mum and watched the color drain from her face. The shock of a legion of unannounced guests may even have surpassed the jolt of meeting her future son-in-law for the first time only six days earlier. We calmed her down, briefed her on the contingency plan, and looked forward to the Big Day.

I'm not going to ramble on about the wedding, but the owner/manager of the Stanley Hotel in nearby Hoylake, where we had the reception, had been a purser on Cunard Lines and was a great fan of Americans in general (and inexplicably, Pittsburgh's baseball team, the Pirates). He made it his mission to put on a helluva show. He succeeded, sourcing the Stars and Stripes from the US Embassy to provide accompaniment for the Union Jack in the decorations, accommodating all my squadron mates in the hotel and arranging a round of golf for them at the world-class

Hoylake course. He also hosted my stag party the night before which, unsurprisingly, involved substantial alcohol consumption and the telling of numerous and sundry war stories. Happily, we were many years ahead of the current fashion of handcuffing a naked groom-to-be to a lamppost or tying him up for a freight train journey to destinations unknown. Indeed, the Wirral being extremely civilized, a somewhat wasted groom-to-be, Ed Thomas, the 'best Bear', and Elaine's cousin Cliff were safely escorted home by the local constabulary.

We had a beautiful, traditional English white wedding at the 900-year-old St Hilary's Church. The wedding breakfast and evening buffet went without a hitch; not a punch was thrown and the 'Spanish Flyers' behaved impeccably except for my buddy John, whose thunderous fart in the midst of a dignified group photo brought the house down. The guys did leave their mark on the distinguished guests, however. As we were chatting about the events of the day with the family, Elaine's grandmother, stone deaf since she was a teenager, revealed a less significant but enlightening episode. In her quavering, high-pitched voice, she said with obvious good nature: 'They were lovely boys, the Americans, but you know, after dinner, one of them ate my corsage.' Exit the 'Spanish Flyers', stage right. I expected nothing less and hey, I've got to say, it was the best wedding I ever attended.

SOS (No, not *that* one)

At this point, I'm compelled to make another brief diversion from the thrust of my story to report one of the low ebbs of my career: a fourteen-week pause in the action known as the Squadron Officers' School or SOS (not to be confused with the renowned military delicacy of creamed beef on toast or, more commonly, Shit on a Shingle). Professional military education is a necessary Air Force evil if you are to make any progress at all and, while the preferred (read 'painless') method for achieving it is by correspondence, some are shanghaied and I was 'it'. Despite spirited evasive maneuvers, I was tagged for this ordeal by my boss, 'The Rabbit', shortly after Elaine and I were wed.

I'm not going to dwell on SOS, but it was, as best as I can describe it, a Scout Jamboree with mandatory academics. I shouldn't be so harsh; some of the courses were interesting, but the structured games and compulsory camaraderie were cringeworthy and the program was about four times as long as it needed to be (this was remedied, unfortunately after I left. It's now six weeks long). The final nail in the coffin, as far as I was concerned, was the fact that all this enjoyment was conducted at Maxwell AFB in swingin' Montgomery, Alabama, home of brown bag liquor laws and the Bible Belt; not the recommended setting to introduce your British bride to the good ol' USA. We were both seriously underwhelmed, but true love prevailed.

Despite our overall disenchantment with the program, there were a couple of high points worthy of note. Most of us brought our wives and they were 'encouraged' to join the fun. We were split into sections and each section had nicknames ('Tigers' for us) and colors (neon orange, naturally). The wives were responsible for coming up with uniforms which could be worn on sports days for cheerleading and other buffoonery. Our group of wives agreed on loose-fitting big girls' pants and floppy sweatshirts which made them look like orange Teletubbies. Elaine was happy with this outcome for about thirty seconds, but she was young, shapely, free-spirited and handy with a pair of scissors, needle and thread. In a single evening, she had converted her double-knit baggies into a pair of short shorts and a halter top exposing a fair amount of midriff. She wore this outfit to the big volleyball game the next day and, predictably, the other wives were incandescent with green-eyed rage, but my teammates were (secretly) most appreciative and I was very proud indeed.

Nearing course completion, I faced a conflict of massive proportions. There was a class talent show (really!) scheduled on a particular evening. Those of us who had no discernible talent were expected to attend and cheer on our classmates who read poetry, balanced spinning plates, or gargled the Number One hit on the pop charts. On the same evening, a moderately celebrated entertainer named Ray Charles was performing at the Officers' Club. Now I don't know what Ray was doing at an obscure military officers' club either, but I was loath to waste an opportunity to find out. I agonized over this scheduling quandary for as long as it took to dial the 'O' Club and reserve a table for eight.

The following morning I was summoned to have a chat with my section leader, Captain Reggie Williams. For a shoe clerk, Reggie was categorically a good guy, intelligent, enthusiastic and motivated by his role within the SOS staff. He appealed to my sense of loyalty to the team, my innate sense of duty and honor and chided me for leading three other class members and their wives astray by skipping the mandatory function. Reggie was right, of course, and I apologized but I'm only slightly embarrassed to admit that I walked out of his office cheerfully humming *Hit the Road, Jack*.

Just as SOS drew to a close, our South-East Asia PoWs were released by North Vietnam and returned to the States in what was designated Operation HOMECOMING. Groups of these guys fanned out to share their experiences with those of us who had been luckier. Among those who visited Maxwell AFB was my best friend from high school, Tom Hanton. His wife Pat accompanied him and Elaine and I 'sponsored' them for the few days they spent with us.

Tom and I went way back; notably, we (and a couple of cronies) were suspended from Lakenheath High School in England for setting 'The Queen's' outhouse alight on school property, but that's another story. Tom's visit was the most worthwhile event of our time in Alabama and we still renew our bond regularly to this day.

Having endured the indignities of SOS, I was delighted to return to Spain and the challenge of being a fighter pilot.

Deterrence

Autumn 1971; 0743 hours (7.43 am in civilian time). Eight young men begin the day in a prefabricated four-bedroom building adjacent to the end of the 12,000ft-long runway at Incirlik Air Base near Adana in south-eastern Turkey. A few are wide awake, draped over old overstuffed chairs with cracked faux leather upholstery reading yesterday's *Stars and Stripes*, the daily Yank newspaper printed overseas for America's military. Others (myself included) begin to emerge from their double bedrooms (no more than cubicles with two single beds, really; this is not opulent accommodation). This securely-fenced enclosure is home sweet home for the 401st Tactical Fighter Wing (TFW) Victor Alert force for the next three days and nights. Outside the spartan accommodation block and a similar structure housing our alert maintenance crews there are four hardened aircraft shelters (HAS). Each of these houses a McDonnell Douglas F-4E Phantom II fighter-bomber. The aircraft are simply configured with two 370-gallon fuel tanks on outboard wing pylons, an inboard Electronic Countermeasure (ECM) pod and the sole reason we are here: a single centerline-mounted B-61 Y3 thermonuclear weapon with yields selectable up to 345 kilotons (or 345,000 tons of TNT destructive power). By way of comparison, 'Little Boy' detonated over Hiroshima in August 1945 yielded only 16 kilotons of fire and brimstone.

It is my first tour on Victor Alert as an aircraft commander. I'm paired with an experienced weapons systems officer (or 'GIB', 'Guy in the Back') who will, no doubt, give me lots of good advice if/when the klaxon goes off. Our job will then be to get airborne within five minutes, follow a predetermined (and meticulously planned and studied) route and deliver our sleek aluminum weapon with a very chic mahogany nosecone against a tactical target in southern Russia. We can expect to be tested once or twice a tour with a simulated scramble order which sends us sprinting to our steeds to await a valid launch message. We cannot enter the 'No Lone Zone' in which the nuke-loaded aircraft is housed without the other crew member. We can never start engines using the explosive cartridges fitted for that purpose until the two of us have authenticated such a message individually and compared the lengthy alphanumeric code inside the sealed 'cookie' we each have in our cockpits. There are armed security policemen at each HAS to ensure we do not violate any of the myriad rules governing handling of nuclear weapons. They are not, in this environment, impressed by the officers' rank on our shoulders and they will use their weapons without hesitation if we are assessed to be infringing the deadly serious protocols under which we operate. As the only 'FNG' ('Fucking New Guy') on this week's alert team, I'm determined to perform flawlessly and, as we never know when the balloon could go up for real, I'm spending the day in an uncomfortable state of barely disguised exhilaration tempered with a deep abiding dread.

I don't have long to wait. As I settle down in an easy chair with a newspaper and start to trade banter with my comrades, the door is flung open and our senior crew chief breathlessly appears ringing a large, extremely loud cowbell. Eight of America's finest leap to their feet and jostle for position heading out the door where we begin the sprint start to the aircraft. My heart pounds, adrenaline literally spurting through my veins, and I move significantly faster than I have in many years. It's roughly 50 yards to my aircraft and I quickly overtake the two pilots who beat me out the door. As I approach the bright red line painted across the mouth of the HAS, my path is barred by a security policeman brandishing an M16 automatic rifle. I quickly comprehend that I'm going to have to wait for my GIB so we can enter the No Lone Zone together. I decelerate abruptly, wondering just where the ponderous bastard is. Breathing hard and itching to get on with our deadly mission, I wheel around, ready to elicit a large chunk of my GIB's ass for his unforgivable lethargy in this most urgent of scenarios. He's lounging there, arms folded casually with an enormous grin on his face. Gathered around him are my comrades – six other would-be warriors – all in various stages of mirth as they focus on the incredulous, angry, and yes, *desperate* expression on my face.

My GIB takes a step forward: 'Lesson number one: we only scramble on a klaxon; the cowbell means the coffee's ready. Welcome to Victor Alert, Rookie….' The blood drains from my face and I wheel back to confront the Sky Cop who waved the M16 at me; he's now grinning as well. As I regain enough composure to survey the area, I'm painfully aware that everyone within the confines of the fenced alert facility has turned out to watch the show. In addition to the crews, the entire maintenance contingent, security police detachment, and even the cooks are enjoying my abject humiliation. Oh, yeah, and my GIB lied about the coffee: as I discovered later, the cowbell's only used to embarrass FNGs like me. This is a stark reminder that there's no slack in my world; I give none, and I certainly cannot expect any in return.

My ritual mortification is followed by a return to our shabby but comfortable living quarters where, much to my chagrin, the banter at my expense will continue sporadically for some considerable time. It's a vigorous roasting, but most valuable for morale in an otherwise deadly serious environment.

We eight are on alert for three days and nights. We will be replaced by eight more crew members and so it goes, 24/7, 365 days a year. Every month, one of three 401st Tactical Fighter Squadrons (TFS) rotates from our home base at Torrejón Air Base, Spain to Incirlik Air Base, Turkey to keep the chain linked. We are but one of our country's many deterrent forces in a Cold War that has been unremitting since the end of the Second World War. We like to think we are unique: irreplaceable modern-day crusaders primed for a mission only we can achieve. We rarely discuss it among ourselves, but the facts are contradictory. If we are launched, Armageddon is undeniably upon us and the immense nuclear arsenals of the US and USSR will have been irretrievably committed. We, the proud fighter pilots of the 614th Tactical Fighter Squadron will deliver the fifth, sixth or even seventh nuclear weapon against our assigned target, having been preceded by US Army Pershing missiles based close to the Iron Curtain, ICBMs launched by lurking Allied nuclear submarines and those unleashed from underground silos in our American homeland. Indeed, every few months senior officers will 'certify' each aircrew as having committed virtually every detail of our top secret combat mission profile for a specified target to memory. The certification is not a million miles away from a kangaroo court, and there's one 'quiz' question that will invariably surface: 'OK, Captain, you've made it to your target, but your first sighting of it reveals only a large, smoking hole; what are you going to do now?' There is only one correct answer: 'I'll make it a bigger smoking hole, Sir.' The resulting pat on the back from the presiding officer signaled a successful certification and formal approval to join the ranks of nuclear troopers at Incirlik, waiting for the fabled balloon to go up.

Of course, 'making it a bigger smoking hole' was not an easily attainable result. There were a few minor hurdles between us and the billowing mushroom cloud we will proudly watch as we egress the target area, or not (more about that later). First of all, when Armageddon ensues, the skies will literally be filled with airborne vehicles. Ours will be heading east or north-east and theirs winging their way westward to obliterate places like Incirlik and dozens of other airfields, missile batteries, headquarters and yes, gentle reader, major towns and cities that used to ring Eastern Europe and the Soviet Union. The likelihood of running into one of these large metal craft, while not inevitable, was significant, particularly during the initial, medium-level segment of our journey which was required to conserve fuel for the last few miles, euphemistically known as the 'Run for the Roses' flown very, very low and very, very fast, burning jet fuel at a colossal rate (and more about *that* later).

The mid-air collision threat was not something we discussed often, but it did occasionally surface and when it did, someone would come up with a limp joke: 'If you've got to run into something, make sure it's got red stars on the wings.' Then we'd quickly move on to the subject of women or booze or more likely all of the above.

There was another awkward topic that everyone thought about but rarely brought up. Flying an aircraft at 100ft or so above the ground and 540 knots (if we couldn't get more out of her) was an integral part of survival on that last historic bomb run. Such a feat required great reflexes, coordination and *visual acuity*. Herein lies the rub: given that we will be proceeding towards Mother Russia at a great rate and we are far from the first to arrive at the party, we will no doubt be confronted with a dazzling array of nuclear explosions. Many of these are likely to be right in our faces. A nuclear blast directly observed at a range of many miles will burn the retina, instantly blinding the unfortunate observer.

The good news for us is that the Air Force has anticipated this peril and equipped us with a couple of items to mitigate our dilemma. Our helmets are equipped with a large visor which slides down from its housing and virtually covers the face from the bridge of the nose where it meets the oxygen mask to the forehead. Visors are useful in a number of ways, whether deflecting an unfortunate bird that has crashed through the canopy or simply serving as the world's biggest sunglasses. They are also interchangeable: dark shade for sunny weather, clear for night-flying and, our ace in the hole, vivid reflective gold to shield us from all those nuke detonations en route to the target. The second piece of vision-retentive kit provided by Uncle Sam is the simple yet effective cotton eye patch, donned before the helmet during a scramble. The eye patch is there because we know a close-in, face-on nuke detonation will overwhelm the reflective properties of the gold visor so the eye patch will guarantee vision is at least retained in one eye. The bad news you've been waiting for is the fact that this guarantee only works once. After a few beers, the jesters among us would postulate that your gold visor and eye patch would keep you heading safely inbound through one debilitating blast but after a second dose of nuke on the nose, Stevie Wonder might as well be flying your jet.

There's one more sobering thought I alluded to earlier. This one wasn't included in bar banter, because there simply wasn't anything droll you could offer up. To a man, we were keenly aware that an active nuclear scramble from Incirlik was a one-way trip. There were no ifs, ands or buts, the laws of physics and jet fighter fuel consumption were irrefutable. In many cases, even reaching the target would require all the skill and cunning the crew could muster. In most others, there was just enough fuel to do so and perform the weapon delivery, normally an automated loft maneuver predicated on time and distance from a known point with an automatic weapon release. Detonation of the parachute-retarded weapon was assured by sophisticated ground proximity radar under that stylish mahogany nosecone. Engine flameout due to fuel starvation in some cases would dramatically take place during recovery from the bomb delivery. If you were luckier, there was adequate fuel to fly an escape maneuver from the blast from your own weapon, leaving the crew to ponder just what the hell they might do with the very few minutes of powered flight they had left.

In any event, there wouldn't be a triumphant return home to Mom and the kids. Indeed, within the overall concept of Mutually Assured Destruction (MAD) that characterized the Cold War stand-off between East and West, it's highly unlikely there would be any moms and kids to come home to. As you will appreciate, we didn't have a dinner table chat with the family about this particularly dark aspect of our profession. Forty-odd years on, I've never even shared this cheery little piece of information with my own wife until now. With the benefit of hindsight, I'm awfully glad it didn't happen. If things had gone differently, I wouldn't be writing this book and it is equally unlikely that you would be reading it.

Night of the Donkey

After spending three days and nights on alert status contemplating a one-way trip to Armenia or Georgia, with the best possible outcome being a parachute let-down into an area on which we had just dropped 345 kilotons of fire, brimstone and radiation, we naturally looked forward to blowing off a bit of steam. The environment was perfect for this kind of mischief; there we were, two dozen 'fun-loving fools' far away from home and family for a month at a sprawling air base in south-eastern Turkey. As was the norm with American bases, we were afforded good facilities: billeting, movie theater, bowling alley, swimming pool, various dining establishments (although in those days the Big Mac and Pizza Hut had not yet reared their ugly heads in the European Theater of Operations), a Base Exchange and Commissary complex (modest department store and supermarket) and most importantly, an Officers' Open Mess (better known as the 'O' Club).

The club was an oasis no matter where we were in the world: cheap booze, reasonable food, cheap booze, a relaxing environment to unwind after a long day with colleagues and did I mention cheap booze? At Incirlik, it was a very basic structure – primarily a bar and dining room – but it was our very own watering hole away from home and we supported it to the hilt.

Having said that, we also occasionally abused this concession, which was established solely for our entertainment, relaxation and recreation. Although I am thoroughly mortified to this day, I'm compelled to relate one of these heinous abuses to you now.

We had completed our three-day tour on the Victor Alert facility, defending freedom as part of America's nuclear arsenal. Our replacement crews arrived at the appointed hour and we went through the ritual of signing the aircraft, the bomb, the top secret mission planning folder and the awesome responsibility over to the fresh-faced fighter pilots who would now spend the next few days and nights waiting for that klaxon to sound. As was the tradition, they did not appear empty-handed. Each two-man crew brought a congratulatory bottle of Cold Duck, purchased at the Class VI facility (the base liquor store, a function of the retail facilities mentioned earlier) and presented as tribute to our successful completion of a Victor Alert tour. Cold Duck is very charitably defined in Wikipedia as 'a beverage made of sparkling Burgundy and champagne'. It is, in fact, one of the most loathsome concoctions on the face of God's green earth and as I research this digest, I find, even now – forty-odd years of inflation later – it routinely sells for less than $5.00 a bottle.

I have no idea why Cold Duck was the accepted memento of a triumphant tour on the alert pad – 'It's what we always did' – but I can tell you that it always came with an unspoken challenge. The changeover ritual culminated with the return of our flying gear – helmets, 'G'-suits, checklists and other paraphernalia – to the Squadron Operations building, 2 miles distant via the perimeter road that paralleled the runway. Our replacements had brought their own kit with them in a panel truck we called the bread van and we would return using the same vehicle. The bread van was unremarkable: accommodation was a driver's seat and two long benches on either side extending back to a double-door entry point at the rear. It was painted dark blue and had United States Air Force stenciled on the side, ostensibly to give it street cred. The challenge was for each crew to finish off their congratulatory bottle of Cold Duck during the 2-mile drive and it was a source of pride to achieve it (never mind the damage inflicted on digestive system, liver and brain cells).

On this particular occasion, however, a distraction occurred and the Cold Duck challenge was relegated to a lower priority. As we navigated the perimeter road, our driver, one of the GIBs and renowned prankster, called our attention to activities on the side of the road. As the bread van was devoid of passenger windows, we loudly cast aspersions on his own intelligence and his parents' marital status, but when he pulled over, we all had a look. There, in an adjacent field, was one of the many wild donkeys that inhabited the air base environs (and paid no heed to the earth-shaking din of F-4 take-offs and landings). This one was contentedly munching the grass and appeared completely docile. We eight looked at each other; fighter pilot conniving combusted spontaneously and, as a team, we began formulating a conspiracy that would surely bring us immortality in the annals of fighter aviation history.

Although the nuclear alert commitment was 24/7, for those of us not 'sitting on the bomb', the weekend was still a couple of days away from the job and, as luck would have it, we had finished our tour on a Friday afternoon. When deployed (to Incirlik or around the world) this meant one thing: Happy Hour at the club. In the '70s, although the forces of political correctness and moral posturing were beginning their dreadful onslaught, we were still able to celebrate the arrival of the weekend with some panache and eagerness. Drinks at the bar, already cheap by civilian standards, were further discounted by half, and small-time gambling (Liar's Dice and other games of chance) ensued. Most importantly, in terms of contributing to the success of our plot, many Incirlik-based officers brought their wives and significant others to the club for an evening of relatively sophisticated enjoyment, as music was often provided during the evening. At Incirlik, the feminine turnout consisted of wives and girlfriends of officers permanently stationed there, the nurse contingent and a few feminine administrators. Because we were deployed from Spain, we had no such accompanying diversions and indeed, one of the most inviolable imperatives of deployment came into play: 'What goes on TDY (temporary duty), stays TDY.' Woe betide the fighter pilot who returned home to regale his wife with tales of squadron mates' indiscretions while he himself was THE paragon of virtue.

As Incirlik hosted aircraft from other locations, it had no flying organizations of its own. There was a smattering of unfortunate aviation-rated staff officers there, but the vast majority of permanent residents consisted of support types. There were administrators, maintainers, air traffic controllers, doctors, nurses, security policemen, and services officers such as the guy who managed the club to name just a few. Most uncharitably, we assembled all these good folks into one mammoth stereotype and referred to them as 'shoe clerks'. This may sound a bit harsh, but consider, if you will, the Army's designation for their similar group of non-combatants: REMFs, or 'Rear Echelon Mother Fuckers'. As you will now appreciate, the Air Force is much more urbane.

On this Friday night then, the club was beginning to fill with pre-weekend revelers: deployed fighter crews and our accompanying maintenance and support officers and Incirlik's broad spectrum of shoe clerks and their ladies. The hour approached seven o'clock.

Back on the perimeter road, our most gentle conspirator approached the grazing donkey, holding out the only inducement we had available: a plastic cup full of Cold Duck. The donkey, apparently possessing far better judgment than we did, scorned the horrible brew, but remained calm and responded positively when he was gently guided towards the open doors of the bread van. Upon reaching the point of no return, he looked around frantically and attempted an escape, but as there were eight of us and only one of him, the outcome was never in doubt. We then replicated the old 'How many clowns can you get in the driver's compartment of a bread van?' trick, while leaving the increasingly apprehensive donkey in the rear between the benches. We quickly completed the trip to Squadron Ops, dumped our gear, and moved forward with Phase 2 of our planned Friday night folly.

The Incirlik Officers' Club was entered via a main front door and immediately thereafter, a left turn took you into the dining room, while a turn to the right through a pair of western movie-style swinging doors got you into the bar. It wasn't enormous, but the room was spacious enough to accommodate a horseshoe-shaped bar with a dozen or so stools, a number of small tables and a reasonable dance floor. At the far end of the room in a corner was a door leading to a small alcove which housed the men's room and also a fire door to the outside, which could only be opened from within.

I was elected to trigger the action. It was now 7.30 and, as I entered the bar, the familiar sights and sounds swept over me. The bar was heaving: fighter pilots in flight suits surrounded the bar, two deep in many places, ordering (cheap) drinks, telling war stories and ogling the growing throng of shoe clerks' wives. They were seated at small tables with their husbands and had no intention of mingling with the uncouth animals from the Iberian Peninsula who had invaded their cozy environs. Indeed, as previously mentioned, we had christened ourselves collectively as the 'Spanish Flyers'. The ladies were, for the most part, dressed up for the biggest night of the week and many looked, as Billy Crystal used to put it, 'simply marrr-vellous'.

The bar was manned by two Turks: Emin, who had presided over bar operations for many years and was a large, quiet, friendly man who doted on his family, ably assisted by Mike who moonlighted as a taxi driver. More than once Mike had recognized inebriated fighter pilots wandering the city streets of Adana and returned them safely to the base. On a Friday night they were maxed out, but seemed to enjoy the revels as much as the participants. They were supplemented by two or three bar waiters, only one of whom was regularly employed on nights other than Friday, and went, for some reason lost in the fog of time, by the nickname of 'Shotgun'. He was a nervous little man who scurried about, carrying drinks and had mastered a single line of English he employed monotonously with every single delivery: 'Yes sir, *Habi* [Turkish for brother], who's *payfer*???' More often than not, because we were all kind-hearted and sensitive creatures, one of us would come back with something like 'Time for you to *payfer* a round, Shotgun' which would result in his eyes rolling, hands shaking slightly, and little beads of sweat breaking out on his forehead. Although we always kept this dodge going for a while, we never actually stiffed him, but he was unable to grasp that inevitable outcome and his discomfiture provided additional light entertainment.

I strolled into the bar, soaking up and returning ribald banter from my mates already assembled and doing a little ogling of my own. I ordered a beer, exchanging pleasantries with Emin, left it on the bar (as I fully intended to return to it to watch the merriment unfold), and strode purposely towards the alcove and the fire door. No one was en route to the toilet, so I left the alcove door open, pushed the handle on the fire door, swung it open and there as planned was the bread van, reversed onto the grass a couple feet from the entrance. As the fire door opened, so did the van doors and in one flawlessly choreographed movement, our now terrified donkey was propelled through the alcove and into a crowded bar full of fighter pilots, shoe clerks, wives, girlfriends and Turkish bar staff, all talking and laughing with absolutely no premonition of what was about to occur. Appropriately, musical accompaniment for the main event was *Eli's Coming* by Three Dog Night, blaring out of the big Wurlitzer jukebox adjacent to the dance floor. I closed the fire door as my partners-in-crime left the bread van where it was and hot-footed around to the main entrance (a rapidly-emerging donkey with eight fighter pilots in hot pursuit would a) give the game away prematurely, and b) incriminate the conspirators). I then innocently followed the donkey into his arena.

He had, momentarily, frozen and was surveying the carousing in progress before him. He swung around, frantically seeking an escape route, but finding none available behind him he tossed his head, brayed loudly and began formulating his quest for freedom.

The braying immediately drew attention from the shoe clerk tables surrounding the dance floor. Then, as if by magic, the happy by-products of letting the good times roll – laughter and general good cheer – were replaced by one, then three, then an entire chorus of discordant high-pitched feminine screams and (slightly) lower-pitched exclamations of 'What the fuck?' and similar disbelieving observations. The bar was instantly transformed from relatively sophisticated cocktail lounge to a microcosm of the *Titanic*'s first-class lounge immediately following impact with the iceberg. Disbelieving patrons – even the 'Spanish Flyers' – were caught in a moment of indecision, unlike the donkey, who had apparently settled on Three Dog Night as the source of his predicament and headed for the jukebox. On my way to that nice cold beer, I watched him glance off the offending jukebox, which resulted in the horrible sound of a needle scraping through *Eli's Coming* and the Wurlitzer sliding across the dance floor on its little wheels.

The mayhem accelerated: the donkey set sail for a cluster of tables adjacent to the dance floor and inhabited by shoe clerks and spouses, most of whom were now galvanized into some form of frenetic action. I saw one fetching young thing climb onto her chair and thought: 'Questionable move sweetheart, this is a donkey, not a mouse.' Her husband/boyfriend was trying to coax her down without much success. Fortunately, she was saved the embarrassment and potential damage of going ass over teakettle by our friend the donkey, who took a slightly different route, bypassing her completely. In a number of cases, shoe clerks were gallantly defending their womenfolk, but I saw at least two instances where a lady was left screaming and/or crying in dismay as the man in her life *un*gallantly headed for the exit, alone but obviously not unafraid. I can only imagine the conversation that ensued when they were reunited.

Other more tactical thinkers had placed the tables between themselves and the marauding donkey who now caught a glimpse of light through the smoky semi-darkness of the bar area. This light originated from the swinging doors to the main club entry corridor. The good news was that this was a potential escape avenue for the donkey; the bad news was that fleeing shoe clerks and wives had effectively jammed the passageway and as the donkey headed for the light, knocking over tables, drinks and the occasional shoe clerk/wife/girlfriend it became obvious to him that this wasn't an option. He abruptly reversed course and headed back into what had now become a scrapheap. Tables, chairs, glasses and bottles littered the floor, along with the occasional high-heeled shoe. It was at this point I noticed the pandemonium had altered slightly. Screams and anguished cries were still in evidence, but these sounds were now being drowned out by a growing cacophony of unabated laughter. The 'Spanish Flyers', clustered around the bar, hadn't budged and the floor show they were witnessing was obviously providing the best entertainment most of them had seen in years. They were, to a man, immersed in raucous mirth, tears rolling down their cheeks and banging on the bar behind which Emin and Mike wisely continued to preside while Shotgun and his colleagues feebly attempted to corral and then eject the donkey. They were woefully ineffective in this tasking, alternately cornering him and then retreating in terror when he lurched towards them. The laughter from the bar was reaching a crescendo, but with the bar almost completely cleared of shoe clerks and their ladies, the conspirators finally decided that the donkey had performed admirably and it was time to bring his torment to a merciful end. A few of us again detained him and maneuvered him back from whence he had come, out of the fire door and into the waiting bread truck.

Our donkey was obviously distraught, but one of the guys had taken the time to liberate a few carrots from the kitchen and during the egress from the Officers' Club, these were employed to soothe the little fella and he responded well. The boys had had a little time to think about things and it was decided there was one more performance left for the donkey. One of our colleagues was a bit of a *bon vivant* and certainly a legend in his own mind. At the time, he was romancing an Air Force nurse and had little time for the sophomoric antics of his peers. Fred wasn't really a bad guy, but he was somewhat arrogant and narcissistic. Consequently, it was decided that some form of mild but noteworthy maltreatment might be appropriate. Besides, it was Friday night and after our spectacular at the club neither we nor the donkey had anything better to do.

We located the nurse's apartment which was fortunately on the ground floor of the officers' quarters and confirmed that Fred and his lady friend were tripping the light fantastic elsewhere. One of the boys was pretty handy with a screwdriver and presto!, the door swung open. With the aid of a carrot, we gently led our donkey into the young lady's boudoir, wished him a fond goodnight and disappeared into the darkness. Sadly none of us witnessed the return of the lovebirds, but we understand that the donkey had made himself completely at home, lounging on various articles of furniture, moving freely about the apartment and attempting, unsuccessfully, to properly use the en suite toilet. Consequently, Fred and an extremely irate nurse spent most of the night in damage limitation mode. One of the guys awakened early the next morning, found our four-legged friend contentedly munching the grass outside the nurse's quarters and escorted him back to his patch. He seemed to be none the worse for his adventures and in fact, once released, I'm confident he forgot all about it.

On the following morning, our squadron commander and operations officer were summoned to the Incirlik commander's office to explain their charges' abhorrent behavior (not the nurse's quarters incursion; she wisely kept that to herself). Exemplary fighter pilots both, they had been in the bar the preceding evening, witnessed the entire event, joined us all in side-splitting laughter and gone to their beds well-oiled and happy.

As they solemnly explained to the group commander (a full colonel who outranked them both), they had no idea who had perpetrated this outrage and, indeed, there was no evidence tying it to any of the 'Spanish Flyers'. The good colonel wasn't buying that one for a minute and so, for the sake of continuing cordial relations with our hosts, our bosses forged a diplomatically acceptable covenant that would satisfy nearly all injured parties (shoe clerks were not considered in the deliberations). Any resulting damages would be paid for by the 'Spanish Flyers' in exchange for amnesty for any culprits who might be identified in the future. The option of barring the perpetrators from the next deployment to Turkey was considered but quickly abandoned as that would have been punishment very much akin to Br'er Fox tossing Br'er Rabbit into the briar patch. Instead, our boss would read the riot act to us all and we would, forever more, be model citizens whenever we deployed to Incirlik.

We all cheerfully chipped in for the broken chairs, tables and glasses, satisfying the contract. In these, the good old days, this was part of the fighter pilot creed and no one ever quibbled about coughing up when they had caused damage through exuberance, mischief or any other factor which contributed to the character and spirit of those who flew fighters for a living.

The position adopted by our commander and ops officer was also typical of the era. We'd have been astonished if either of them had thrown us to the wolves and in return for their unyielding top cover, we all reciprocated with an undying loyalty I've never seen outside the Air Force fighter fraternity.

In today's Air Force, although there are still charismatic leaders and fighter jocks with spirit and panache, the changing culture has severely dented the qualities that transformed mere airplane drivers into fighter pilots and the ethos that resulted. I have no doubt that the adventure related above in the current environment would result in serious sanctions for the perpetrators. The abysmal pressures of rampant political correctness, moral posturing and endemic covering of backsides have resulted in an environment that, at very best, stifles the *joie de vivre* and boundless initiative that once defined the successful fighter pilot.

I'm confident in saying that the ringleader (and co-conspirators) in a 2020 'Night of the Donkey' event would be facing at very least an Article 15 (non-judicial punishment) administered by his commander. At worst, a commander heavily engaged in the aforementioned covering of his/her backside might opt to have the unspeakable offender court-martialed. All this would be accompanied by the disgrace of being branded a troublemaker, a trip (or trips) to some form of counselor (whom you can no longer refer to as a shoe clerk), and a very real likelihood that a promising young pilot's career would now come to a screeching halt because of nothing worse than a surplus of spirit.

Times have certainly changed, but IMHO (in my humble opinion), not for the better.

(Disclaimer: No animals, Turks or shoe clerk's wives were injured in the conduct of this extravaganza.)

Chapter Six

The Wonderful World of Instructing

The adventures you've been reading about involved the 614th Tactical Fighter Squadron based just outside Madrid with quarterly deployments to Turkey. Life in an operational fighter unit like this one was subtly different from toiling in a training squadron. Objectives and motivations were different for a start. The operational world encompassed maintaining a high degree of readiness to go to war. As an experienced pilot, the task was honing the skills developed over time to be the best you can be among others striving for the same result. In the Phantom, this was a Jack-of-all-trades exercise as the Phantom did it all: air-to-ground (nuclear and conventional weapons) and air-to-air, employing long- and short-range missiles and in some aircraft models a seven-barrel Gatling gun. If, as a pilot, you were second-rate in any of these regimens, you were, to be blunt, mediocre.

So it was to follow, on completion of my tour of duty with the 'Lucky Devils' at Torrejón. I was assigned to the 307th Tac Fighter Squadron, Homestead AFB, south of Miami as an instructor pilot, molding recent pilot training graduates and others (known as re-treads; more to follow) into competent fighter pilots. Because I was going into a specified role as an instructor, the Air Force mandated that I should attend a course designed to school the experienced pilot in how to teach other pilots. Consequently, Elaine and I embarked on a temporary stopover to sunny Phoenix, Arizona for a six-week-long instructor training program at nearby Luke AFB. This involved a lengthy journey from Madrid to Miami to Phoenix and back to Miami, but since we were not under time pressure for arrival, it afforded an opportunity to show my British bride a reasonably good slice of America.

This is probably an opportune time to make another of my brief off-piste diversions and give you a brief seminar on the bittersweet experience of Air Force long-distance moving; bittersweet because for many of us, travelling the world was one of the most exciting aspects of our military existence. At the other end of the satisfaction spectrum, the physical performance of packing up our worldly goods every two or three years in order to experience this excitement could best be described as a recurring pain in the ass. The Air Force process for moving is actually quite reasonable. Unlike some countries whose military families are required to live in furnished quarters, Uncle Sam sanctions shipping of automobiles, furniture and household goods to most installations, foreign and domestic, and off-base quarters of our choice were often available. This policy was most valuable in terms of morale, providing the family with a sense of 'home' we could take with us on our travels.

The shipping weight limitations are levied according to rank and I cannot complain about our allowance at any point in my career. Of the nine 'permanent' moves Elaine and I made, all except a couple of inter-European moves were long-haul overseas: USA to Europe and vice versa. Achievement of the moves by contracted companies varied, but again, with some notable exceptions (the lethal forklift stabbing of our bed and immersion of much of our stereo gear in seawater en route from Germany to Las Vegas spring to mind), we were reasonably fortunate.

There was one aspect of moving I always found ironic. We were allowed two shipments for a Permanent Change of Station (PCS) move. The first, known as Hold Baggage, was a relatively small consignment, theoretically shipped via the fastest means available in order to provide timely arrival of necessary items (dishes, pots & pans, bed linen, towels, etc.) to survive while waiting for the bulk of our belongings to arrive by slower containerized shipment. This substantial consignment was designated as Household Goods and consisted of furniture and other sizable items and was normally sent via surface container (from overseas locations). Murphy's Law was certainly in evidence as, on every occasion, the slow boat Household Goods reached us before the expedited Hold Baggage.

Military family travel is rarely a straightforward point-to-point exercise because en route complications always get in the way. This time, on arrival in the States, we collected the Porsche at Norfolk, Virginia, its port of entry and dropped it off with friends in Florida before starting our journey. We then flew to Phoenix, hurriedly rented an apartment and I set out to learn how to be a mentor. Elaine had never driven, so I sought to remedy that by acquiring a sturdy, reliable new German Opel Manta (as opposed to the bright red Mustang with white vinyl top and shag carpet that she actually coveted). This was probably the last marital debate I ever won, but nevertheless she enrolled in a motoring course and off she went while I was happily flying airplanes at Luke AFB.

When the course ended, we launched on an extensive trip back to Miami, spending a week in Las Vegas (which was much more stylish when the Mafia ran it), visiting friends in Lubbock, Texas and searching for traces of John Wayne at San Antonio's Alamo. We also spent a few nights in New Orleans, where Elaine tipped a delighted waiter in Brennan's $20 for serving us a couple of $2 drinks ('Your money all looks the same,' she explained). We survived coastal flooding in Biloxi, Mississippi, turned southward at Tallahassee and headed for the next three years in the land of debilitating humidity. Here endeth the diversion.

Instructing in a Replacement Training Unit (RTU) is a different kettle of fish. The name of the game as an instructor pilot is to coach a novice (or 2 or 3 of them in a class of 15 to 20 students). These greenhorns are invariably naïve, slow-witted and uncoordinated, just like I was when I pitched up immediately following pilot training. At the end of four months' training, the desired outcome is a competent fighter pilot with sufficient tactical skills to cultivate further specialized expertise and enough basic savvy and situational awareness to stay alive while proceeding with the cultivation.

RTU covered the gamut of fighter aviation: basic and tactical formation flying, tactical navigation, conventional and nuclear air-to-ground gunnery, air-to-air tactics and weapons employment, and air to-air refueling. Most students are fresh out of pilot training, excited about being in fighters and enthusiastic about learning this stimulating new trade. A few, however, are recycled: funneled into fighters from assignments in transports, tankers, even the occasional bomber. Finally, there are upgrading fighter folks, transitioning from older jets or simply moving sideways into another fighter aircraft because of personnel assignment requirements.

Each of these categories provides a different challenge for the instructor. The brand-new pilots are not unlike sophisticated puppies. Eager to learn but short on experience, they are readily stage-managed, compliant and normally quick on the uptake. Consequently, they are typically a pleasure to fly with and provide a great deal of satisfaction to the instructor who guides them along the way.

Recycled aviators (re-treads) often fall into one of two categories: they are either delighted to leave the comparatively routine world of driving a large aircraft from point A to point B to experience the diversity and complexity of fighter aviation, or they have been diverted by an impersonal personnel system into something they don't want to pursue. In a few cases, recycled many-motor guys are seriously uncomfortable due to lack of competence or genuine apprehension. Pilots in the first category present themselves as older, wiser puppies, possessing abundant basic aviation experience and know-how but soaking up the specialized knowledge. They are keen to adopt new skills, increasing both the quantity and quality of the arrows in their quiver. They, like the FNGs out of pilot training, are receptive, avid learners who tend to make the instructor's task a rewarding experience.

The second category of recycled flyers proved far more problematic. Reluctant transitioning 'many motor' pilots, regardless of the causes of their disinclination, can cover the spectrum from technically competent to point-blank dangerous in the air. The vast majority are clearly professional and strive to master the aircraft and the roles it performs, but many lack the drive and ambition that defines the classic fighter pilot. This is a real challenge for the instructor who, in the F-4, had the dubious pleasure of riding around in the back seat trying to convey both essential skills and inspiration. Most half-hearted recycled pilots managed to complete the training program but, it has to be said, without distinction and it's likely they went on to achieve that mediocrity I alluded to above.

The final category of RTU student is perhaps the most disconcerting for an instructor. Fighter pilots moving on to another fighter can be a pleasure or a pain, depending on personality and disposition. For an instructor, there's nothing better than being tasked to mentor an upgrading fighter pilot who possesses both the motor skills necessary to fly the bird as it should be flown and the propriety that allows him to realize he doesn't have all the answers when it comes to operating a new piece of kit. The good news is, the majority of transitioning fighter folks exhibit this agreeable blend of technical skills and humility.

Instructing upgrading fighter pilots with diverse backgrounds and varying skills was always challenging and almost always rewarding, but it lacked the cut and thrust of working in an operational unit. The competition was always there: a gunnery range mission included the standard fighter pilot bet: 'Quarter a bomb; nickel a hole.' Translated, the pilot, student or instructor who dropped the most accurate bomb on every pass collected 25 cents from each of the others. If strafe was on the agenda, the high-scoring shooter collected 5 cents per hit from all the rest. Not enough to retire on, but a good day on the range would fund a couple of beers at Happy Hour and, more importantly, provided just a touch of extra incentive. Speaking of Happy Hour, Friday nights at a training base were always entertaining, thanks primarily to the first group of young Turks, fresh out of pilot training and ready to assume the fighter pilot image in a big way.

Instructing new fighter pilots was a stimulating and gratifying role, but it had its drawbacks. For example, those of us in the RTU instructor role missed out on operational deployments to faraway places with strange-sounding names (and all the delights that accompanied such boondoggles). Nevertheless, the Air Force ensured we would be ready if the Mongol hordes streamed across Asian borders and we were required to answer the call at short notice. This readiness – real or imagined – was partly achieved through an authentic ordeal known as the Mobility Exercise which tested our squadrons' ability to pack up and move at very short notice. We never actually went anywhere, of course, but had recurring opportunities to 'practice bleed' in the name of flexibility.

These occasions were heralded by the dreaded Wing Mobility Recall: a pyramid summons of all aircrew and support personnel initiated by the boss that cascaded down through the ranks with a call to congregate at a predetermined venue. This invariably occurred in the middle of the night. Had it not, many of the intended participants would have been working – which would have been far too easy – or out carousing which would have negated the entire exercise due to inability to round everyone up. To add to our delight, they usually kicked off at Oh-Dark Thirty hours on a Saturday; this designed to complete in time for us all to go back to work, 'rested' and ready to fly by Monday morning.

Anticipating these occasional nocturnal fandangos, we all maintained a 'grab bag' with underwear, a couple of flight suits and other necessities which we could throw into the trunk of the car, even while bleary-eyed after being awakened by a 2.00 am call from an equally enthusiastic colleague. We then hustled to the designated aircraft hangar where we knew we would spend the next twelve to fourteen hours in a state of near terminal boredom while we played the mobility game. We were designated as either flyers (who would simulate taking our fighters to whatever simulated destination the exercise demanded), or passengers (who would simulate riding in simulated transport aircraft to the same simulated destination).

While we waited for all this simulation to take place, we were all 'processed' for this imaginary expedition by teams of shoe clerks who, to be fair, weren't any happier to be involved in this debacle than the aviators. Processing involved queuing up to prove to the shoe clerks that our 'i's' were dotted and our 't's' were crossed. We had to review our personnel records, including wills and established financial allotments, produce a set of dog tags and an immunization record and generally flaunt our personal details on paper for someone who had no business delving into it.

As you might imagine, this exercise brought out the 'fun-loving fool' in many of us and we took great delight in manufacturing whatever light-heartedness we could muster under the circumstances. I can vividly recall turning up one humid South Florida Saturday morning and finding my place in the queue in front of Stan Hallam, an instructor from a sister squadron. I didn't know Stan well, but he had a reputation as one of the steady guys and when I had a good look at him through groggy eyes, I doubled up with laughter. There, pinned to the front of his flight suit, was a large note done, as I recall, in bold green ink. It read 'Stanley's lunch money is in his pocket. Please make sure he gets in all the right lines and call me if he causes any trouble.' It was signed simply 'Mrs Hallam'. I never met Stan's wife, but I wish I had; she was obviously a real treat. To his credit, Stan wore this badge for the duration, providing a bit of levity to many during a long, boring day.

It was during this same mobility sham that I managed to have a little fun with political correctness. As mentioned earlier, one of the items checked prior to clearing us for our simulated trip to Never-Never Land was a set of dog tags. These little rectangles of tin defined our existence in fewer characters than a Twitter message:

Last Name, First Name, Middle Initial
Rank
Service Number
Blood Type
Religion

The tags were worn on a metal beaded chain around the neck and designed for one sole purpose: to identify a casualty in combat. Because they were considered essential for deployment, each tortuous processing line included a small embossing machine which manufactured them via a typewriter-style keyboard, just in case one of us was thick enough not to have brought a set along.

On this particular bogus deployment, I was that thickhead. As I approached the dog tag station in the queue, a simple but, at least in my mind, somewhat amusing wind-up came into focus. I stood in front of the kid wearing two stripes behind the keyboard and, in a voice full of remorse, said 'Sorry, airman, forgot my tags today.'

He looked at me with an expression of undisguised disdain; after all, he was at least as bored as I was and I was breaking into what was obviously a significant trance. 'OK, Sir, last name, first name, middle initial.' Clickety-clack went the machine as it pounded out my identity, and so it went through rank, service number and blood group. He was obviously trying to guess when he asked for my religion, but was never going to succeed.

'Cult of the Toad,' I told him, in the same monotone as before. His head snapped back slightly, his eyes widened and he groped for something to say. When he spoke, I was ready for it: 'I can't put that on the tags, Sir,' he spluttered, looking around for help should it be necessary to subdue the madman standing before him. I looked at him severely and somewhat disbelieving. 'You're not *really* going to mock my religion, are you son?' He met my gaze briefly, then averted his eyes. Clickety-clack, clickety-clack went the embossing machine and he reluctantly handed me what I believe to be a totally unique set of dog tags. I've still got them somewhere and you can bet I'll want them buried with me, along with my world-class baseball card collection.

Having done my bit for civil impropriety, I continued through the processing line, perched on my duffle bag within a grouping of fellow malcontents and waited for the non-existent transportation to arrive. Some hours later, the powers that be decided we had proved, beyond a shadow of a doubt, that we were capable of surviving boredom on a grand scale. Given the opportunity to actually go somewhere as a team, we could probably do so without embarrassing ourselves or the United States Air Force. As we shuffled out of the hangar to head for home and ready ourselves for our day jobs in a few hours, one of the guys loudly summed up the experience for all to enjoy: 'There's no more mail and the beatings will continue until morale improves.'

Chapter Seven

FWIC: The PhD in Fighter Aviation

I've alluded to the competitive nature of the fighter jock a number of times in this dissertation, but probably did not give this characteristic the emphasis it deserves. Fighter pilots like to WIN, whether they are in the cockpit working to convert an ammunition dump into a smoking hole, exterminate Vietnamese MiG pilots or in the bar rolling from the dice cup.

So it was in the autumn of 1974 when I was toiling as an F-4 instructor pilot (and enjoying mobility exercises) at Homestead AFB, just south of Miami. I was a fairly senior captain and had finagled my way into a flight commander position. This was not as difficult as I'm trying to make it sound. We were woefully undermanned and there weren't many of us qualified enough in flying hours and experience to take on the role. It was this combination of flying time and proficiency that opened two doors to opportunity. The competitive aspect was making sure the right one opened. My squadron commander Lieutenant Colonel Dick Fisher and operations officer Lieutenant Colonel Duke Terry told me to get ready because they were fighting my corner and I *WOULD* be going through one of those doors within a month or two.

On the one hand, there was a class slot available in the USAF Safety School at Kirtland AFB, New Mexico. This training would qualify me to manage an aviation safety program at unit level, conduct accident investigations, compile copious safety records and statistics and process great consignments of data supporting the worthy cause of flying safety. I considered this option thoroughly (really, I did), and I finally determined I would rather stick pins in my eyes or toboggan naked down a mammoth razor blade.

The second alternative was the USAF Fighter Weapons Instructor Course (FWIC, or Fighter Weapons School for short), a six-month PhD in fighter aviation conducted at Nellis AFB, Nevada on the northern periphery of Las Vegas. I spent all of a heartbeat thinking about this one. I wanted it, badly, and at the time would have sold my immediate family into slavery (sorry, sweetheart) for a class slot and a crack at the toughest and most prestigious flying school in the world.

My competition for this sought-after plum (and the Safety School as a consolation prize) was a young captain in one of our sister squadrons. He had a great reputation for instructional skills, good hands and could also claim a South-East Asia combat tour. He was good, but IMHO not quite as good as I was. (You didn't expect me to comment otherwise, did you?)

The matter would be contested not in the air, but around the Wing King's conference table, where my champions Dick and Duke would debate his bosses using relatively benign weapons: our personnel and gunnery records. Importantly, the ability of the combatants to sell their boy to the boss with stirring tales of aeronautical excellence and a vivid portrayal of the individual's standing among his peers and bosses as a fighter pilot was significant. I'm told that, on this particular occasion, the deliberations took up most of an afternoon, fuelled by numerous beers. The Wing King ruminated and came to his decision the following morning. My adversary and I were none the wiser.

That evening the phone rang in our lavish (not) Air Force quarters kitchen and I picked it up. A deep, rich voice intoned: 'Steve, this is Duke, the bad news is you're *not* going to Safety School.' I'm not sure how long the rusty wheels turned in my head while I tried to decipher this tiny, bewildering morsel, but it had to be a while because the next thing he said was 'Are you still with me?'

Assuming the role of village idiot, I finally blurted out: 'Does that mean....?' and ran completely out of the ability to communicate. He laughed and, putting me out of my misery, said: 'You're going to love Las Vegas, but you're not really going to have much time to enjoy it.'

I managed to corral my patrons the following morning and after declaring my undying gratitude and devotion for their efforts on my behalf, I asked about the negotiations and which of my numerous and abundant talents had won the day. Dick Fisher laughed and said: 'You're old.' 'What?' I stared at him as I would have if he'd told me I was pregnant. 'I haven't reached my 30th birthday. Old?' and they both laughed. As it turned out, 'old' was relative and technical. Eligibility for attending the

Weapons School expired when the applicant reached seven years as a rated pilot. I was rapidly approaching that milestone and the wily Dick and Duke had used that hastily-closing window to convince the Wing King that I had to capitalize on this opportunity *right now*; after all, even though we were fairly evenly matched in the aptitude, skill and cunning departments, my slightly younger opponent would have at least a couple more cracks at it.

I reported in to the Weapons School in January of 1975, at once extremely proud to have been selected and also apprehensive to be embarking on what was universally accepted as the toughest, most demanding training process in military aviation. We were facing six months of academic rigor artfully linked to various fighter roles and missions and a golden opportunity to combine the concepts with practical training in the air. At the end of the journey, assuming we successfully completed it, was a small shield-shaped patch depicting a red bullet impacting a bulls-eye target and a small banner below that reading 'Graduate USAF Fighter Weapons School'. Only those who had ploughed these furrows were authorized to sport this patch and it conveyed a prestigious message: this guy is *the* expert in weapons and tactics; pay attention to him, he knows what he's talking about. In the years since I earned the patch, times have changed, the program has grown to accommodate numerous other weapons systems and at some point the powers that be surgically removed the 'Fighter' from the patch. I'm not going to rant here, but when the 'Fighter' designation was exorcised, something sacred died.

Our 'classroom' was phenomenal: 4,531 square miles of the Nevada Test and Training Ranges comprising the 'largest contiguous air and ground space available for peacetime military operations in the free world'.[1] This real estate provided numerous basic and realistic tactical gunnery ranges, many instrumented and configured to score weapons deliveries and provide electronic feedback of operations. Overhead 5,000 square miles of restricted military training airspace kept us far removed from our airline brethren ferrying passengers between east and west coasts and points in between. The result was a training scenario which allowed training operations that stretched the performance envelope to its limit without endangering the general public.

The FWIC instructor corps was renowned throughout the Air Force as being the cream of the crop: virtually all combat veterans and hand-picked for their assignments to Nellis, they were going to be knowledgeable, skilful and experienced. They also had a reputation for being demanding and uncompromising, so it was obvious the course wasn't going to be stress-free. I was also aware my classmates were going to be at the top of their own totem pole and that competition would be both fierce and constructive. I was confident my flying skills would meet or exceed standards, but was slightly less self-assured about some of the academic demands the course promised, mainly those centered around the mystifying world of mathematics. To ease my anxiety, my wife invested a relatively large sum in a Texas Instruments hand-held calculator, which today could be purchased for pennies. As it turned out, the math wasn't that challenging, but her concern was appreciated.

There were twenty-four in my class, assigned for training to the 414th Fighter Weapons Squadron: fourteen pilots and ten navigators (the Air Force had finally ceased the irrational practice of populating the back seat with a pilot). We'd been sourced from F-4 training and combat-ready units all over the world. We also had an exchange officer: a Navy RIO (Radar Intercept Officer) who was delighted to find that Air Force F-4s, unlike the Navy version, had a stick in the rear cockpit. He didn't get to use it much, but every now and then one of us would give up control of the bird and let him flail around a bit, always cautioning him not to hit the other airplanes (which never failed to raise his ire).

The curriculum was challenging in every way. Academics covered, in great and copious detail, every weapon and supporting weapons system employed by the F-4, including weapons planning and effects, tactics for employment in all areas of fighter operations, including those of our adversaries, and mission planning. Half a day, every day, was devoted to academics and, whenever there was a free half-hour or so, we were trained in how to teach the art of advanced instructorship. Each course element brought with it the joy of written examinations. There was very little scope for relaxation and if you breathed a small sigh of relief walking out of the classroom, it didn't last long because the flying program was every bit as punishing. The fact that the advanced flying was exhilarating – what we lived and breathed – didn't alter the fact that meeting the FWIC standards was hard, hard work.

Again, the F-4 was an extremely capable jack-of-all-trades and the flying experience at Nellis explored each and every one of them at a level of difficulty we never anticipated. The flying syllabus covered air-to-ground gunnery (conventional and nuclear weapons), intercepts, air-to-air tactics, low-level and medium-level employment tactics, precision-guided munitions delivery and how to combine any and all of the above into complex mission employment. The course was based on a building block approach which meant we started with relatively simple concepts working towards far more demanding tactical employment exercises later in the program. Although varying in personality and approach, the instructors were uniformly unyielding in terms of enforcing the standards and demanding performance as befitted the skills we were alleged to possess by virtue of being there.

I vividly recall one mission I flew late in the program with then-Captain Joe Henderson in the back seat. Joe was a typically gifted instructor and an extremely likeable individual, but he was no pushover. As we were nearing graduation, despite my good intentions not to succumb to complacency, I obviously lost concentration on this particular day. The mission was part of the Ground Attack Tactics phase, flown as a strike package with a number of other F-4s. We were subject to interception by some extremely realistic aggressor aircraft (more about that later), and were tasked to put actual bombs on target at one of Nellis's superb tactical gunnery ranges. To succeed, we needed to avoid being whacked by the aggressor force or successfully targeted by any of the sophisticated (and tantalizingly authentic) Soviet ground-to-air defense systems 'protecting' the target area. I won't go into great detail (because it's embarrassing to do so), but I will admit my performance in that very demanding scenario was well below par on this occasion. FWIC instructors rarely lost their cool in the air as they afforded us a generous amount of respect for reaching the Weapons School in the first place, but this was to be an exception. From his perch in the back seat, Joe was on my ass (figuratively *and* literally) throughout the mission, with very good cause. Despite my shoddy performance, we managed to get back to Nellis and land safely.

The verbal debriefing was justifiably brutal: it was held in a large briefing room with all participants present (except the aggressors, who tuned in by phone) and my buffoonery was covered in excruciating detail for all to hear. I wasn't the only one who screwed up that day, but I have to admit I was clearly at the top of the list. Following the public flogging, Joe and I retired to a smaller briefing room where he proceeded to take me down a number of notches, documenting each and every clanger on the grade sheet which would become a part of my performance record. When he finally finished tearing strips off me (this was truly a one-way conversation), he handed me the grade book (which I had to sign off), and departed for a well-earned beer.

I sat there alone for a few minutes, severely disappointed with my performance and worn out from absorbing relentless flak for the past couple of hours. I read through the grade sheet entry from the beginning, growing gloomier by the minute. I waded through the catalogue of errors and omissions and when I finally reached the end, I blinked, did a double-take and laughed out loud. After a masterful job of documenting my failures through the instructor's full repertoire of fear, ridicule and abuse, Joe softened the blow: his last entry read 'Engine shutdown was excellent.' Sarcasm at its very best, but believe me, I got the point.

Don't let Maverick, Goose and that Hollywood crowd hoodwink you; I have no doubt the Navy's Top Gun course is challenging and extremely valuable to those who spent a short stint at Naval Air Station Miramar, California. The Navy course was four weeks long in the 1970s, five weeks in the 1980s, and all about air-to-air stick and rudder work with a similarly focused academics program in between; IMHO not nearly as grueling or fulfilling as the six-month Air Force version.

The FWIC Academic program was – and there's no other way to put it – a bitch. We'd spend four hours or so a day in a classroom, trying desperately to absorb vast quantities of very technical information about weapons, weapons release systems, delivery parameters, tactics; ours and the bad guys'. For a bit of icing on the cake, we learned how to effectively pass this cornucopia of knowledge on to our squadron mates when we returned from the course with that well-respected bulls-eye patch velcroed on the upper left sleeve of our flight suits. It was this academic pressure cooker that provides some of the most vivid memories of the fighter pilot's unique interpretation of teamwork v. individuality.

Virtually every Air Force program concludes with the awarding of gongs for exceptional individual performance. The Weapons School was no exception, but there were no awards for 'Captain Congeniality' or 'best polished boots'. Weapons School honors hit only the high points: the Academic Award, the Flying Award and the Overall Top Graduate. I've mentioned the fighter pilot penchant for competition and the man-sized ego that goes with the job and these factors were clearly in evidence throughout the Fighter Weapons School program. The element you might not expect to read about is the one I was most impressed with: the spirit of teamwork within the group. We studied together for the numerous academic tests thrown at us every couple of days and I cannot recall a single instance of advice or assistance requested by one of us that wasn't enthusiastically provided by another, even though it may have added a point or two to the requestor's test grade. The competition was never far below the surface, but the cooperation benefited us all.

Now That's What I Call Realism

By far the most remarkable aspect of flying at Nellis was the ability to push the operational envelope not only of the aircraft but of our own capabilities as a pilot. The 'classroom' as mentioned earlier was not only vast, but also remote and consequently the rules and restrictions did not have to be structured around safety of the public, noise abatement and similar non-operational considerations. We could fly tactical low-level missions at 100ft above the ground, 150ft lower than our brethren in squadrons elsewhere. Now 100ft may not seem that low at first blush, but at 540 knots, the earth below is a disorienting blur and a very few seconds of inattention can (and has) resulted in a smoking hole and two guys who won't be home for dinner.

The remoteness of the Nellis Range complex also lent itself to the pursuit of exotic weaponry and 'black' programs that needed to be shielded from public scrutiny in order to be effective. Although virtually all the flying experiences I had during this course were remarkable, one stands out as the defining event…and we didn't even see it coming.

We'd had another stressful day, about two-thirds of the way through the program. I had afternoon academics (including a test on Soviet fighter capabilities, which we were studying at the time) so we wandered back to the squadron building around 6.00 pm just to check any last-minute scheduling changes for the next morning. When we entered the squadron building, the other half of the class (who had completed the afternoon flying schedule) were milling around near the operations desk and most of them were bitching. There's an old adage in the military: when the troops (and that includes anyone from the general on down) stop bitching, there's real trouble afoot.

In this instance, the grousing was centered around a no-notice mandatory meeting the operations officer Major Larry Keith had just called. After another twelve-hour+ day, the last thing any of us wanted or needed was a bit of administrivia, but when the boss directed a gathering, we shut up and sat down in the auditorium, albeit amid much muttering.

Major Keith (none of us would dare call him 'Larry' at the time) took the stage in front of two large projected photos: one each of the Russian-built MiG 21 and its older cousin, the MiG 17. The message was brief: 'For the last week, you've been studying the performance, strengths and weaknesses of these two aircraft.' Yeah, we know, we know, come on, Boss, time for a beer. He paused briefly for effect and quietly stopped the bellyaching in its tracks: 'Starting tomorrow, gentlemen, you will fly against these aircraft.'

Bitching ceased abruptly, the room went silent, jaws dropped and there wasn't one of us who could utter a word, but we were all thinking the same things: how could we possibly fly against Soviet equipment? Who would the pilots be? Russians? Where would these airplanes come from and why didn't we, the fledgling golden boys of fighter aviation, know all about it?

On that day, in that auditorium, F-4 FWIC Class 75CID was introduced to and became part of Department of Defense Project 'Have Idea'. We were the first class of students to have an opportunity to fly dissimilar air combat training missions against the actual aircraft we would expect to encounter in virtually any conflict around the world.

We were extensively briefed on the security requirements that came with participating in this program. At the time, 'Have Idea' was shrouded so completely that we were totally unaware of the bustling operations being conducted daily by the 4477th Test & Evaluation Squadron known as the 'Red Eagles' in Area 51 of the Nevada Test and Training Ranges. We were told in no uncertain terms that we knew all we were going to know about the operation itself and one misguided comment about the training we were about to take part in would be a career-ending event.

'Have Idea' was the initial exploitation of Russian-built fighters; originally a few MiG 21s and MiG 17s that mysteriously became a part of the USAF inventory. Our exposure to these assets was an ad hoc precursor to a structured training program which was renamed 'Constant Peg'. The difference was that, thanks to Larry Keith and others who got the ball rolling, we weren't constrained by a syllabus requirement or limited to a single sortie as would be the case in 'Constant Peg'.

Managing this unique experience must have been a significant challenge for the commander and ops officer. The sensitivity of the existence of the assets being flown in itself was a major security issue and you could add to that an extremely awkward internal morale matter: within the 414th Fighter Weapons Squadron were a number of flights whose instructors specialized in a particular aspect of training. For the 'Have Idea' exercise, instructors in the air-to-air flight were 'read in' to the existence of the MiGs and the training to be flown; other instructors (air-to-ground, nuclear weapons, etc.) were not. This meant their fellow instructors and even we as students could not discuss any aspect of the project with them. I wasn't privy to squadron politics in the 414th, but I'd be willing to bet the farm there was some world-class animosity at work in the background. To their credit, outwardly, they maintained a professional posture throughout.

Project 'Have Idea' was declassified in 2006 and a number of excellent books have been written since about the program itself and how it was developed and conducted. I'm not the right guy to relate those historical details, so I'll stick to my experiences and those of my classmates.

Our briefings for these special missions were minimal. After all, a significant objective of the mission was how we would react to an unannounced appearance of a MiG 17/21 (or a combination of the two). An hour or so before take-off we'd get on the phone with our adversaries who were ensconced in Area 51. We had no idea who they were, but they sounded suspiciously like USAF and US Navy or Marine fliers (which, of course, is exactly who they were). We covered basic safety considerations: everyone's responsibilities in case of accident or emergency and a titillating bonus; the rejoin after our air combat mission as we would be escorting the MiGs back to their base and dropping them off before we returned to Nellis. This would give us an opportunity to fly in close formation with the MiGs and get a REAL good look at these airplanes. A helluva lot more exciting than a trip to the circus when I was 8!

We then briefed within our own two-ship flight and covered the routines of start, taxi, take-off and departure and our role as fighter-bombers ingressing to a target area likely to be protected by enemy aircraft. We also discussed some fascinating security requirements to be adhered to while working with the Red Eagles. We learned, for example, the training schedule was sacrosanct and any delay in getting to the area would likely result in a cancelled mission. This was based on a concept called 'cover times' and referred to the fact that the MiGs had to either be airborne or hangared whenever any of the numerous existing Soviet intelligence satellites was due overhead. Now why didn't I think of that?

Additionally, harking back to the premise that 'loose lips sink ships', we were briefed to take extra care with radio transmissions that might compromise these sensitive assets. Consequently, the MiG 17 was to be referred to as a Type One in any transmission and the MiG 21 was a Type Two.

This communications pronouncement burned into my mind, we headed out to do mock battle with Types One and/or Two in the skies over southern Nevada. One of each bounced us shortly into the scenario, splitting our formation and requiring, at least until we got our act together, an 'every man for himself' situation. I managed to use the F-4's vertical climb superiority to temporarily shake the Type Two off my tail and, as I rolled off the top of an Immelmann turn, I found myself behind but slightly offset from the Type One who had been chasing my wingman. As I was accelerating on the way down, I was able to close on him and set my armament switches up for a simulated gunshot. Heart pumped, adrenaline gushed and within seconds, I had a turning Type One nailed in the gunsight superimposed on my heads-up display. My instructor in the backseat had locked him up on the radar and a sliding bar on the right edge of the gunsight reticle told me I was rapidly approaching gun range. I took a breath and, as was the custom in a training environment, simultaneously squeezed the trigger on the stick, keyed the microphone button on the right throttle and proudly announced to the waiting world

'Vegas One, Guns, Guns, Guns on the **MiG 17**, left turn through heading 330. 5 miles east of Pahute Mesa at 12,000 feet.'

The instant the words were uttered, I fervently wished they hadn't been. My slip of the tongue wasn't a hanging offense, but as a professional, I'd let the side down. Did anyone notice? I had my answer in a heartbeat. In a measured tone that came out sounding a little like Will Rogers, my instructor summed it all up on the intercom: 'Asshole,' he muttered.

As luck would have it, my loose lips sank no ships and I was awarded the coveted FWIC graduate patch a few weeks later. Flying against the Red Eagles was the zenith of realistic training, but there are other facets of keeping ahead of the bad guys that contributed to the knowledge base.

The Petting Zoo

Most militarized nations will have one or more museums designed to proudly show off their war-fighting hardware. Not nearly so common are exhibition halls which display the adversary's tools of the trade. Knowing your enemy and his capabilities is one of the greatest advantages available to the modern warrior and it is on this premise that the Nellis AFB Threat Training Facility was established in 1976. Operated by the 547th Intelligence Squadron (whose motto is 'Our Adversaries Have No Secrets'), the very existence of the 'Petting Zoo' was highly classified until 1993. I suspect much of the strict secrecy surrounding the facility was attributable to how, when and where the various exhibits were acquired. Suffice to say unless you sported at least a 'Secret' security clearance, you weren't going to have a chance to poke around the archives. Ironically, if you knew what you were looking for, a stroll past one end of the facility revealed the business end of a Russian-built SA-2 Guideline SAM prominently looming above the high walls surrounding the main building. My wife once asked me what 'that chimney' was for; I couldn't tell her then and it was years before the classification was relaxed and I could give her an explanation and show her around.

Far more than a museum, 'The Zoo' formed a foundation for the development of a research department to provide hands-on assessment of the capabilities of enemy military equipment. In the Cold War's pressurized cat-and-mouse technology superiority sweepstakes, the ability to peek at the other guy's hardware was invaluable. The 'Petting Zoo' uniquely made that ability available to those of us who might face that equipment in anger. Within the main building and in a mammoth courtyard surrounded by a substantial wall were Soviet aircraft, vehicles, surface-to-air missiles and anti-aircraft artillery plus numerous items of support equipment, all available for close scrutiny.

There's only one source of intelligence better than having your adversary's weaponry available to study and evaluate and that is an opportunity to talk to someone who has operated that equipment professionally. I'm going to depart temporarily from the chronological flow to describe such an encounter, which took place in late 1977 as the result of a significant Cold War defection.

Fraternizing with the Enemy[1]

On 6 September 1976, a twin-engine jet abruptly appeared out of thick clouds near the Japanese city of Hakodate on the northern island of Hokkaido. It was an enormous, hulking gray aircraft emblazoned with the red stars of the Soviet Union on wing and tail. No one in the West had ever seen one before.

The aircraft, a MiG-25P (NATO code-name: Foxbat) touched down on Hakodate Airport's runway, which unfortunately was not nearly long enough to accommodate its landing roll. The jet departed the runway end, ploughing onwards through the turf for hundreds of feet before finally coming to a stop near the airport perimeter.

After the engines had wound down, the pilot climbed out of his cockpit and fired two warning shots from his service pistol to warn off Japanese motorists who had been, as you might expect, taking pictures of this strange drama from the public highway just outside the airport perimeter. When police and airport officials finally reached him from the terminal, the 29-year-old pilot, Flight Lieutenant Viktor Ivanovich Belenko of the Soviet Air Defense Forces, dropped his pistol, raised his hands and announced that he wished to defect to the USA.

Adhering scrupulously to international law and convention, the Japanese government returned the aircraft to the Russians, but not until US intelligence operatives had pored over every plate and rivet and actually operated many of the aircraft systems, including the engines and avionics suites, to determine just how good this super-fighter really was. It turned out to be underwhelming in a number of important areas, thus mitigating to a large degree the insecurity surrounding Soviet aircraft capabilities within the Department of Defense. The sleek and impressive MiG-25, delivered so dramatically to the West by Flight Lieutenant Belenko, was subsequently shipped back to its rightful owners in forty oversized containers.

Within three days of his defection, Viktor Belenko was spirited to the US, where he was intensively debriefed by the CIA, DIA and Air Force Intelligence about every aspect of his life, career and psychological make-up. His interrogations revealed an unusual picture of the life of a Soviet fighter pilot, characterized by what one official called 'brutal discipline, distrust, extraordinary concern with safety and spartan living conditions.' A bureaucratic military, tightly controlled by senior officers with little scope for innovation or independent thinking. In terms of intelligence value, Lieutenant Belenko's testimony surrounding the appalling training, morale and living conditions within the Soviet military was far more lucrative than the aircraft he flew.

Consequently, it was obvious that sharing his thoughts with fellow fighter pilots would be a most valuable use of what was clearly a unique 'asset'. I was running the Wing Weapons and Tactics Division at RAF Bentwaters when I got a call to report to the Command Post, a secure venue where the Wing Deputy Commander for Operations briefed me on the imminent arrival of one Flight Lieutenant Belenko and two CIA minders from London. Flying had been cancelled for the following day and I was tasked with setting up an appropriate program of events to introduce Viktor to his American counterparts. Unfortunately, the Officers' Club bar wasn't large enough to accommodate all the interested parties, so I settled on an aircraft hangar with one of our F-4 Phantoms as a suitable backdrop and the wheels started turning to notify the troops and set the stage.

I called Elaine and told her not to wait up. Trooper that she is, there was no interrogation and immediate acceptance that I was doing something important and would tell her what I could, when I could. Viktor arrived and joined us for drinks and dinner at our Officers' Club, a converted Second World War Quonset hut that was short on splendor but absolutely brimming with fighter aviation atmosphere. He walked in, we shook hands and the bond was immediate; Russian or not, here was a fighter pilot.

We (and the CIA babysitters) shared numerous drinks and, as is the custom in our fraternity, traded several war stories. Viktor's English was basic but improving and he clearly had an active sense of humor. He had, for example, given his minders the slip in London on the day prior, spending the afternoon and most of the evening exploring the city as a free man while they frantically attempted to reacquire the potential Soviet target under their care. He'd been given a moderate amount of cash and spent it like a typical tourist, enjoying the delights of a great Western city. He and I laughed long and heartily; the CIA guys did not and looked extremely stressed until we both made a solemn promise to forget the episode entirely (which I've honored until just now).

The following morning, Viktor briefed our aircrews in the hangar and hung around to shoot the breeze with the troops. As they would at any fighter base Happy Hour anywhere in the world, topics ranged from flying (US and Soviet style) to women and back again with very little divergence from those themes. Viktor was in his element, as were dozens of American aircrew who shared the event with him and we all gained something important from the experience.

Obviously, he now maintains a relatively low public profile but Viktor, wherever you are and whatever you're doing, it was an honor to have met you. *Na Zdorovie* (*На здоровье*) from one fighter pilot to another.

Chapter Eight

Death and Related Unpleasantries

There's an axiom in the fighter community: as a fighter pilot, only two *really* bad things can happen to you and one of them most certainly will:

1. One day you will walk out to the aircraft knowing that it is your last flight in a fighter.
2. One day you will walk out to the airplane NOT knowing that it is your last flight in a fighter.

Despite the fact that aviation – particularly fighter aviation – is generally considered to be more hazardous than, say, herding goats or dealing blackjack, I can count the number of friends, *close* acquaintances and squadron mates who met their Maker in aircraft accidents or in combat on my combined fingers and toes. That might seem remarkable given a twenty-eight-year flying career including a 204-mission combat tour, but I'm confident most of my colleagues would tell a similar story. Overall, the mishap rate for fighter aircraft – in peace and war – has plummeted over the past fifty years. As an example (and this will likely be the only concentration of statistics you see in this publication as they tend to put you – and me – into a deep slumber),[1] the US Air Force flew 5.25 million sorties over South Vietnam, North Vietnam, northern and southern Laos and Cambodia, losing 2,251 aircraft: 1,737 to hostile action and 514 in accidents; 110 of the losses were helicopters and the rest fixed-wing. A ratio of roughly 0.4 losses per 1,000 sorties compared favorably with a 2.0 rate in Korea and the 9.7 figure during the Second World War. Nevertheless, fighter flying is a highly charged environment characterized by large, powerful jets operating in close proximity to *terra firma* and/or each other. In this setting, some aircraft will unquestionably be damaged or destroyed and lives will be lost. The fact that this is the exception and not the rule is testimony to the aircraft we operate, the expertise of those who maintain them, and the proficiency and judgment of those who fly them.

The Blue Sedan

The culture of the fighter pilot as discussed earlier also includes certain customs and traditions that wouldn't be appropriate in civilian life. The fact is that, from time to time, in war there is attrition and in peacetime accidents occur. These tragedies must be dealt with quickly in a highly dignified manner and the Air Force has developed precise and sensitive guidelines for handling them.

Fighter units have always prided themselves on taking care of their own. This includes the military members themselves and their families. Breaking bad news comes with the title 'Commander' and is arguably the most difficult task a boss must undertake. The ritual is well-established and, although never rehearsed, is always performed with extreme decorum and solemnity.

Aircraft combat losses and mishaps are invariably unforeseen and abrupt and, in this age of the internet and twenty-four-hour news, very difficult to keep under wraps. Nevertheless, the commander's overriding responsibility when a fatality occurs is to reach the family first and personally assume the supportive role, preventing the news being dropped on loved ones, inadvertently or otherwise, via gossip, newsflash or (today) tweet or email.

This mission involves the very rapid assembly of the commander, an appropriate clergyman and a medical professional. They'll don the class 'A' blue uniform (when I was a commander, this was always hanging in my office for just such a disheartening contingency), then climb into the commander's staff car, invariably a dark blue sedan. The drive to the home of the family is awkward and stressful while the boss tries to organize how he will compassionately deliver the worst message he could possibly convey.

The unsuspecting wife or partner, witnessing the arrival of the sedan, will instantly be keenly aware of the implications of three officers in Dress Blues making their way to her front door. Her initial response is often either denial, hoping against hope that a dreadful mistake has been made, or a complete and utter collapse.

Circumstances will dictate the approach to be taken and the scenario from this point cannot be adequately defined. Appalling news having been delivered, the wheels of a well-oiled support system will already have been set in motion by the commander's staff. Devastating though the situation is, the family will now be assisted throughout the long ordeal of closure by friends and Air Force 'extended family'.

I've witnessed this ritual a couple of times, although I was never directly involved. The process never failed to impress and the result was as positive as the situation allowed.

Chapter Nine

Iran: Training Fred's Air Force

Y ou may recall a brief anecdote about a pilot training colleague from Iran earlier in this volume. Young Afsar was among those individuals brought to the US by our government (in concert with his own) to undertake American Air Force training, in this case of the undergraduate pilot variety. The flip side of that concept was our responsibility, as leader nation of the Free World, to arm and train our allies in the art of warfare. International politics being what they are, today's allies are tomorrow's potential foes and we have seen this concept in action more times than I care to remember.

So it was in early 1976, as a recent graduate of the F-4 Fighter Weapons School instructing at Homestead AFB, I was offered the opportunity to join a small hand-picked team of specialists who would provide an intense course of flying training to a group of equally hand-picked Iranian fighter pilots. The nature of the course was driven by the fact that the Imperial Iranian Air Force (IIAF) was equipped with American fighter aircraft: the F-5 Freedom Fighter (as noted earlier, the combat-ready basis for the exquisite T-38 trainer) and the newest addition to their inventory, the F-4E Phantom II. Our charter was to develop and teach a syllabus of dissimilar air combat training involving these two aircraft types.

What's dissimilar air combat, you may ask. Well, during the Vietnam War we discovered early on that we were regularly getting our butts kicked by smaller, more agile Russian-built MiG 17s and 21s flown by the Vietnamese (oh yeah, and maybe by the occasional Russian as well). There were a number of reasons for this, but without going into laborious detail, one of the most prominent was the fact that we trained only against similar adversaries (other F-4s or F-105s, for example) that had comparable flight characteristics and performance to our own steeds. Consequently, the training was less than effective in operating against aircraft that turned tighter, accelerated quicker and presented an additional challenge due to their small size and our resulting difficulty in obtaining early visual acquisition.

The solution to this dilemma was to begin training our fighter pilots to fly air combat maneuvers against smaller highly maneuverable aircraft such as the F-5. We began to develop tactics to exploit the American fighters' clear advantages – superior thrust, climb capability and more versatile weaponry – to level the playing field (or, as actually occurred, tilt it in the other direction). As a result of this change in training and emphasis, by the end of the war we were clearly on the offensive against the MiGs and the concept of flying air combat sorties against dissimilar adversaries was firmly embedded in our training culture.

It was this concept which spawned our mission to Iran, providing the IIAF with a foundation upon which to build a lasting training regime, using the wisdom and expertise we would impart to their instructor pilots and the compact, professional syllabus we would design to achieve this end. However, it didn't turn out to be quite that straightforward...

We were particularly well-suited to the task. Led by an experienced F-5 instructor pilot, Major Skip Harbison, there was a second F-5 instructor, myself and another F-4 instructor pilot plus an F-4 Weapons System Operator (navigator) and a tactical weapons controller. He was a non-aviator highly skilled in the art of tactical radar control of aircraft operating in a combat environment. This added dimension established us as state-of-the-art, and we embarked on the project with abundant enthusiasm. Like most assignments of this kind, we didn't just hop on an airliner for Tehran and get on with it. The Air Force planned these things properly: we attended a course at Hurlburt AFB in Fort Walton Beach, Florida designed to prepare us for the significant differences between our culture and that of the Iranians and how to (and not to) behave as guests in a Muslim country. The course was taught by Air Force specialists who knew their stuff, academically. It gave us a grounding in the language, the customs and the culture of Iran, but as we were to discover, there was a helluva lot more we needed to learn and many things we would never, ever completely understand.

The project started with a pre-deployment trip to Tehran. The objective was to coordinate our program and syllabus with the Defense Attaché's office and Military Advisory and Assistance Group (MAAG) so we would not step on anyone's (American or Iranian) toes. Tehran was a culture shock in itself for a bunch of American fighter pilots. Most fascinating was our introduction to murky international politics and this manifested itself on Day One. We were told to wear civilian clothes and expect transportation at 08:00 at which time a small minibus promptly appeared. What we *weren't* told to expect were the two Iranian security types with pistols in shoulder holsters that were riding shotgun. For the three weeks we were in Tehran, these guys rode with us daily. Interestingly, we always travelled to the American Embassy at different times and via different routes. This provided a sobering realization that His Imperial Majesty, Mohammad Reza Shah Pahlavi wasn't everyone's flavor of the month. There were clearly serious enemies of his State lurking in the shadows long before today's crop of feral Jihadis began publicly beheading folks on the internet. At the time, we were reasonably relaxed about the security situation, but three years later, the Iranian government was overthrown and a number of Americans lost their lives in the fracas.

The brief interlude with the Air Attaché staff was productive and we picked up a lot about our Iranian hosts and our national relationship with them. For a start, Americans being Americans, the Embassy staff put their own spin on the formalities of Middle Eastern diplomacy. The thought of constantly referring to the Shah as 'His Imperial Majesty' as protocol dictated did not sit well with the comparatively casual Yanks, so when there were no Iranians present he became, very simply, 'Fred'. It always raised a chuckle in me whenever a senior diplomat or two- or three-star US Air Force general came out with something like 'You wouldn't believe what Fred said/did yesterday.' Nevertheless, as far as I am aware, not a single international incident was generated by this irreverent, albeit not unaffectionate lack of respect.

The Attaché team also gave us a more realistic view of the cultural challenges we might face than the ethnicity instructors at Hurlburt AFB. I should explain here that Fred had done a great deal for his country in terms of fostering its belated emergence from the Paleolithic age. With massive US financial and technical assistance, he engineered a national development program known as the White Revolution. This championed construction of a developed road, rail and air network, a number of dam and irrigation projects, the eradication of diseases such as malaria, the sponsorship and support of industrial growth, and land reform. He also established a literacy corps and a health corps for the enormous but isolated rural population. That's the good news. The bad news was that in encouraging the nation to adopt these predominately Western initiatives, he incurred the wrath of fundamentalists who then, as now, had no desire to ascend out of the Stone Age. They posed a significant threat to the Shah's ongoing vision for Iran, not to mention his very existence. Consequently, he ruled the former Persia with an iron fist and his tolerance of those who opposed him was monumentally lacking.

We learned, for example, that virtually every military unit had, infiltrated within its structure, at least one member of Fred's Secret Service, *Savak*. No one knew who this person was, so we were cautioned that the pilots we would be training would be very reluctant to exhibit any level of open-minded thinking as, paradoxically, this kind of initiative would be viewed as suspicious. Thus, at least in public, the highly-educated, intelligent and articulate Iranian fighter pilots we were there to train withdrew into a kind of politically correct shell. They were unwilling to debate fighter tactics and concepts to any degree and therefore reluctant to participate in the freewheeling critiques we were used to conducting at home. In addition to this paranoia, they were virtually all enslaved by the Eastern tradition of 'saving face' and this detracted immeasurably from the quality of training we were able to impart. When debriefing a complex mission with fellow Americans (or Brits, Germans, Dutch and I'd suspect Russians as well), it was customary not to bar any holds. Such mission analysis sessions were sometimes brutally direct and at times bordering on the pugnacious. For example, if I flew an instructional ride with Bill or Bob or Charlie and they had made a (potentially) fatal mistake, I'd feel obligated to diplomatically drive that home: 'How am I supposed to tell your widow that you got blown away because you fucked up the simplest gun tracking conversion in the book by overshooting and becoming the world's most inviting target? Try to pull your head out of your ass so you don't become just another statistic!' (or something equally motivational). With the Iranians, we quickly learned how counterproductive that approach was. Applying a far less blasphemous but equally critical comment to one of our Iranian students would result in him immediately switching out of 'receive' mode, staring at the wall or out the window in a massive sulk, and the end of productive training for the day. Consequently, a similar scenario with Ahmed would necessarily go something like this: 'Ahmed, what you did in the guns tracking exercise was OK, but please try to remember the objective is to remain *behind* the enemy and not fly out in front of him where he can shoot you down.' This soothing bit of cajoling would probably keep Ahmed from getting his panties in a knot, but it was unlikely to leave a lasting impression and therefore was fairly counterproductive in a training environment.

Clearly, our primary challenge in this educational process was dealing with a culture we then (as now) failed to understand. There were many examples of this conundrum of comprehension; some mildly interesting, others of significant importance in completing our task. A few brief illustrations follow.

The day before we arrived at Shahrokhi Air Base, the IIAF had managed to run two airplanes together à la airborne bumper cars. One crew jettisoned their brand-new F-4E in the desert, parachuting to safety, while the others nursed their somewhat bent bird back to base for a safe landing. This airplane had not been hopelessly damaged, having suffered some damage to the nose-mounted radar dome and other superficial cuts and bruises. When I pitched up for my project in-brief with the director of operations, I asked him how long it would take to put the bird back in working order and get her back into action. In the USAF, this would happen in a matter of days: access the parts, reassemble the broken bits, run a number of technical tests and test-fly the aircraft under a specific profile to ensure airworthiness.

His response staggered me: 'No, that airplane will never fly again. It is jinxed and last night our pilots gathered to sacrifice a lamb to guarantee better luck in future for the flying Wing and Shahrokhi Air Base.' This pronouncement from an American-trained, university graduate lieutenant colonel fighter pilot and commander rocked me somewhat. Atypically, I had the presence of mind to keep my mouth shut. Nevertheless, I suspect my expression was one of great skepticism, similar to the one I might display if told that the sure-fire resolution to Islamic terrorism is an evening holding hands around the campfire and a few rousing verses of *Kumbaya*.

One of our trainee pilots told me (when we were alone, of course) a story about an IIAF C-130 Hercules that landed for an overnight stop at one of their more remote desert bases. When the crew went to their quarters, the airplane was left to be guarded by a young conscript, fresh out of his desert mud hut village. When the crew arrived to fly the following day, they cranked up the airplane and noted there was no fuel in one of the internal wing tanks which had been filled the night before. Investigation showed that during the night, overcome by boredom, the curious conscript had poked the underside of the wing with his bayonet and the resulting drip, drip, dripping, which I'm sure amused the lad, ultimately drained the tank. Allegedly, he was summarily shot for his innocent naivety.

A modern fighter aircraft is a marvel of technology and the brand spanking new McDonnell Douglas F-4Es flown by the Iranians were, for their day, the top of the totem pole. In order to keep them flying at the peak of efficiency, it's necessary to maintain them meticulously. As a part of the Military Advisory and Assistance Program, the United States provided maintenance contingents that would have been the envy of any American fighter unit. The Yanks that serviced Fred's aircraft were the cream of the crop: senior maintenance technicians with bags of experience. As they weren't flying with us, however, the onus for giving them the ability to fix things properly rests with the aviator, whose description of faults and discrepancies is key to analyzing the problem and taking the proper action.

Recalling an example of how important this information is takes me back to a mission I flew in the back seat with one of the brighter IIAF pilots. As this is not meant to be a technical manual, Wikipedia describes the situation adequately: 'A compressor stall is a local disruption of the airflow in a gas turbine or turbocharger compressor.' That's the definition; the reality is that hard maneuvering can cause this disruption and the name of the game in air-to-air training is hard maneuvering. A compressor stall is not a catastrophic occurrence, nor is it rare in fighter aviation. What it is, beyond a shadow of a doubt, is an attention-getter. A tight, high 'G' turn is followed by Thor's hammer abruptly and intensely striking the side of the aircraft; the result is not unlike an unexpected collision with a metal vehicle going very fast and it is invariably followed by an exclamation of surprise and dismay. 'Shit!!' is the traditional utterance. After the stall, the engine's power will abruptly roll back but, in most cases, it will rapidly clear and recover without prompting. If not, an engine restart is almost always successful.

On this particular occasion, we were engaged in a spirited battle with one of the sister squadron's F-5s high above the desert floor. My Iranian student in the front seat was pulling hard to attempt to put his gunsight aiming reticle on the tightly-turning F-5 when it happened. Thor's hammer smacked into us on the left-hand side: BAM! My student emitted a high-pitched yelp in Farsi which I didn't understand (but I'm willing to bet it would have translated as 'Shit!!'), the engine rolled back and, as he relaxed his turn, it quickly recovered.

At this point, as there were very few engine instruments in my back seat, I was expecting the student to do the same thing his American counterpart would have done: make a note of every parameter he could think of to assist the maintainers in thoroughly investigating the problem. I had jotted down those indicators I could monitor in the 'pit' – airspeed, altitude, throttle setting, RPM, 'G', angle of bank and so on – but I didn't have some of the critical instruments that would provide important clues as to the cause of the stall: temperatures, oil pressures, angle of attack, etc.

When we landed, the first port of call (after a quick diversion to the toilet) was maintenance debrief. Each aircraft had its own maintenance record – Form 781 – in which discrepancies and faults were described and the steps taken to rectify them were catalogued. A senior American technician presided over the debrief and was there to discuss the problem(s) in detail, clarify and add any pertinent information before sending the form to the hands-on guys to start working on the problem. I anticipated a relatively lengthy debrief as the compressor stall, although not particularly dangerous, was relatively complex and required some discussion. I was therefore a bit surprised when my student scribbled a few words in the form and pushed it over to the debriefer, an Air Force chief master sergeant with stripes all the way from his elbow to his shoulder. He glanced at the entry, raised his eyebrows and pushed it back over to me. My student had written, in the perfect English he was capable of: 'Left engine makes funny noise.' Knowing, as I did, the unpleasant cultural ramifications of verbally disembowelling the student in the presence of a US non-commissioned officer, I told him I'd see him in the flight debriefing and, as an aside to the debriefer, said: 'Chief, I'll be back in a half hour and give you something to work with.' He looked grateful.

Our contract stipulated that training would be conducted in English, as our students all possessed a reasonable working knowledge of the International Language of Aviation, at least while they were in a tranquil environment. Once airborne, in the heat of mock battle, however, the rush of adrenaline took hold and, try as they might to honor the language decree, their communication degenerated into excited Farsi gibberish. The critical radio calls to other aircraft and within the cockpit to us as instructors became an incomprehensible cacophony as useful for imparting vital information as the proverbial tits on a boar hog. Skip the Skipper called us together after only one or two missions and we unanimously decided that the only solution was to quietly advise our students they should communicate with each other in their native tongue (Farsi) and try to keep us in the loop in English. I say quietly, because we realized that making this concession public would undoubtedly cause great ructions among our American project administrators. This would reverberate through the halls of the Pentagon itself, if not scuppering the whole project, at very least resulting in interminable delays, debates and bureaucratic buffoonery we could ill afford. In the final analysis, our flexibility worked well and the Iranians were far more relaxed in the air. On the down side, those of us who had to instruct from the back seat while Ahmed flew the bird and chatted to his colleagues in modern Persian could look forward to every mission being an utterly terrifying and exhausting hour or so while we strained every muscle, sinew, eyeball, audio and brain cell to

1. Keep up with what was happening around us at 600 knots or thereabouts, despite being bombarded with high-intensity Farsi babble and
2. Ensure that Ahmed and his buddies weren't going to run into each other, subsequently transforming us into an insignificant grease mark on the desert floor below.

The Iranian pilots were a bewildering paradox. Highly intelligent, educated, articulate and generally well-trained, they occasionally reverted to the Stone Age culture of their religion, leaving us to shake our heads in astonishment. One of these regressions involved their unwillingness to accept an aircraft equipment upgrade provided by good ol' Uncle Sam. The aircraft they were receiving were brand spanking new and had all the bells and whistles (other than some highly classified US eyes-only gear we kept to ourselves). From 1974 the IIAF employed improved F-4Es with leading-edge maneuvering slats and TISEO (target identification system, electro-optical). TISEO was a Northrop-built long-range television camera lens in a cylindrical extension from the Phantom's port wing. It was slaved to the radar image and provided the aircrew with an extended range visual identification of a target to circumvent restrictive rules of engagement for identification of friend or foe. Despite the fact that the F-4, with its drooping tail section and upturned wingtips, was perhaps the least visually appealing fighter aircraft design of its time, the insignificant physical wing extension was the source of great consternation among the Iranian pilots. It was around 18in in diameter, protruded about 2ft forward from the wing root and looked like a telephoto lens (which, of course, is exactly what it was). The Iranians interpreted it as an airflow disruptive protuberance which under certain circumstances could cause the aircraft to spin, crash and burn. Aerodynamically, this is ludicrous. The F-4 has often been described as indisputable proof that if you bolt enough thrust onto a brick it will fly and TISEO wouldn't affect this postulate in any way. Nevertheless, our Iranian colleagues grumbled, moaned and became embarrassingly timid when contemplating a hard left turn. No matter how much we demonstrated the rock-hard stability of the aircraft in a break turn to the port side, the Iranians remained squeamish. As fighter pilots, we all made a mental note: when the political climate shifts (as indeed it *has*) and we're at war with the IIAF's Phantoms, remember to maneuver Ahmed into breaking left (gingerly), and chalk him up as an easy kill.

For all their idiosyncrasies, the Iranians were agreeable colleagues in the fighter business. They were friendly (unless you embarrassed them; see above), welcoming and generous as befits their culture. They obviously appreciated our efforts to impart training and reciprocated with an impressive kindness and eagerness to please. On a number of occasions, one or more of our students would take us into the city of Hamedān, some 30 miles away, to shop for Persian gifts: jewelry and other artifacts for our wives and partners at home. These trips invariably included a (non-alcoholic) drink or two and a meal along with the visit to the bazaar and, much to our relief, our hosts always managed to find restaurants serving food which did not result in rampant 'Iranahreah'. It is somewhat ironic to note that our only serious bout of gastro-intestinal catastrophe during the six-month-long deployment resulted from a lunch we all had together in the American Embassy in Tehran as guests of the Military Attaché. This resulted in nearly a week's delay in training while virtually the entire team was forced to lie in state in darkened rooms except for numerous and sudden forays to the toilet where, to a man, we hoped for a swift and merciful death.

On the other side of the coin, when our students took us to dinner in Hamedān, we found that Iranian cuisine is rich and varied, if very different from our own Western staples. Typical Persian main dishes are combinations of rice with meat, such as lamb, chicken, or fish, and vegetables such as onions, various herbs and nuts. The ubiquitous kebab was often in evidence and much more agreeable than the Western equivalent. Fresh green herbs are frequently used, along with fruits such as plums, pomegranates, quince, prunes, apricots and raisins. To achieve a balanced taste, characteristic Persian flavorings such as saffron, dried lime, cinnamon and parsley are mixed delicately and used in some special dishes.

Senior IIAF officers were impressively hospitable as well. Shortly after we arrived at Shahrokhi, we were invited to the commander's quarters for a meal. He lived in a lavish bungalow, beautifully furnished with quality fittings. We were bemused to note that, in a devoutly Muslim country, he was using bottles of Chivas Regal as bookends. Unlike his pilots, the boss offered alcohol before, during and after the meal. This loose interpretation of 'The Rules' by more prominent members of Iranian society was a feature often noticed and discussed among the Westerners. On the night we visited it was quite chilly and we hadn't brought appropriate clothing for the outdoor barbecue. The commander passed around a number of impressive leather jackets and, when I mentioned casually how nice it was, he followed Islamic tradition and said 'It's yours.' Oops, something they didn't tell us about at 'Culture School' prior to deployment. I found a quiet way to return it to him some weeks later, saving face all round.

Not everyone in Iran appreciated the resurgence of their military and those who made it happen. Shahrokhi's base commander was a gentleman; personable, generous and articulate and a capable leader in the air. A fighter pilot firmly in the mold of the people I'm writing about here. It was therefore unsettling at best when I came upon a photograph of him in a national news magazine being summarily executed by one of the Ayatollah's wild-eyed radical Islamists during the Iranian Revolution of 1978/9.

In addition to our positive social relationships with the Iranians, we had other colleagues nearby. For example, the Brits had sold Fred's army state-of-the art Chieftain battle tanks and supported their maintenance and training programs with top-notch technicians and mentors in a similar manner to our own provision of expertise for the F-4E sales and service project. On 4 July 1976, the Brits surprised us with a bicentennial bash that reinforced the 'Special Relationship' in a big way, albeit on a very small scale. We enjoyed the celebrations with our allies immensely, if not the throbbing heads and nagging nausea that resulted on 5 July.

Chapter Ten

Enter the 'Hog

Shortly after my temporary 'consultancy' in Iran, I reached the end of my tour as an instructor pilot at Homestead. Having become an Anglophile (and not only through marriage), I lobbied for an assignment to the UK where there were F-4s at RAF Bentwaters/ Woodbridge. I was delighted to receive a validation of my 'Dream Sheet' and orders to the 81st Tactical Fighter Wing (TFW), RAF Bentwaters. Consequently, in the summer of 1977, I reported to the 81st and was appointed wing weapons and tactics officer. I had achieved just about everything a captain fighter pilot could aspire to: a combat tour in South-East Asia, instructor and flight commander in a fighter training squadron and a graduate of the distinguished F-4 Fighter Weapons Instructor Course. In short, I was having about as much fun as was possible with my clothes on and enjoying my lot in life immensely. It was at this point that rumors began to circulate within the F-4 community that the venerable old war horse was being considered for the glue factory. There were new kids on the block: in the air-to-air world, the F-15 Eagle was McDonnell Douglas's sexy air superiority fighter and all the bright young sparks were chomping at the bit to saddle up on this sleek charger. The rumor mill gained momentum and it soon became likely that F-4 units based in Europe would gradually be phased out. Many of us had stimulating (if unrealistic) visions of climbing out of a tired old Phantom on a Monday and into a bright shiny Eagle on Tuesday.

Although the F-15C would go a long way towards ensuring NATO's air superiority in a future conflict, there was one vital piece of the puzzle missing. The F-4 was a remarkable air-to-ground machine – a role the early F-15s couldn't handle at all – and the Russian adversary we faced in central Europe possessed an awesome land army capability – armor and infantry – which would need to be blunted decisively if we ever came to blows. It was this threat that kept the folks in the Pentagon awake at night, but on the periphery of the well-hyped introduction of the F-15 into Europe was another new aircraft, unobtrusively being developed out of the limelight.

The A-10 was conceived in the wake of the relatively large numbers of ground-attack aircraft shot down in South-East Asia by small arms, surface-to-air missiles and low-level anti-aircraft artillery. Attack helicopters flown by the Army were effective for supporting troops on the ground, but not against a substantial armored threat. We were seeking an aircraft better able to survive such weapons and provide a credible capability against armor. Air Force planners weren't asking for much: a low-cost ground-attack bird possessing long loiter capability, excellent battlefield visibility, low-speed maneuverability, massive cannon firepower and extreme survivability. The prototype was produced by Fairchild Republic Aircraft in the mid-'70s and 'flown off' against the Northrop YA-9 (which bears an uncanny resemblance to the Soviet Sukhoi-25, NATO code-named 'Frogfoot'. Just sayin'…).

The rumors of the F-4's demise in Europe persisted, and finally we were advised that a force structure announcement was imminent. The ubiquitous F-4 was based in a number of European locations. In England, in addition to my own unit at Bentwaters/Woodbridge, there was the 48th TFW, flying F111s, 60 miles up the road near Newmarket and Cambridge. We waited expectantly for a couple of weeks and then the wing commander assembled us in the base theatre to present 'the Plan'. The powers that be in the Pentagon had rolled the dice and the 81st Wing at Bentwaters had been selected to host not the sleek F-15 ballerina of the skies, but the A-10 Thunderbolt II.

At this point, I need to explain yet another influential trait of the fighter pilot: rampant narcissism. As F-4 pilots, we were proud of the image our aircraft conveyed. It was not aesthetically appealing (for example, F-15s are elegant and slick; F-16s are cute) but the Phantom always looked like what it was: a consummate weapon capable of inflicting massive destruction on an enemy. It was in some respects asymmetric with a droopy tailplane and bent-up wingtips, but by God it looked mean…and we liked that a lot.

We didn't know a great deal about the single-seat A-10 (as we'd all been banking on the sleek and sophisticated Eagle and there was no Google available for us to conduct in-depth research), but there's one thing we knew for sure: the A-10 – and there's really no other way to put this – was Butt Ugly.

It was a big gray airplane with straight wings and two fanjet engines which sounded not unlike massive sewing machines that appeared to have been mounted high on the fuselage just forward of the twin tail as an afterthought (more about these later). We were horrified by the fact that the main wheels retracted forward and not completely and the bottom half of the tires hung inelegantly from big ungainly pods under the wings (there's a damn good reason for this too, but remember, we're talking vanity here). The bulbous nose housed a seven-barreled Gatling gun, which poked out from underneath like some kind of monstrous carbuncle. I don't believe any aircraft ever lost its official title as quickly as the A-10. The Air Force had designated the airplane Thunderbolt II after the Second World War's P-47 – a powerful and capable attack and pursuit airplane – and this tag was a logical choice. It took the community of A-10 pilots less than a heartbeat to bestow the unofficial nickname which was instantly adopted and will never be superseded: Warthog.

To add insult to injury our initial perception of the 'Hog's performance was underwhelming. There were no afterburners and top speed was less than 400 knots. We were used to mounting a steed whose afterburners would push us to and through Mach 1 effortlessly; a bird that generated noise and power in abundance and garnered respect wherever we went.

We left the base theatre in a state of numbness. The 48th Wing at Lakenheath would be transitioning to the urbane and classy F-15 Eagle (albeit many years down the road), while we were to be relegated to the slow, clumsy, repulsive Swine of the Skies. As a group, we were not happy bunnies.

In the weeks to follow, we learned that there was an element of choice attached to this evolution. Within certain constraints, if we so desired, we could either upgrade (well, at that moment we considered it downgrading) to the A-10 and complete our tour with the 81st in the new aircraft and role. Alternatively, we could remain with the F-4, taking our chances in terms of assignment location and available job opportunities. As an F-4 Weapons School graduate, I was confident of a reasonable flying billet elsewhere in the Air Force, continuing to fly my beloved Phantom until we were both too old to continue functioning. Consequently, as was my custom in those early days, I applied virtually no logic, reason or forethought and decided unequivocally that my bright future would be fulfilled by maintaining the status quo and moving on with the Phantom. My wife, who has always been far superior in foresight, held her counsel and continued to give me rope, hoping I wouldn't hang myself with it.

The Bear Checks In

Sometime during these deliberations, just before I could sign on the proverbial dotted line, my back-seater from a previous life with the 'Lucky Devils' in Spain came to visit us in England for a few days. Ed Thomas had been an F-105 Electronic Warfare Officer (EWO) in the Wild Weasel program in South-East Asia. These guys went hunting for North Vietnamese surface-to-air missiles (SAMs) and used sophisticated acquisition equipment and beam-riding missiles to locate and exterminate the SAMs. The mission was dangerous but rewarding and relied heavily on the technical skill of the EWOs (known universally as 'Bears') to achieve successful outcomes.

When Ed left South-East Asia, he transitioned to the F-4 back seat and ended up with me as a formed crew (bringing the 'Bear' nickname with him). We bonded immediately; he had my total respect as a professional and as a drinking buddy and confidant. I took great pleasure in letting him land our airplane from the back seat (illicitly; as good as he was, the Bear was a navigator and not authorized to land the bird) and he was best man at Elaine's and my wedding in 1973. We were – in every respect – a formidable team.

As happens less often than it should have in the Air Force, the Bear's talents were finally acknowledged and he was selected to go to pilot training. He departed Spain shortly after we did and a couple years later was flying the single-seat LTV A-7 Corsair in the close air-support role. Therein lies the reason for including this anecdote.

When the Bear pitched up at Bentwaters, I was merrily proceeding with my mental plan to follow the F-4 wherever she would take me. I brought him out to the house on a Friday evening, where Elaine had prepared dinner and we all had a lively chat about old times with the

'Spanish Flyers' – parties, road trips, mutual friends and foes and flying – notably the time we (oh, all right, 'I') dropped a 600-gallon centerline fuel tank on a Spanish gunnery range instead of the intended 25lb smoke bomb.

The hour grew late, the single malt whisky appeared and Elaine decided we were becoming unintelligible and she would leave the boys to their own devices. The conversation moved entirely to aviation. I told the Bear about the impending transition and gave him all my logical, painstakingly reasoned and compelling arguments on why I would be snubbing the 'Hog in favor of a few more years of flying Phantoms. The 'Hog was slow, the 'Hog was terminally ugly, the 'Hog failed to support my enthusiastically-cultivated image as a dashing fighter pilot; I would be mortified to climb out of this ungainly beast at a strange airfield. Having run out of logical, painstakingly reasoned and compelling arguments and lubricated with another double shot of Glenlivet, I started the list all over again.

The Bear shook his head and looked at me with an imposing blend of benevolence and pity. 'Steve, for a reasonably perceptive individual, you can be awfully stupid,' he began gently. The Bear had always been a straight-shooter and the respect I had developed for him over the years kept me from tossing my toys out of the playpen in response to this blunt indictment. I poured us another round and he began his monologue.

Although he, too, only had a basic working knowledge of the A-10, his argument was cleverly constructed around a number of factors near and dear to the heart of a fighter pilot and robustly supported by the magic of Glenlivet. Why, he asked, would I want to continue to fly in an airplane with a built-in backseat passenger when I could be master of all I surveyed in the single-seat 'Hog? Without directly referring to yours truly, his former FUF (Fuckhead Up Front) he lauded the delights he had discovered since earning his pilot's wings and subsequently swapping me for a couple of hundred pounds of JP4 jet fuel to venture forth in the land of single-seat flying.

He then switched his argument to the mission: the F-4 had been the consummate Jack-of-all-trades and he, like me, enjoyed the variety that role provided. Since joining the single-mission close air-support world, however, he had found genuine satisfaction in specializing and becoming very, very good at a single, complex and demanding mission. Close support of troops on the ground brings with it a powerful element of responsibility: that of delivering lethal weapons in very close proximity to those friendlies you are supporting and the unparalleled sense of achievement that follows when you've whacked some bad guys and saved friendly lives.

It's not completely noble in nature, however. The Bear went on to remind me of the somewhat selfish benefits of getting close to your work in an attack aircraft and getting instant feedback on your performance. 'Dogfighting makes movies. Close air support wins wars,' he said, and I started to believe him, although I have no doubt that there is job satisfaction in hurling an air-to-air missile at an enemy which is visible only as a blip on the radar screen many miles distant, and even a bit more when that blip goes 'poof' and disappears, alleging a kill.

That admittedly lofty level of video game feedback cannot compare with the air-punching elation that comes with rolling in on an armored column. You ignore the incoming tracers whizzing past in your peripheral vision, put the gun cross on an advancing tank a mile or so distant, squeeze off a few rounds and watch said tank explode as a combat mix of armor-piercing and high-explosive incendiary 30-millimeter rounds drives home and detonates. That, ladies and gentlemen, is feedback at its very best and this was the prospect the Bear laid out before me as night transitioned into dawn.

I was a beaten man. My old friend the Bear had left my feeble line of reasoning in tatters and by the time I had recovered from my raging hangover, my chosen career path had been irreversibly altered and resolved. 'We' came to a splendid decision that night. Thanks again, Bear; I owe you another one.

Firmly persuaded, I strolled into our Base Personnel Office on the Monday and signed over my hard-earned entitlement to awesome power, blazing speed and the admiration of fast jet aficionados the world over in exchange for a 350-knot airplane that sounded like a huge ceiling fan and looked very much like a slug with wings.

Conversion

It would be quite a while before I appreciated exactly what I gained when I signed that upgrade (downgrade?) request. In the meantime, there was the dual task of preparing the wing for departure of the F-4s over a period of a few months and readying myself and my colleagues to change horses in mid-stream and check out in the A-10. As the wing's weapons and tactics officer, I was fortunate enough to be tapped for the first upgrade class, which we attended en masse in the traditional fighter unit, the squadron. The 92nd TFS 'Skulls' got the nod and in the early winter of 1978, those of us who had opted for life in the slow lane packed our bags and headed west, not in our own aircraft but in a Boeing 747 out of Heathrow Airport, London.

There were, I'll have to admit, worse places we could have been sent for our training. Three months at Davis-Monthan AFB in sunny Tucson, Arizona was a welcome diversion from the bleak winter of 1978 in rural Suffolk, England. Indeed, most Air Force fighter training bases are situated in relatively pleasant locations, primarily to exploit good weather conditions. Through the years, I've trained (or been trained) at bases in Florida (Homestead near Miami, MacDill in Tampa and Eglin in Fort Walton Beach), Arizona (Davis-Monthan in Tucson and Luke in Phoenix) and Nevada (Nellis in Las Vegas), but no matter where we checked out in the A-10, we would need to develop thick skins. Because of its comparative speed and power shortcomings and not-so-sleek appearance, at the beginning of the Warthog era the banter dispensed by everyone else in the fighter community was relentless. A few examples follow:

- The Warthog is the only aircraft that takes bird strikes from the rear
- The A-10 doesn't have an airspeed indicator; instead there is a calendar installed on the instrument panel
- There's no need for a two-seat A-10 trainer. The instructor just plugs in a microphone and runs along outside (nearly true, more later)
- You're going to take a lot of hits – the A-10 simulator is a dumpster – the pilot climbs inside and people throw rocks at it.

...and my own personal favorite:

• You can't base the A-10 near a swamp; the frogs will try to mate with it.

The Air Force master plan was for the squadron to check out in the airplane in the States, then ferry the birds across the Atlantic to arrive in England with basic skills developed. Then, in a highly-concentrated local training effort, attain combat-ready status as the very first Europe-based A-10 unit in minimum time.

From the pilot's point of view, the transition was relatively uncomplicated. Certainly we had to check out in the new bird and start modifying our tactics and techniques to employ it effectively. This process comes naturally to the pilot, similar to the progression from T-41 to T-37 to T-38 in pilot training. It's far more complicated for those who maintain the jets and the organizations that support that effort: supply and logistics.

The evolution of a maintenance unit from one aircraft to another is incredibly complex and our conversion from Phantom to Warthog is an appropriate time to recognize the army of talented folks that kept the transition on track. Aircraft maintenance is a far cry from your local service station and the mechanic who can readily turn his hand from Fords to Chevys to Buicks without a great deal of difficulty. F-4 maintainers don't magically morph into A-10 specialists, so most had to be imported to support the aircraft swap. Our maintenance organization had to spool up from building knowledge on the three test aircraft that arrived months earlier to a full squadron of A-10s. Inherent in this evolution was the process of adopting a complete new set of technical orders and procedures to maintain, arm and nurture a totally different breed of bird. There was also the small matter of building a complete inventory of parts and equipment for the A-10. In order to achieve that, for months there had been a steady stream of F-4 maintainers departing and A-10 specialists arriving. These folks and their families had to be housed, fed and looked after properly if they were to carry the heavy load we were expecting them to shoulder.

The personnel transition alone was exactly the same as moving a small town's population into new homes and starting life more or less from scratch. Say what you will about the military, this kind of conversion is not at all uncommon and we, as a mammoth bureaucracy, handled it pretty well.

As there were no A-10s based in Europe when we transitioned from the F-4, our first glimpse of the 'Hog came when we arrived in Tucson for training. We were taken aback by the size of the airplane, not necessarily because of sheer length, width or girth; more in terms of how conspicuous a target we were going to be lumbering slowly around the sky in this behemoth.

Virtually all Air Force flying training courses follow a similar profile. There's always a certain amount of ground-based academic training required before they let you anywhere near an airplane and the A-10 course was no exception. We were quite amazed at the simplicity of the Warthog. Having flown a fighter developed in the '60s for many years, we were acquainted with outdated technology but at least there was some technology to be acquainted with. The A-10 in most respects appeared to be a Second World War machine, tarted up with two fanjet engines. These didn't seem to have much effect on the speed of the bird, but at least no one had to prime propellers to get it started.

The good news here was that pre-flying academics were relatively benign. The airplane was simple, operating systems and limitations were straightforward and, compared to learning the idiosyncrasies of the Phantom, getting ready to climb aboard the 'Hog was a piece of cake. What gnawed at us all a bit (although none of us would ever own up to it) was a slight twinge of apprehension about the crew configuration on the first hop. There were no two-seat training versions of the A-10 with space for a guardian angel to ride along. As much as we were exhilarated by the prospect of flying a single-seat fighter, none of us had ever taken a first flight in an Air Force aircraft without an instructor pilot in a second seat, just in case. This applied to all three pilot training birds and every aircraft thereafter. As motivated, confident and yes, arrogant as we all were, there was a small seed of 'What if?' lurking inside us. While the instructor didn't exactly just 'plug in a microphone and run along outside', he'd be chasing us in another aircraft and therefore unable to provide much more than verbal technical (and moral) support.

Don't get me wrong, this brief bout of trepidation was far from gut-wrenching fear, for me at least. It equated to the butterflies flapping around in the solar plexus region before I took the field for an important football game or grabbed the microphone to brief a number of high-ranking officers and/or politicians. Well under control, but providing a shot of extra adrenaline for sallying forth without adult supervision.

As it happened, the single-seat debut proved to be an anti-climax as the Warthog was easy to start, taxi, take-off and land. The difficult bit, as any fighter pilot would attest, was employing it as a weapon, and that proficiency would be built up gradually as the training program progressed.

As we began learning more about the bird and how to use it, our initial observations revolved around what helpful utensils we no longer had at our disposal and we began thinking about other ways to get the job done.

Probably the most significant example of the lack of vital kit in the 'Hog was the navigation system. In essence, there wasn't one. The airplane was designed to fly very low, using the terrain to mask our position and shield us from enemy gunners. This required hard, abrupt maneuvering in an environment that was terribly unforgiving in terms of even the most fleeting mental lapses. From 100ft above the ground, an inadvertent shallow descent will result in ground impact within a very few seconds. Add to this the 'distractions' of planning and executing tactics on the hoof, evading enemy defenses and managing fuel, weapons switches, flight integrity and discipline, it becomes obvious that just a little help in navigating would not go amiss. The venerable old F-4 had an inertial navigation system (INS), primitive by today's standards, that featured programming of turn points and targets and provided steering to these points. Because it was reliant on constantly spinning gyros, a certain amount of precession was expected over the course of a maneuvering flight and the INS was routinely a mile or two off at the end of a mission. Nevertheless, it kept you in the ballpark and gave the pilot a tool to supplement his visual navigation problem and would have proven invaluable in the kind of ultra-low, terrain-masked adventure that A-10 flying involved.

The first model of the A-10 had none of this archaic but helpful wizardry on board. Instead, some of the original A-10 instructors, applying the ancient principle of 'Necessity is the Mother of invention', came up with a cleverly improvised method of staying alive at low level and having a fighting chance of actually arriving somewhere close to the desired turn point or target. It was dubbed Low Altitude Tactical Navigation (LATN) and employed the most sophisticated aids we had at our disposal: a heading indicator, a clock and a large-scale map, covered with clear adhesive plastic and festooned with course arrows, headings, times and indecipherable doodles applied with a grease pencil before and during flight. LATN was a bastardization of the old reliable time, distance and heading concept employed by the likes of Charles Lindbergh to go directly from point A to point B and within these boundaries it was perfectly adequate. Once introducing trivial distractions such as lousy weather, enemy defenses, aircraft emergencies and so on, it became clear that a whole lot of flexibility would have to be incorporated if the process was going to work.

Even our most valuable tool, the map, could be extremely problematical. Depending on the 'area of the sky' we were to patrol, as Baron von Richthofen put it, our meticulously tailored map could reach dimensions of 4 or 5ft square. We took great pains to fold this in the most efficient manner: accordioned, sectioned, separated into two or three separate parts; everyone had their own technique. At the end of the day, it made very little difference. Have you ever wrestled with a professionally fabricated, ring binder roadmap while driving your car? If so, multiply your speed by six, map size by eight, the level of frustration by a factor of twenty and you'll gain some appreciation of using a large folded section of plastic-covered paper to conduct ultra low-level navigation.

Believe it or not, this scenario could actually deteriorate. Imagine, if you will, the intrepid A-10 pilot hugging the terrain at 100ft above the ground and 300 knots, navigating with his once precisely folded map, which by now has somehow been unfurled to fill most of the cockpit. The following happened to me many times; a result of my mediocre technique, probably. As I reached a turn point (or what I thought might be a turn point), I pulled into a hard turn to set the next course heading. As soon as I did, the increased 4 to 5 'G' forces wrenched at me and everything in the cockpit, including my map which was deposited on the floor at my feet. You know what I said then, don't you? 'Ahhhhh, shit!'

In your living room, or even in the car, this would be a non-event. You would simply lean forward and pick up the map, right? In a fighter cockpit, there is a slight complication to achieving this simple solution: you are tethered to your ejection seat by two snug shoulder straps which limit forward movement to approximately 18in; enough to reach your cockpit switches, but not nearly enough to scoop up the map now resting on your boots.

At this point in the proceedings, there are four options available to the hapless 'Hog driver:

1. He can simply choose to leave the map on the floor and press on with the mission. If he is familiar with the terrain and geography of the area he's operating in, this is undoubtedly the best alternative. If, however, he is either 'temporarily disoriented' (read 'lost') or in a combat scenario, working with live ammunition and friendly troops in close proximity to the bad guys he must keep track of, it is a non-starter.

2. He can retrieve the map by unstrapping from his life-saving ejection seat long enough to grope for the map at his feet. Believe me when I tell you there is not a man among us stupid enough to unfasten his parachute risers at 100ft above terra firma and 300 knots just to salvage his wayward map.

3. He can roll the aircraft inverted and gently push forward on the stick to exert mild zero 'G' conditions, much like you see in the films of astronauts floating around in a large airplane experiencing zero 'G' flight. He can then snag the map that gently floats up in front of him, roll the airplane upright and continue on his merry way. Aggressive upside-down flying for a brief moment in time can be an exhilarating experience, but when sustained, particularly at zero or negative 'G' is both uncomfortable and unnatural. Additionally, very low-altitude inverted flying is for the poster boys (and girls, these days) in aerial demonstration teams who practice it with great regularity. Finally, in that combat situation we were discussing earlier, pushing forward on the stick while inverted causes the airplane to climb, albeit upside down. If your objective is to remain very low, using the terrain to obscure you from enemy defenses, you have spectacularly failed to achieve it using this option.

4. Finally, in a variation of the above, he can abandon the soft and gentle approach and use a bit of aggression to reacquire his precious laminated chart. This technique more closely suits the *modus operandi* of the fighter pilot as the distractions of trying to remain graceful and dexterous are eliminated. Throttles are shoved to the firewall (granted, in the A-10 this has little immediate effect, but every little bit helps), the stick is pulled abruptly aft but only for a fraction of a second; this pitches the nose up enough to keep the next step from driving you into the ground. Now, the stick is snapped forward even more severely, instantly pitching the nose down, resulting in a sudden *negative* 'G' situation and, as if by magic, the pilot's butt is lifted briskly off the seat. The errant map, along with dust, bits of paper and anything else that might have been nestled on the floor fairly leaps into the upper reaches of the cockpit. Cigarette butts are a rarity today, but in the F-4 a similar maneuver would unearth a number of them. Like the nose-up preparation move, this aggressive thrust needs only to be held for an instant, and that's good news because abrupt negative 'G' is, for most pilots, the most unpleasant sensation of all. Despite the momentary discomfort, advantages of this technique are the fact that it can be accomplished in little over a heartbeat with very little gain or loss of altitude. One cautionary note, however: while performing the maneuver, the pilot must be spring-loaded to catching that map with his left hand as it launches upwards from the floor; a fumble means having to do it all over again.

As the German philosopher Friedrich Nietzsche famously pointed out: 'That which does not kill us makes us stronger.' I can't conclusively say the lack of a sophisticated navigational system has ever killed an A-10 pilot; I'll cover one possibly related incident later. What it did achieve is bringing us back to basics in terms of piloting skills and fostering a resurrected breed of fighter pilots, no longer totally reliant on electronic wizardry to find the target or home plate, as our base (site of the Officers' Club bar) was referred to.

Falling in Love with the 'Hog

While we were busy getting accustomed to this kind of Second World War-era technology, another subtle and insidious event was taking place. We began to learn a bit more about the Ugly Duckling we were inheriting, and what was at first a slightly grudging acceptance of some of the less glamorous features of the aircraft began to grow into something much more substantial.

The folks that designed the 'Hog were well aware, as we all were, that an aircraft that big and that slow was going to take hits in a combat environment. It began to dawn on us that our little tantrums regarding the appearance of our new steed were a bit unfair and maybe, just maybe, there were some very positive features we were ignoring while focusing on the aesthetics, or lack thereof.

For example, the two enormous fanjet engines apparently added as an awkward afterthought to either side of the aft fuselage had one or two redeeming features: these were relatively quiet and bad guys with AK-47s were unlikely to hear us coming until it was too late to react. They burned much cooler than conventional turbines and were therefore far less susceptible to ground-launched heat-seeking missiles. Indeed, the awkward positioning of the engines just forward of the twin vertical tailplanes meant that the reduced heat signature was actually shielded by these appendages, further reducing our heat 'signature' and lessening the risk of being tracked by a heat-seeker. Finally, unlike other jet's engines snugly enclosed in the airplane's fuselage, they could be readily swapped right to left or vice versa if damaged. This capability to 'switch hit' also applied to the main landing gear, primary aircraft flight controls – ailerons, rudders and elevators – and many external aircraft panels. This unique versatility proved invaluable in later years when aircraft parts were commonly switched back and forth to repair battle-damaged birds in the Gulf War and subsequent mêlées.

As I mentioned earlier, the aircraft was fitted with wheels which protruded slightly beneath their housings rendering them aesthetically repugnant and therefore of no real value. *Au contraire!* I was forced to recant when I learned they were designed that way to lessen aircraft damage from a wheels-up landing necessitated by battle damage or

Smashing Bugs, the Air Force way! (*Public domain*)

Being some…body! Moody
AFB, Georgia, 1967.
(*Author's photo*)

Post-flight debrief preparation, Moody AFB, Georgia, 1967. Left to right: Chris Weeber, the author, Lang Morris, Bill Jones, Rich Van Veen. (*Author's photo*)

Post-flight debrief, Moody AFB, 1967. Left to right: The author, Lang Morris, Bill Jones. (*Author's photo*)

Tuning up the 'Dog Whistle', 1967. (*Public domain*)

Student B, sporting Mickey Mouse ears, preflights the Tweet. (*Author's photo*)

Bonehead of the Week, Bill Jones, Moody AFB, June 1967. (*Author's photo*)

'White Rocket'. (*Public domain*)

White Rockets in Echelon Formation. (*Public Domain*)

Boy Wonder Moody AFB 1967.
(*Photo credit Carl Ramsey*)

Enter the 'Phabulous Phantom', MacDill AFB, Florida, 1968. (*Original Painting by Blake Morrison, editor of* USAF Fighter Weapons Review)

'The College of Jungle Knowledge', Clark Air Base, Philippines, January 1969. (*Author's photo*)

Dad goes downtown, Ubon Ratchathani, 1969. (*Author's photo*)

Loaded for Bear and Refueling (without the vertigo), 1969. (*Colonel Joe 'Gork' Gorecki USAF (Retired)*)

Unloaded and heading for home, 1969. (*Colonel Joe 'Gork' Gorecki USAF (Retired)*)

The author in full fun-loving fool mode, Ubon, 1969. (*Author's photo*)

El Bufon meets his match, Madrid, Spain, July 1970. (*Author's photo*)

MEDICAL RECOMMENDATION FOR FLYING DUTY

Elaine and the Porsche, Segovia, Spain, 1973. (*Author's photo*)

The REAL Special Relationship, Wallasey, Wirral, England, 6 January 1973. (*Author's photo*)

Spanish Flyers behaving
badly (smug young man
in white coat transforms
poignant moment with
thunderous fart), 6 January
1973. (*Author's photo*)

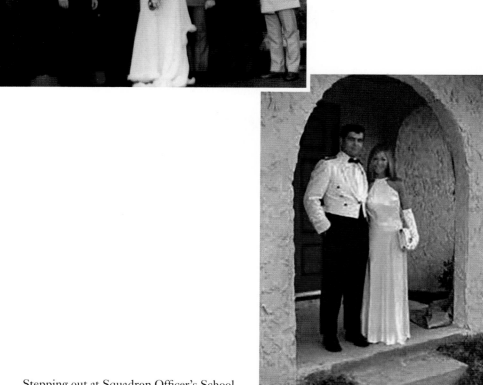

Stepping out at Squadron Officer's School,
Montgomery, Alabama, 1973. (*Author's photo*)

'The Home of the Fighter Pilot', Nellis AFB, Nevada, 1975. (*Hamodia.com 2016*)

The Prize: Graduate Patch 1975. (*Author's image*)

MiG 25 as flown by defecting Russian fighter pilot Viktor Belenko. (*Dmitriy Pichugin, http://russianplanes.net/id42977, GFDL 1.2, https://commons.wikimedia.org/w/index.php?curid=20269571*)

Imperial Iranian Air Force plaque, Shahrokhi, Iran, 1976. (*Author's image*)

'Hog popping flares to spoof heat-seeking missiles. (*Matt Ellis, Flickr Commercial Authorized*)

'Hog at the trough: refueling from KC-135 tanker. (*Kārlis Dambrāns Flickr Commercial*)

Perspective: Gun meets Beetle. (*Photographer unknown – US Air Force/National Museum of the US Air Force*)

Note the offset nosegear: making room for the gun. (*LoadedAaron Flickr Commercial*)

Third Squadron, German Fighter
Bomber Wing 31. (*Author's image*)

JaboG 31 patch: the inspiration for
Detachment 4 emblem. (*Author's image*)

A-10 Division patch, Nellis AFB,
Nevada, 1983. (*Author's image*)

81 TFW 'Pizza patch' showcasing all six A-10
Squadrons, RAF Bentwaters/Woodbridge,
ca. 1990. (*Author's image*)

Author in the office, Air Warrior Commander, Nellis AFB, Nevada, ca. 1992.

The Dream Team, Ramstein AB, Germany, ca. 1991. (*Author's photo*)

hydraulic catastrophe. If that wasn't impressive enough, the quirky landing gear retracts forward. Why? Without hydraulic pressure, you can unlock the gear and the combination of gravity and your headwind will help them fall into place and lock down. Oh, me of little faith!

We made more significant discoveries while we were checking out in the airplane. We were, for example, riding around on 1,200lb of molded titanium known as the bathtub. This handy bit of kit was inserted there to protect vulnerable flight control cables, fuel hydraulic and electrical lines and other components from ground fire. The most vital of those components, in my book, is my chubby pink ass and the reduced probability of being disemboweled by some Jihadi's AK-47 round clearly trumped the flak we often caught from F-16 and F-15 drivers: 'Going out to take another bath today, Steve?' It was best to ignore the taunts; mincing ballerinas, all of them.

The fighter pilot's worst nightmare, other than a fire in the cockpit, was that 'golden BB' (lucky shot) that penetrates the main hydraulic lines and freezes up all your flight controls with only a 'step over the side' option remaining. The 'Hog was designed with numerous features, not one of which improved its appearance (I keep coming back to this; what a pompous bastard I was) but instead were installed to bring us back alive from a thoroughly unpleasant outing in some Cold War or Middle Eastern shooting gallery. A few of them are outlined below.

Fighter aircraft have had dual flight control systems for a long time, but prior to the A-10 they were designed to compensate for system failure and consequently weren't physically separated. The engineers who designed the 'Hog thought to themselves: 'Man, the bad guys are going to beat this big, slow airplane like a red-headed stepchild; how can we get it home in one piece?' so they set about fitting separate and distinct flight control channels on opposite sides of the aircraft which couldn't both be taken out by the golden BB. Control inputs are transmitted to the flight controls by cables rather than the traditional rods. They are less likely to be taken out by a single bullet or jammed by structural damage. As noted above, the dual control systems are physically separated to further lessen the likelihood of catastrophic failure due to ground fire. Either system can be locked out from the cockpit, enabling degraded but controllable flight. If the proverbial shit really hits the fan, the last port of call is the manual reversion system, which provides limited control inputs to small trim tabs on the flight controls in the case of no hydraulic boost whatsoever. This operation is so physically demanding and delicate that practicing it is strictly prohibited and the stick forces required are likely to be possible only for a relatively large, very fit fellow.

I now take a moment to a) bite my tongue, b) abandon my lifelong chauvinistic tendencies, and c) apologize profusely because, at the time of this writing, the only successful A-10 manual reversion recovery and landing in combat has been achieved by a relatively petite but obviously very fit young lady. Captain Kim Campbell (aka 'Killer Chick') managed to locate a competent Iraqi gunner over Baghdad in the Gulf War and consequently soaked up some serious flak. She brought the bird back to a coalition airfield and after contemplating the alternatives she landed a severely disabled bird with no hydraulic boost to the flight controls rather than jettisoning the entire airplane.

Similar survival-oriented thinking went into the fuel system. Except for benign ferry missions, all fuel is carried internally. Fuel lines are protected by running them through the tanks and those tanks are lovingly cared for: they are tear-resistant, self-sealing and fitted with folded flame-resistant foam panels which expand when the tank is breached to limit fuel spillage and airflow to the damaged tank.

All the while we were learning about the survivability features the 'Hog afforded, we were undergoing a subtle but undeniable mental metamorphosis. Our going-in position of 'I don't want to be seen anywhere near this dreadful collection of bumps, lumps, angular irregularities and grotesque features' was gradually being replaced with the steady emergence of an entirely different attitude. There was no denying it, flying this airplane was kicks and the more we sampled the instantaneous control responses, spectacular roll and turning capability, magnificent external visibility and efficient radio communications equipment, the more we began to appreciate the 'Hog (or, dare I say it, be seduced by her). Our training, as always, was a stair-stepped approach and, although it was sandwiched into a short period of time, the basic simplicity of flying the bird allowed relatively rapid progression. It wasn't long before we had all mastered the nuts and bolts of getting it into the air and getting it back down again, at which time we were able to work on the fun stuff in between those two important events: employing the Warthog tactically. This involved another progression, first involving missions to the Air Force's gunnery ranges to explore and then perfect our weapons delivery skills. In almost all respects, this phase of training was very similar to weapons programs in any other tactical fighter capable of delivering air-to-ground weapons. We carried weapons dispensers, each with six cute little 25lb blue bombs fitted with charges which discharged equally adorable little puffs of white smoke on impact. These puffs could be plotted on the target we were aiming at on the ground and a score provided; instant feedback (and something we could bet on within the flight – big stakes, normally – a quarter a bomb).

Note I said that the training was comparable to any other weapons programs *in almost all respects*. There was one significant difference. Shoehorned under our titanium bathtubs and occupying most of the fuselage real estate between nose and trailing edges of the wings is the most fearsome forward-firing weapon ever mounted in an aircraft. It was officially designated the Gun, Aircraft Unit (GAU) 8 Avenger. We just called it…

The GUN!

I'm not going to reel off dozens of technical specifications; Google 'GAU-8' if that's what you're looking for. No, I want to tell you what it does, how well it does it and how it makes us feel to pull that trigger.

When we were introducing the 'Hog to Europe, we often briefed NATO Military and European political leaders and we never failed to impress with a comparison photo involving a Volkswagen Beetle. This was a graphic demonstration of the dimensions of the Gun. The large cylindrical drum at the rear holds 1,170+ linkless rounds, which are cycled into the firing mechanism: a seven-barreled Gatling gun arrangement. After firing, the empty casings continue the cycle back into the drum so spent rounds are not ejected from the aircraft.

Built by General Electric, the Gun has always generated rumors. Let's get those out of the way first:

- They designed the gun, then built the airplane around it. Not exactly, but there were numerous accommodations built into the airplane to allow the big boy to fit snugly and work properly. More later...
- Due to recoil, the airplane actually slows down when a prolonged burst is fired. It probably would, but prolonged bursts aren't part of the game plan because they don't need to be. Read on.
- The pilot can only fire short bursts because gun exhaust gases will flame out the engines. Again, less than totally accurate, although over time, gun gases can build up on engine fan blades and affect performance. Diffusers which dispersed gasses were tested on the business end of the Gun with mixed results. In keeping with the aesthetics of the airplane, these looked a lot like chimney baffles adding yet another amusing protuberance to the 'Hog's sleek exterior.

In my day, the GAU-8 was optimized to fire 4,200 rounds per minute (that's 70 per second for those of you who are math dunces; don't get upset at the label as I am among you). It has since been limited to 3,900 rpm, but let's discuss the Gun at its peak.

The ultra-clever among you will have already noted the disparity between rounds carried (1,170) and 4,200 rpm. You are correct, but when you're hurling seventy 30mm projectiles weighing just over a pound per *second* at a hapless enemy tank, size matters more than numbers, hence my comment above about the lack of necessity for prolonged bursts. Tests indicate the GAU-8 will routinely put around forty of those seventy rounds smack dab in the middle of a vehicle, unquestionably ruining a tank crew's day in less than the blink of an eye.

These projectiles aren't just long-neck beer-bottle-sized hunks of metal either. Going to war in the 'Hog means saddling up on a combat mix load of five armor-piercing incendiary (API) rounds to one high-explosive incendiary (HEI) projectile. The API rounds are the much-maligned depleted uranium rounds which are actually less radioactive than the average shovel full of earth from your garden, but have received lots of bad press simply because no one thought to call them something else.

The API rounds are designed to punch large holes through the substantial armor of a tank, followed in very close proximity by HEI.

This does an excellent job of ricocheting around the interior of a tank, causing the crew, in their very last thoughts, to wish they had become insurance salesmen.

The Gun is optimized to fire most accurately at around 4,000 ft from the target. This range is less important than it is for many guns because the extremely high velocity of the GAU–8 round when it leaves the barrel and the weight of the round mean they don't decelerate rapidly. This results in a flat trajectory and an exceptionally accurate firing solution well beyond the optimum 4,000 ft.

I promised to elaborate on a couple of gun rumors and so I will. Nose gear positioning is one example of modification to accommodate the gun. This was not an afterthought, but the offset nose gear was an obvious 'must' for siting the GAU–8 in the aircraft. Other internal organs were shifted here and there to make room for the big fella, but none quite as dramatic as this one.

Our training program swiftly brought us to the long-awaited opportunity to pull that trigger and there wasn't a man among us disappointed. The gunsight in early A–10 models was primitive, but one item in the Heads–Up display was constant: about 2 in from the top of the gunsight was a small cross projected on the display. This wasn't adjustable, but set permanently at 41 mils depression it was the aiming point for the gun and spoke volumes about its accuracy.

TLAR

Manual gunnery (and I'm referring primarily to bombing here) in a fighter is a challenging experience. When accomplished skillfully, it is also tremendously satisfying but it involves coordinating a number of shifting parameters simultaneously. As understandably as I can put it, an accurate weapons delivery requires selecting a suitable dive angle, airspeed and release altitude for the chosen weapon. The gunsight is then manually depressed to pre-calculated margins in order to give the pilot an aiming reference (known as a 'pipper') for that dive angle, airspeed and altitude. That's the easy part. Once ready to deliver the weapon, the pilot must fly his airplane to a point in the sky where his dive angle, airspeed and altitude are precisely as calculated at the instant the aiming reference reaches the target. Piece of cake, eh? Oh yes, a couple of other little things: one must compensate for wind and make adjustments for any of the parameters that aren't 'wired' when it's time to let that baby go.

Today's digital weapons systems do virtually all of that magic for the pilot, including the wind corrections, but in the early A-10, we had pretty much the same technical wizardry as the guy who dropped his bomb over the side of his biplane in the First World War. Consequently, fighter pilots – starting with the guy in the biplane – have sought a technically sound process to compensate for the lack of technical magic that could solve his bombing solution dilemma. That methodology was conceived a long, long time ago and has been endlessly tweaked over the years. It is discussed quietly in cool dark places that serve alcohol and is respectfully called **TLAR**: an acronym which stands for 'That Looks About Right'.

The difference between a skillful and a mediocre manual bomber is his talent for applying TLAR correctly. I'll give you a broad example, and then we'll move on. If, in hurling your body at the earth to deliver a Mk 82 500lb general-purpose bomb you are a few degrees shallower than say the 45-degree dive you meticulously planned, your bomb will impact short of the target when you release it with your pipper on the bull's eye and all other parameters right on the money. You can compensate for this error via TLAR in a couple of ways. If you recognize your shallowness early, you can boost the speed because fast counteracts shallow. You can also delay your release until you are a bit lower than planned which has a similar effect. How much? Damned if I know. When 'That Looks About Right' you hit the release button (colloquially known as the 'pickle' button) on the stick and hope you've 'calculated' correctly. When you've done it enough you develop a sixth sense, hence TLAR, but I'll share a little secret with you: in the movies, when the Second World War fighter pilot (or 1980s Warthog driver) rolls in and puts every bomb right down the destroyer's smokestack or into the enemy commander's living room, that's not TLAR, it's Hollywood.

What has all this got to do with that wonderful gun? The complexities of meeting all these parameters required to master accurate dropping of free-fall weapons are largely irrelevant when you turn that bad boy on. The aiming reference (not a pipper now, the gun cross) is fixed and the projectiles are fired with it on or very near the target. The size, weight and mass of the projectiles coupled with a muzzle velocity (speed of the bullet when fired) of 3,500ft/second ensure that near-level track. As a result, 70 bullets per second travel the optimized gun range of 4,000ft in 1.2 seconds and approximately 40 of those will impact an area roughly the size of a Russian T-80 tank (other Soviet battle tanks are available). Unlike the complex freefall bombing example above, it matters not if you are steep, shallow, fast, slow or any combination of the above. As long as the gun cross is on the target when you let rip, you won't be embarrassed by the results. The only TLAR required when employing the 'Hog's pride and joy is a very minor adjustment to compensate for longer range (gun cross a smidgeon above the target), or a crosswind (a similar smidgeon right or left), hence 'on or very near the target' above.

Having mastered that very simple firing solution, all that's left is squeezing the trigger and the first time you do it is a genuine revelation. The noise in the cockpit, even while wearing a custom-fit helmet with excellent sound-limiting properties, can only be described as breathtaking. **BRRRRRRRRRRT!!** roars the gun, the airframe shudders and 4,000ft downrange, directly behind a parachute-sized target on a frame, a neat cluster of 60 to 70 impacts appears almost instantaneously. There's only one thing to say: 'Oh, shit!' Uncharacteristically, this time it's uttered reverently, reflecting the respect due to this awesome piece of artillery.

You may have noticed a subtle U-turn in my attitude towards the A-10 in the past few pages. Those of us who were flying her experienced the same relentless seduction as we became more and more enamored with the bird's capabilities and unique character. Don't get me wrong, the ugly duckling wasn't getting any cuter or cuddlier; on the contrary, the more we experienced her capabilities, the meaner and more aggressive she appeared and the better we felt about climbing aboard.

Probably the most gratifying reversal of attitude from a 'Hog driver's point of view came from the boys (well, prima donnas actually) who flew the lithe and eminent air superiority machines: F-15s and F-16s. Although they always maintained a certain arrogance around 'Hog drivers, these poster boys, like any other competent fighter pilots, were keenly aware of the capabilities of potential adversaries. This mindfulness applied to friendly aircraft they might oppose in training encounters as well as actual enemy equipment. Thus they developed a healthy regard for the 'Hog in one very important respect. Everyone who flew a fighter was cognizant of the fact that a Gatling gun capable of punching large holes in a heavily-armored tank at a mile plus was able to whack even bigger holes in a thin-skinned F-15 or F-16. Consequently, despite its acknowledged deficiencies in speed and aerial ballet, the 'Hog was a force to be reckoned with and flying one's sleek air superiority fighter within range of that gun, even in a training scenario, was to be avoided at all costs and due respect was established.

All the while we were being seduced by the 'Hog, most of us were completely oblivious to one distinguishing characteristic of the airplane that would provide immense fulfillment in years to come. The Warthog is undoubtedly the last true 'stick and rudder' fighter; i.e. flown entirely by a human being with little if any assistance from the myriad automated electronic systems and artificial intelligence features which do the job for you (and take much of the fun out of it).

Flying the 'Hog demanded physical and mental agility that will no longer be required as evolution provides more and more electronic aids to lighten the pilot's workload. There's nothing wrong with progress, of course, and today's (and tomorrow's) fighter pilots will need a totally different type and level of skillset to operate the modern warbird, but the cut and thrust of 'stick and rudder' flying will be lost forever and to those of us who had the opportunity to employ these skills, it will be a great loss indeed. This DIY dimension of the 'Hog, in our opinion, established us as superior pilots to our pinball wizard colleagues and this burst of self-esteem more than made up for the derision they often heaped upon us and our unsightly airplane.

The Transatlantic Shuffle

Our training program at Davis-Monthan AFB in Tucson was unique. The Air Force wanted an A-10 force that was ready to go almost as soon as we touched down in Europe. This was part Hollywood, part saber-rattling as we wanted our potential adversaries the Russians to be aware that we could get an anti-armor force up and running in no time at all and poke some significant holes in their attack strategies from our arrival on the scene. Consequently, our training package included concentrated emphasis on close air support tactics in a European scenario.

The concept, code-named 'Ready Thunder', was to deploy our squadron to the 'twin bases' of RAF Bentwaters/Woodbridge, then almost immediately undergo a NATO Tactical Evaluation (TacEval) which would certify the squadron as combat-ready in the European theater. Visualizing the North German Plain while flying low-level over an Arizona desert required significant imagination, but as training approached its conclusion, we began to bond rather well as a fighting force and confidence that we could pull this off was growing.

The next step was to move the entire squadron to Europe. Three aircraft had deployed some months earlier to enable maintenance training to take place at Bentwaters. Our cadre of 92nd Squadron pilots was joined by two 'Ready Thunder' instructor pilots, Dean Dodson and Chuck Haberstich who had flown other aircraft in the European environment and were now A-10 instructors. They would spend a few weeks at Bentwaters assisting the 92nd Squadron's rapid upgrade to mission-ready status. Planning for the main deployment thankfully was not down to the airplane drivers, but we would have to execute the plan. The first leg of this excursion would take us from Davis-Monthan AFB in Arizona to Myrtle Beach AFB in South Carolina, an A-10 base. This would have been a relatively mundane event except for one slightly contentious issue. Overall command of the Bentwaters deployment was given to Colonel Mike Dugan, vice commander of the 355th Tac Fighter Training Wing at Davis-Monthan. Dugan looked and sounded a lot like Jimmy Cagney and had the same aggressive tendencies as many of Cagney's characters. Years later, as a four-star general he was fired by the Secretary of Defense for publicly announcing that the US would be targeting Saddam Hussein, his wife, family and even his mistress during the Gulf War, but that's another story.

The comparatively small bone we had to pick with Dugan was his bright idea to convert a protracted and tedious cross-country flight from Arizona to South Carolina into something far more miserable. To explain this properly, I need to give you a brief tutorial on the anti-exposure suit. Known to all who wore them as a 'Poopy Suit' because of the odor generated after wearing them over an extended period, this form-fitting torture chamber is made of rubber with tight seals around the neck and wrists. There are integral booties to keep your feet dry, a single straight zipper across the chest which enables you (with a little help from your friends) to peel the damned thing on or off over your head and a smaller horizontal zipper at the crotch (more about that later). The requisite layers of clothing involved are underwear, thermal underwear, Nomex fire-retardant flight suit, anti-exposure suit, harness and 'G'-suit. Consequently it is very low on the list of comfortable lounging apparel. It has its advantages, however: if you are forced to eject over very cold water (60 degrees Fahrenheit or less) it keeps you relatively dry and, with a bit of luck helps you live a few minutes longer until you're picked up by someone who just happens to be in your vicinity. We routinely wore them when flying training missions over the North Sea or North Atlantic and certainly expected to tolerate them when crossing 'the Pond' to England. What we *didn't* expect was to be directed to wear them from Arizona to South Carolina in order to 'get used to them', as Dugan put it, and we were not happy bunnies. We bitched, moaned and whined, pointing out that we were all 'used to' the poopy suit and wearing them across the contiguous United States was roughly equivalent to practice bleeding. The chain of command prevailed, however, and wear them we did, but it took a bit of sparkle out of the deployment and Dugan dropped right down to the bottom of our list of respected leaders.

Fighter aircraft trans-ocean deployments are not uncommon but rarely are they conducted as a full squadron unit and this was the first ever such venture for the Warthogs. You may wonder 'What difference does that make?' Well, most modern fighters cruise at somewhere around 500 nautical miles (knots) per hour, thus being able to cross the Atlantic in something like six hours. As we've already discussed at length, the A-10 may be ugly, but it's also very slow and that means significantly more time airborne to cover a similar distance. Like the fast jets, we would rely on air-to-air refueling to keep the engines running, but to combat the effects of aircrew fatigue and provide an opportunity to perform any required servicing en route, we would stop over midway across the Pond, at Lajes in the Azores. Here, we would refuel with excellent Portuguese beer, a couple of good meals and a reasonable night's sleep before continuing on to Bentwaters.

The orchestration of a fourteen-ship fighter deployment is worthy of discussion. We were shepherded across by two KC-135 tanker aircraft that acted as airborne gas stations and command and control centers. The good Colonel Dugan was on board one of these, undoubtedly plotting additional ways to make our journey more arduous and uncomfortable. Also we were accompanied by a C-130 'Duckbutt' aircraft (defined without further explanation by the DoD Dictionary as 'An aircraft assigned to perform precautionary search and rescue (SAR) or combat search and rescue missions, support deployment of single-engine aircraft, or meet other specialized situations.'). In plain language, this means search and rescue experts who could locate a downed pilot and toss us a reasonably robust life-raft to keep us afloat until help arrived. They would then coordinate a rescue effort to fish us out and take us home.

These shepherd aircraft also provided a much more sophisticated level of navigation than the A-10s had onboard and additional travel aids such as weather avoidance radars and long-range radio communications. We were very slightly jealous of these goodies, although not one of us would have sacrificed one pound of JP4 jet fuel to have them installed in our jets. What we *did* covet in a very big way was one of the most basic features of any large aircraft: a toilet. In a very cramped cockpit, we could always find room for a bit of food and liquid, but unlike our Big Buddies the tanker crews, there was no short stroll to the conveniences to dispose of the natural consequence of our sustenance. As always, the Air Force had found a way to cater to our biological needs, at least in terms of liquid waste. Long ago, in the dawn of time, some clever boffin had come up with a contraption which allowed fidgeting aircrew in a tiny cockpit to relieve themselves. Known officially as a 'Urine Collection Device', this gadget was undoubtedly renamed by a pilot in less than a heartbeat and was universally renowned as the 'Piddle Pack', essentially a thick vinyl bag tapered into a handy receptacle at the top. Inside the bag were three or four highly-compressed sponges which looked like thin cardboard when dry but would expand dramatically when liquid was added. On mission completion you rolled the open receptacle end closed and clamped it shut with heavy twist ties. The bad news, if you recall the last couple of pages, is that maneuvering through the varied and numerous layers of clothing, including the Poopy Suit, to locate the necessary appendage for insertion into the Piddle Pack was about as close to Mission Impossible as it comes. The final blow to carefree long-distance flying was the fact that the A-10 had no credible autopilot. Therefore, in order to make any reasonable attempt at using the Piddle Pack it was necessary to use hands, knees or in some cases feet to fly the airplane safely while working on Mission Impossible in the background. A few of our number who suffered from TBS (tiny bladder syndrome) actually gave this a try en route and we added insult to their obvious injury through unrestrained harassment on the radio as they fell out of formation while fumbling with the aircraft, the Poopy Suit and their appendages, not necessarily in that order. Fortunately, on the deployment, none of them actually hit the water while flailing about, but reported success rates for Mission Impossible were inconclusive. The rest of us managed to hang on, painful though it was, until we were able to sprinkle the tarmac after landing.

Our Poopy Suit 'orientation' over the Arizona Desert, Great Plains and America's heartland was largely successful (we transited a number of small lakes and rivers without a single cold-water exposure incident), and we all arrived on the East Coast suitably acclimatized to the unpleasant confinement of the rubber suit of armor. We spent a couple of days preparing for the big push across the Atlantic. We had two nights' layover scheduled in South Carolina but, in another small dose of Dugan-induced practice bleeding, we were told to get to bed at 1700 hours (5.00 pm) and wake up at 0100 (1.00 am), once again to adjust to the scheduled sleep pattern for launch day. There wasn't much chance of this exercise being successful without help, so the Air Force had laid on a flight surgeon; our very own doctor who had trained extensively in the domain of aviation medicine. For this deployment, he temporarily abandoned his specialism and became a common drug-pusher, dispensing downers that would assist us into the land of dreams in the early evening. We then popped uppers which, combined with copious quantities of coffee, were designed to stimulate us after an ungodly early wake-up and keep us from nodding off in the cockpit. This, in reality, wasn't much of a threat but Uncle Sam wasn't taking any chances with his first European squadron of Warthogs nosing over into the cold Atlantic with dozing pilots at the controls.

On the second day, we rolled out of bed at Oh-Dark Hundred, popped our uppers, began our coffee transfusions and schlepped off to brief the Atlantic transit. This was not to be. Because of atrocious weather over the mid-Atlantic we went through this drill three times and on the fourth attempt a broken Duckbutt aircraft further delayed our departure. We were getting very sick of popping pills, drinking coffee at 0200 and even the excellent high-protein breakfasts the Myrtle Beach mess hall laid on, but at the fifth attempt, the pieces finally fell into place.

Lajes was about six hours to the east as the 'Hog flies, but the most challenging event of the day would be take-off, join up and rendezvous with our KC-135 tankers. Most of this fandango would be accomplished in the dark and I regret I must once again reflect upon the 'Hog's limitations in describing it.

Most modern fighters are equipped with air-to-air radar systems which take a great deal of guesswork out of a tanker rendezvous. They are also capable of sprint speeds which allow them to chase and overtake a tanker effortlessly. Alas, despite the attributes that were rapidly winning us over, the 'Hog had neither of these advantages and so getting together with our airborne gas station/command and control center was a far more demanding proposition.

Fighters normally travel in flights of two or four. Our fourteen-aircraft deployment package dictated three four-ships followed by a two-ship. We started together and taxied to the active runway in the dark, a long hulking queue illuminated only by the taxi lights of the aircraft behind us. Yours truly was leading the second four-ship, so we and the preceding flight would link up with the first tanker in the cell, while the six aircraft following us would accompany the second KC-135.

Both tankers were already airborne and flying racetrack patterns off the South Carolina coast as we took the runway (God only knows what time *they* had to get up). The tanker racetracks were north/south, perpendicular to our easterly course to facilitate the join-up and after rendezvous, the entire gaggle would proceed eastbound, towards Lajes, tankers in the lead.

We received take-off clearance for the entire flight and took the runway, four aircraft at a time for a sequenced departure. Just before take-off roll we switched on our position lights: red on the left (port) wingtip; green on the right (starboard); white on the tail; and flashing anti-collision strobes atop the twin tail booms and on each wingtip. We rolled twenty seconds apart and the sensation, unlike that of the sleek White Rocket in pilot training or the muscular Phantom, was a lumbering, excruciatingly sluggish canter with airspeed increasing but very slowly. Performance was further limited by the two 600-gallon external fuel tanks strapped underneath the wings. These would never be loaded for combat but were very useful for a deployment of this magnitude.

Airborne with gear and flaps retracted, I visually picked up the four-ship ahead of me in a shallow climb, each aircraft slowly gaining on the one ahead of it (a straight-ahead join-up in 'Hogs is not an expeditious undertaking). It was moonless, pitch-black with four lightning bugs strung out ahead of me in a lengthy daisy chain. Behind me, my three wingmen were concentrating on closing the distance to me as I climbed at reduced power to give them a few knots' advantage and the same choreography was taking place with the third flight of four and the trailing two-ship. Myrtle Beach Tower turned us over to Jacksonville Air Traffic Control Center and, in sequence, we changed radio frequencies and checked in as separate flights: 'Hog 11 check' followed by a snappy 'twoop; threep; fourp'…'Hog 21 check – twoop; threep; fourp' and so on.

Radio check-ins, to me, were a reflection of the professionalism and sharpness of the flight. If they were crisp and quick I was happy; on the other hand, if a pilot missed the frequency change or his response in the check-in queue was lethargic we did it again, embarrassing him and alerting him that he'd fallen a bit short of standard. Unlike the F-4, the 'Hog had an FM radio for short-range interflight communications, invaluable for directive conversations that would otherwise clutter up the airwaves. Fox Mike was perfect for these curt little spankings: 'Hog 23 either wake up and join the party or go home.' Only our flight heard the admonishment, limiting but not eliminating the humiliation bestowed on the offender. It was rare indeed for a pilot so humbled to miss another radio call, at least on that particular mission.

Having sounded like fighter pilots on check-in, we began the serious business of getting our gaggle together with our buddy tankers. The good news was that the sun had begun to rise ahead of us and there was a bit of light to use for reference. Unlike their Air Force counterparts, the civilian air traffic controllers at Jax Center were not trained to facilitate tanker rendezvous. They were able to vector us towards the KC-135s in our climb and give us distance and bearings until we were able to pick up the heavyweights visually. At that point we flight leads were on our own to work out the geometry that would link us up with our companion tanker. Paradoxically, we the fighters were flying with throttles to the firewall, battling for every knot we could muster, while the tankers, heavily laden with fuel, were struggling along at the lower end of their flight envelope. Not too far above their stall speed, they were trying to provide us a little bit of speed advantage so we could catch them using angular cut-off as they turned in their racetrack pattern. Damned embarrassing for us but hey, to paraphrase Popeye, 'We yam what we yam!' The tanker crews might have had a chuckle or two watching us struggle into position, but they would be relieved not to have to put up with a bunch of smartass F-15/16 ballerinas barrel-rolling around them after taking their fuel.

Once we finally got our herd of 'Hogs linked with our tanker, the KC-135 pilot assumed responsibility for navigation and turned us eastwards into the rising sun while the remaining six 'Hogs performed a similar fandango to join the second tanker behind us. As we wouldn't require another refueling for nearly two hours, we settled down for a long, long drive towards the Azores.

It is often said that flying is hours and hours of sheer boredom punctuated by moments of stark terror. So it was from the US East Coast to Lajes in the Azores, thankfully minus the moments of terror. We refueled three times en route, providing a break from simply droning along in very loose formation behind our shepherding tanker. Tedium was broken only by the occasional bouts of universal mirth when one of our colleagues put on a display of floundering enjoyed by all while he went through the aforementioned ordeal of trying to use his Piddle Pack in spite of the Poopy Suit and associated layers of parachute harness, 'G'-suit, flight suit, thermals and underwear.

No one actually flew into the sea while performing these theatrics and so we flew individual straight-in approaches at Lajes International Airport and then handed over our birds to the maintenance contingent to bed down. We then spent a few hours unwinding, making ready for a similar excursion on into Bentwaters on the following day. Oddly, no one felt much like carousing (and Lajes, lovely town that it is, was not renowned for its night life), so we made do with a good meal, a couple of beers, and one or two of the Doc's downers to lead us to a little shuteye.

The new day dawned and we briefed the last leg inbound, struggled into our Poopy Suits amid a chorus of enthusiastic bitching and moaning and headed for the jets. As was the case after any lengthy deployment, we were eager to return to wives, significant others and families, left in cold, snowy England while we suffered through our training regime in the sunshine of southern Arizona for three months. The phenomenon known as 'Get-homeitis' is familiar to any military pilot and has been known to result in serious lapses in judgment for the sake of returning to the nest on time.

This experience plays a part in the tale of the last leg of the trip, but I'll return to it. First, I'm going to leave you dangling for a page or so to reflect on another aspect of our trade. Don't worry; it will all come together before we leave the Azores.

Trust

Fighter aviation, more than any other profession I am familiar with, requires the individual to place considerable confidence in fellow aviators and many other members of the team. Being able to rely on your back-seater for accurate information in a two-seat fighter or your wingman in a formation is crucial in a combat scenario. The concept of exploiting additional pairs of eyes when seeking out potential enemies is one of the cornerstones of survival in the world of the fighter pilot. A flight leader must know his wingmen will follow orders instantly and without question. This compliance is predicated on the wingmen having faith that the leader has the skill and judgment to provide directions that are comprehensive and reliable. The mutual trust required to manage a complex fluid scenario involving a number of other aircraft to a successful conclusion cannot be overstated.

Trust also extends beyond the cockpit in the fighter business. Our aircraft are maintained by a force of superb technicians, most of whom specialize in one aspect or another of the bird's systems: engines, electronics, flight controls, avionics, life-support systems, armament controls, hydraulics, pneumatics, fuel systems and on and on. There are specialists who hang the weapons, service the ejection seats and maintain canopies and navigation systems and most of these folks are more or less anonymous as far as the pilot is concerned. There is, however, a single link between all these technicians and the airplane driver and that connection is the crew chief or CC. The CC is normally responsible for one aircraft and it is he or she that ties the efforts of all these other folks together to present a safe, flyable aircraft to the jock when he (or she) strides purposefully up to the bird to appropriate it for a couple of hours' sport. The entire report card for the aircraft is contained in Air Force Form 781. This is a large white loose-leaf notebook which catalogues the efforts of all the aforementioned specialists and culminates in the crew chief's personal certification that the airplane meets all the many prerequisites for flight and is ready to go.

This process would be unremarkable except for the fact that the vast majority of crew chiefs are youths in their 20s or early 30s. In a period when adolescents in the same age group are aggressively demanding $15 per hour for flipping hamburgers, they are performing a far more responsible function for less compensation.

I was always impressed with the professionalism and enthusiasm of the young men and women who kept their airplane spit-shined and serviceable and then loaned it to me to take out, ride hard and bring back wet. There was a ritual that accompanied this transfer of machinery: the CC would salute smartly as I approached, hand me the Form 781 and after I signed it off (the pilot still retains the last formal remnant of responsibility), he or she would follow me around the bird while I preflighted it, follow me up the steps and help me strap in. Then, together, we would step through a start sequence and perform a visual check of those flight controls which I couldn't see from the cockpit. Once accomplished, the CC marshaled me out of the parking spot, ensuring clearance from potential obstructions and snap one more sharp salute as I rolled past. At this point, more often than not, the CC would bless his/her bird and my flight by planting a kiss (via the fingertips) on the passing wingtip. I was always a bit buoyed when receiving this special send-off.

How do you reward this kind of dedication from someone so young? I found unembarrassed respect and a touch of kinship to be effective. After all, we were both in this together. Occasionally, when I wanted to show special appreciation, I would walk up to the aircraft, return the salute and ask, 'How's the bird today, Chief?' If the answer was positive, as expected, I'd sign off the form with little more than a glance, forego the preflight inspection completely and head straight up the steps, leaving the CC watching me in astonishment before hustling up behind me for the strap-in and the remainder of the ritual. While my intentional flouting of established procedures (and admittedly slapdash technique) would have landed me firmly in the shit had things gone wrong, the motivational effect on that kid whose name was stenciled on the airplane was dramatic and IMHO well worth the risk.

As promised, after that brief diversion, we're back on the tarmac at Lajes, starting engines for the last leg of the journey home. The tankers are already airborne, waiting for us to join up our gaggle of 'Hogs and come aboard. We're starting engines and going through the final flight control checks when my crew chief plugs his microphone and headset into the communications port inside the ladder door. 'Sir,' he says, 'I'm sorry to tell you this, but you've got an oil leak on your number one (left) engine.' Employing the most versatile expression in the fighter pilot's phrase book, I reply 'Ahhhh, shit!!' and a number of crucial facts race through my brain:

- Elaine will be waiting at Bentwaters and she'll be sorely pissed off if I don't show (get-homeitis)
- Tankers are airborne, flight plans are filed, international clearances have been approved and there's no way this flight's going to wait for Steve to get his airplane fixed if it ain't *real* quick
- If I get left behind today, God knows how and when I'm going to get home. The whole deployment is based on multi-ship travel with tanker support; there are simply no single-ship trans-ocean deployments so I will have to wait for another organized crossing or go home commercial air and leave my bird behind
- Did I mention Elaine will be waiting at Bentwaters and she'll be sorely pissed off if I don't show?

My crew chief's already on the case. I've shut down the engine, he's popped open the engine nacelle on number one and he and a couple others are feverishly going through the myriad of oil lines, looking for my leak. I can't see their efforts (and wouldn't know what they were doing if

I could), but I can hear metal on metal and I silently will my crew chief to find a bigger hammer, if that's what it takes.

All around me, A-10s are beginning to taxi. They'll leave my space in the sequence open right up until take-off, but significant delay is simply not an option. The end of our departure window is minutes away and I am in real danger of becoming an unwilling tourist in the Azores. My crew chief comes back up on the headset: 'We think we've found it sir, crank up number one and let's run it for a quick leak check.' Engine running, after what seems to be an eternity, he says: 'You're good to go, Sir.' This is where the trust comes in; there's no need for 'Are you sure, Chief?' only the positive inflection on the most versatile phrase: 'Shit hot, Chief; like it a lot! I owe you one', followed by 'Lajes Tower, Warthog 21 taxi to join the flight' and the unsaid 'saved by the bell'. As I rolled out, I noticed the fingertip kiss being bestowed on the wingtip and gave the man of the hour a smart salute and a heartfelt thumbs-up.

The presence of trust doesn't mean you stop thinking. Taxiing out, my mind wanders to 'what ifs?':

• What if the leak returns with a vengeance? It's 2,000 miles over water to Bentwaters and, although the 'Hog will fly on one engine, it won't fly very well
• What if I end up in the frigid Atlantic, a long, long way from home?
• What if the damn Poopy Suit leaks and even if it doesn't, who's going to be out there to pick me up?

All reasonable concerns, I think, but I didn't dwell on them; it was show time! Nevertheless, I spent a lot more time than usual checking the number one engine oil pressure gauge on the way home. I needn't have worried; she ran like the proverbial Swiss watch.

It is probably worth mentioning deployment politics at this point. The arrival of the first designated A-10 Squadron in Europe was a fairly big deal politically. A reasonable number of the good and the great of our major command, US Air Forces Europe (USAFE), and a smattering of NATO dignitaries would be there to meet and greet us. Consequently, the choreography of the deployment arrival was a bit more complex than it might have been. The leader of the gaggle all the way from Davis-

Monthan had been the 92nd Squadron Commander, Lieutenant Colonel Sandy Babos (known to all as 'Sandor the Commandor') but trailing slightly behind in the third aircraft (Warthog 13) was his boss, the wing commander, Colonel Rudy (Pud) Wacker. He was not the designated leader because, as the top Wing Weenie, he lacked the currency and technical flight lead credentials to take a fourteen-ship across 'the Pond'. Nevertheless, protocol demanded that he should be the first to touch down on British soil and so, a few miles out, he and Sandy Babos swapped places. This was a no-brainer, but there was one more slightly thorny problem to solve so Rudy would be *numero uno*.

Following the final air refueling, one of Dean Dodson's external tanks stopped feeding fuel to the engines. This was serious, as he would have 600 gallons of usable fuel less than the rest of us, but not fatal. Time, distance and fuel flows were calculated and it was determined that he had enough to make it to Bentwaters, just. The bad news, in terms of our arrival performance, was that he would have to land first, ahead of both the Wing King and the squadron commander. The weather at Bentwaters was poor, snow flurries and low cloud surrounding the airfield. Ground Controlled Approach elements brought Dean aboard as surreptitiously as possible (a Warthog landing straight in from a 5-mile final approach is difficult to conceal). After landing, Bentwaters Tower banished him to Siberia (a quiet cul-de-sac on the north side of the airfield). He lingered there, wanting very badly to get rid of the Poopy Suit and do what comes naturally, until the triumphant parade of 'Hogs had landed and taxied past and he joined at the end of the queue.

When we had all taxied in and shut down, we were directed to IMMEDIATELY climb aboard a shuttle bus which would take us to a hangar for an arrival ceremony, attended by the NATO and UK bigwigs. Faithful and steadfast soldiers we may have been, but the IMMEDIATE nature of the order given was a step too far. We ignored it, fumbled with Poopy Suits, flight suits, thermal underwear and the rest and spent some considerable time watering the Bentwaters tarmac. This small act of defiance proved most beneficial as the aforementioned ceremony, attended by local dignitaries and lesser of the good and the great representing NATO was protracted as only a gathering of politicians and higher-ranking military officials can be. After six hours in a cramped cockpit, my enthusiasm for stirring words and endless platitudes was rapidly fading.

Our wives and significant others had been provided front-row seats on the opposite side of the hangar from our group of bedraggled aviators. After what seemed like another six hours of what was supposed to be rousing rhetoric, the honored guests finally seemed to momentarily run out of bullshit. Elaine, never a shrinking violet, seized the moment and led a small phalanx of wives and girlfriends briskly across the hangar to bestow long overdue hugs and kisses on the sweaty, disheveled and now thoroughly bored returning warriors. That may not be the way the festivities were planned to conclude, but conclude they did, much to the relief of those of us who had long since lost interest in welcome home orations.

The welcome home party at the array of conjoined Quonset huts we laughingly called the Officers' Club was a good one; a few months away from home makes for a worthwhile celebration on arrival. Nevertheless, we knew that converting a Phantom wing to Warthogs was going to be a big job. We had precious little time to make it happen before the dreaded TacEval inspectors descended from our Major Command Headquarters in Germany to test our capabilities in every conceivable way prior to bestowing the coveted title 'Mission Ready' to the organization.

The transition in itself was demanding, but the details are not of great interest to someone reading this volume. Suffice to say our operations element had to adapt procedures designed for fast-moving, powerful 'Jack-of-all-trades' aircraft to much slower, single-mission close air support practices. Most of us were brand-new to the aircraft and there was a lot of polishing to be done before we were ready to lay waste to battalions of Soviet battle tanks. The upgrade involved lots of low-level flying and in the '80s we were able, legally, to race around within designated low-flying areas in south-eastern England and Wales at 250ft above the ground. The newness of the aircraft resulted in a great deal of interest from the local populace, who had grudgingly become used to the great roar of twin General Electric afterburning engines on the Phantom. The A-10, with its fanjets, was a comparative whisper jet and the good people of East Anglia, Suffolk, Norfolk and Lincolnshire were not unhappy to hear the last of the F-4.

Nevertheless, there were instances of exasperation among the natives and one of these is worthy of note. I was in the Wing Command Post one fine spring morning along with our RAF commander, a squadron leader (major equivalent) named Ian who was Her Majesty's liaison with our flying operation. His role was largely that of a figurehead, but he was a genuinely good guy and we liked him a lot. On this particular day, the internal speaker system had been left on for some reason and when the phone rang, the conversation was broadcast on the speakers. Ian picked up and I could hear a lady with a thick Suffolk accent on the other end of the line:

'One of your aeroplanes just scared the bejesus out of me chickens,' she said, more than a little peeved.

'I see, Madam, can you describe it?' Ian responded with all the graciousness and gallantry that only an Englishman can verbally convey.

'Well,' she said, 'it was big and gray and it had two dustbins on the back.'

Ian beamed at me. 'Did it have red stars on the wings?' he asked innocently.

'No, can't say that it did.'

Ian's tone became very solemn: 'Then Madam, thank your God.'

Stunned silence on the other end. 'Cheerio, Madam,' purred Ian and gently put the phone down. He had my respect for life and we laughed loudly and for a long time.

We spent plenty of time honing our gunnery skills during this transition. East Anglia had several excellent weapons ranges dotted around the coastline. Isolated sites with typically British names: Holbeach, Wainfleet, Cowden and Donna Nook that for years had hosted British and American fighters for the sole purpose of being bombed and strafed. The arrival of the 'Hog was just another purveyor of practice bombs but there was one major difference from aircraft that had visited before: that marvelous gun. For decades, air-to-ground gunnery performance was tracked manually. Large fabric targets were strung up on frames, airplanes fired bullets at them and small groups of lower-ranking soldiers or airmen scampered about counting and marking bullet holes (so they wouldn't be tallied twice). This was obviously time-consuming and feedback to the pilot on his performance was excruciatingly slow to surface.

As technology advanced, so did scoring systems. Modern gunnery ranges use a system known as acoustiscore. The equipment broadcasts an adjustable electronic field in the size and shape of the physical target and sensitivity can be set to score different types of bullets: 20mm for lesser aircraft; 30mm for the A-10's awesome GAU-8. The system senses the shock waves from the supersonic projectiles when they pass through the field. These waves are converted to electronic signals and presto! The number of 'hits' on the target is displayed and instantly passed to the pilot, who is either exceedingly pleased or thoroughly disgusted with his performance.

Cold War Warthogging

During the following year, the wing grew exponentially. The original 92nd Squadron was joined by the 78th and 91st, based at our sister base at Woodbridge and then by the 509th, 510th and 511th. Each of these squadrons possessed 18 aircraft and by mid-1980, Bentwaters' 81st Tac Fighter Wing had become the largest operational fighter organization in the world with 108 A-10s, 18 Aggressor F-16s and all the pilots, technicians, support personnel (and their families) needed to sustain them. Additionally, we began establishing four Forward Operating Locations (FOLs) throughout West Germany. More about that later.

At the same time we were integrating the airplane into the European Theater of Operations, the charisma of the 'Hog had begun to proliferate in bigger ways. Army commanders, witnessing the airplane's performance in gunnery demonstrations and live fire displays could be heard extolling the virtues of the A-10 as a troop support weapons system. She had the ability to keep pressure on an enemy through lengthy loiter time, pinpoint weapons delivery accuracy and an impressive array of munitions, not the least of which was that crowd-pleasing Gatling gun. The grunts who would benefit most from the A-10's act began to appreciate what we could do for them during various exercises which combined infantry and armored operations with close air support. Their enthusiasm would later reach a crescendo during the Gulf War (DESERT STORM) and subsequent skirmishes but getting used to the 'Hog took some time, for them as well as us.

We were spending an increasing amount of time away from home in Central Europe, getting accustomed to the terrain over which we would be flying if the balloon went up.

During the Cold War, the Soviets had built a massive armada of armor and infantry on their side of a divided Deutschland from the far north of East Germany to Bavaria. No one had any doubt that the Russian Bear was posturing for a mass invasion of the West and NATO was badly outnumbered in terms of both manpower and heavy battle equipment. The saving grace (the planners hoped) was NATO airpower and there was lots of it in the '70s and '80s. You couldn't travel anywhere in West Germany without seeing fighter aircraft training for the worst-case scenario. In addition to the now-ubiquitous Warthogs there were American Phantoms, F-15s and Aardvarks (F-111s), British Phantoms, Tornados, Jaguars, and Harriers, French and Belgian Mirages, German Tornados, Phantoms, Alpha Jets and F-104s. A couple of years later, American, Dutch and Belgian F-16s joined the party.

Yes, I DO mean party. Fighter pilots being fighter pilots, any casual sighting of other aircraft in the near vicinity was interpreted as an invitation to start or join a fracas. This was extremely valuable training for several reasons. When flying over West Germany your head was always 'on a swivel' looking for would-be attackers anywhere and everywhere. This is a trait that served well in actual combat flying and was honed under these circumstances. There was a constant threat of simulated annihilation by a NATO colleague bent on pressing the microphone button and announcing to the world (on the emergency Guard frequency) 'Guns, Guns on the Tornado/Phantom/Warthog/Mirage heading 340 six miles west of Münster at 500 feet.' Spontaneity of these mock battles was unsurpassed: they just happened and the adrenaline rush they invariably generated was a wondrous thing indeed. We loved them; there was nothing better than wrapping it up with a number of other fighter pilots thoroughly intent on doing it to you before you did it to them. More times than I can count on both hands, I've been in the middle of a dozen or more different aircraft of varying types wheeling and soaring in tight turns and vertical loops over the North German Plain, all trying to gain the tactical advantage over another aircraft while trying valiantly to keep track of all the rest of them.

There was only one downside to these extremely constructive, stimulating and gratifying aeronautical mêlées: they were strictly illegal and, admittedly, for very good reason. Aerial combat training is demanding, complex and, it must be said, perilous by definition. Aircraft maneuvering to the far edge of the aircraft performance envelope in very close proximity to others doing much the same poses an undeniable risk to the aircraft and the general populace. The military has for years insisted on stringent rules of engagement for mitigating that risk while conducting aerial battles. First of all, they must be thoroughly briefed and then rigorously controlled to minimize the inherent risk as much as possible. Authorized engagements are conducted within exceptionally exacting parameters: minimum altitudes (normally in thousands, not hundreds of feet above the ground) and airspeeds, and proximity constraints (each aircraft is in an imaginary '1000 ft bubble' which cannot legally be infringed). This, theoretically, 'eliminates' the risk of mid-air collision. As the combatants in these spontaneous clashes flew from different bases and in different aircraft there was zero preparation and briefing. About the only area of commonality was the fact that all NATO pilots were competent in English and used that aviation standard language in the air. All aircraft were equipped with a common emergency frequency, UHF frequency 243.0 or 'Guard' and therefore it was technically possible to quickly terminate an airborne fiasco going wrong using the accepted parlance of 'Knock it off!' on this frequency. As a testament to the skill of the pilots involved, I never heard that call during a spontaneous battle over Germany.

If we were discussing the butcher, the baker and the candlestick-maker here, the simple fact that unbriefed, unsanctioned aerial battles were strictly prohibited would have been sufficient to ensure that they never happened. Conversely, we're talking fighter pilots and it is a rare (and in my opinion, fainthearted) specimen that had the willpower to pass up an opportunity to mix it up with his peers over the North German Plain. I can only refer to my own reprehensible lack of discipline, but I believe most of us had a fleeting thought that 'I shouldn't be doing this' at about the same time we were lighting the afterburners (if we had them) and pointing our noses directly into the fray.

Criminals all, in the strict interpretation of the word, we were far better pilots for enthusiastically partaking in these valuable but *verboten* skirmishes.

Forward Operations

The establishment of permanent Forward Operating Locations (FOLs) in West Germany was a totally unique concept. Long before we were bedding down the A-10 in England, Air Force planners had devised a strategy for the 'Hog's employment as a weapons system in Europe. The somewhat daunting numerical imbalance between Soviet Bloc and NATO ground forces meant we had to find a concept other than brute force to blunt a major incursion. For the 'Hog community, this concept took the form of FOLs facing the threat across the Inner German Border (IGB), far enough to the west not to be overrun on Day One of a Soviet onslaught, but well within striking distance of armor rolling eastwards across the border.

The plan involved installation of four FOLs, more or less evenly spaced, spanning West Germany from north to south. These detachments were planned for Flugplatz Ahlhorn, once a German zeppelin base, 50km south-west of Bremen; Fliegerhorst Nörvenich, an active Luftwaffe fighter base 40km west of Cologne; Sembach AFB, an active American base 16km north-east of Kaiserslautern; and Fliegerhorst Leipheim, another active Luftwaffe base, 25km east of Ulm.

The FOL concept was straightforward: forward deployment; rearward maintenance. The four FOLs would be manned and equipped to launch, recover and re-arm A-10s and provide limited maintenance during wartime operations. Aircraft requiring more complex repair and maintenance would be returned to the main operating base at RAF Bentwaters and replaced as necessary at the FOLs. This would have been a nightmare scenario for more complicated fighters, but the 'Hog was, in general, easy to maintain and therefore the FOLs were more than capable of most levels of repair.

As the permanent FOL model was relatively new, planners decided to initiate the project at an American installation where US support, logistics and infrastructure were already in place and so Sembach was chosen as Detachment 1. Preparations began there in September 1978, even before the first A-10 reached the UK. As the facilities, equipment and personnel were readily available, the detachment spooled up quickly and was ready to accept deployed A-10s and their pilots in late 1978. We all cycled through Sembach when it was the only FOL in Germany and began to familiarize ourselves with the terrain in the region just west of the IGB, where we would be expected to ply our trade in the event of a Soviet onslaught. Our aircraft were still devoid of sophisticated navigation equipment and getting used to flying in close proximity to the fabled 'Iron Curtain' could sometimes be a daunting experience.

The IGB was protected by an Air Defense Identification Zone (ADIZ) which extended the full length of the border between East and West Germany. Flight into the ADIZ was strictly prohibited. Unlike the illicit pick-up air battles described previously, we paid full attention to this prohibition because aircraft straying into the ADIZ were in very real jeopardy of being intercepted or shot down by Soviet air defense forces. To preclude such disagreeable incidents, the ADIZ was safeguarded on the west by the Central European Buffer Zone (CEBZ or, more often, just BZ). Operations within the BZ were legal, but only when scheduled, approved and thoroughly briefed. The Buffer Zone was monitored constantly by US and NATO radar and inadvertent incursions were severely frowned upon. In the A-10, while fumbling for the map you had dropped on the floor, the first indication that you might have, perhaps, stumbled into the BZ was a dramatic call on the emergency Guard frequency: 'Brass Monkey, Brass Monkey, all aircraft in the vicinity of the BZ turn west immediately.' You didn't question or quibble with this command; you turned west, as abruptly as possible. Unfortunately, so did a dozen or more other aircraft conducting valuable training operations legally in or near the BZ. The guilty bastard would be identified by radar and faced a brisk knuckle-rapping on return to base, but rarely did this level of offense result in having one's sword broken and buttons cut off.

While the Bentwaters wing was growing to its full 108 aircraft strength, FOL operations continued to ramp up and for reasons I cannot offer, Detachment 1 at Sembach was followed by the inauguration of Detachment 3, far to the north at Ahlhorn. Since arriving back at Bentwaters with the A-10 I had served as the wing weapons and tactics officer and then 78th Tac Fighter Squadron assistant operations officer. Recently promoted to major, I was just settling in to the operations job when I got a message that the wing commander wanted to talk to me. Now this could be good news or it could be very bad news. The message didn't provide a clue so, with more than a bit of apprehension, I headed to his office. When I arrived, the Wing King was having coffee with the Deputy Commander for Operations (or DO), also a full colonel. This again could be positive or negative, so I sat down uneasily and waited for either the glowing accolade or the ritual lowering of the boom.

'Steve,' the Wing King opened, 'we'd like you to be the Operations Officer at Detachment 4 in Nörvenich.' I remember just sitting there gawking at him. Without any forewarning, my mind was racing, but uncharacteristically, my mouth wasn't working. Here before me was a truly golden opportunity. The Detachments were as close as you could get to autonomy in the Air Force and, because there were only a handful of officers running the show, the chance to be your own man was unrivalled.

On the other hand, the fact that there were only a handful of officers also meant that a significant personality mismatch could result in two years or more of stress, frustration and potentially serious professional conflict. Rumor had it that the front-runner for the Detachment 4 commander slot (who would be my direct boss) was 'The Politician', world-class egotist but the antithesis of gifted leadership.

As much as I wanted my chance to shine as a detachment operations officer, I knew that toiling for this guy for a couple years would have proven terminal, for one or the other of us. Consequently, I had to ask the question: 'If I take the job, Sir, who will I be working for?'

The Wing King looked at me curiously, not expecting that response, and advised that there were two lieutenant colonels on the shortlist: 'The Politician', the aforementioned self-publicist, and John Casper, a recently-promoted lieutenant colonel I didn't know well, but whose reputation was that of a talented aviator with a positive attitude and an all-round good guy.

I took a deep breath and said: 'Well, Sir, one out of two ain't bad.' I proceeded to tell him, as diplomatically as possible, that I couldn't and wouldn't work for 'The Politician' because in order of increasing priority a) I didn't like him, b) I didn't respect him and, most importantly, c) I didn't trust him and finally, if he got the nod, I would have to decline.

The Boss glowered at me again, more intently this time, and said: 'Thanks for being candid, Steve.' Reasonably sure the conversation (and my candidacy) was finished, I replied 'Yes, Sir' and walked out of the office, closely examining my flight boots for the self-inflicted gunshot wound I was pretty sure I had just administered.

I wasn't too devastated because I was pretty satisfied with my lot in life as it stood, but I was disappointed because I was convinced I had just trampled upon the best major's job in the Air Force. Never mind. As Doris Day so aptly put it: '*Que será, será*, whatever will be, will be.'

I was therefore surprised and delighted when, a few days later, John Casper was designated Detachment 4 Commander and yours truly was named Robin to his Batman. John and I hit it off well, and there was plenty to be done prior to raising the curtain at Nörvenich. Unlike the US operation at Sembach's Detachment 1, we were well outside the normal Air Force supply chain and, although the personnel people in Texas were busy selecting our seventy-odd maintenance and support contingent, we were well behind the power curve in terms of putting together an efficient flying operation.

Farewell to Ashbocking

Despite the rapid tempo of preparing for the assignment at Nörvenich, day-to-day life still went on and that meant continuing the day job: flying routine training sorties and advising the boss as the wing weapons and tactics officer. My wife and I had spent the past three years in our home in Ashbocking, a tiny Suffolk village (population ca. 200) at the crossing of two minor roads about twenty-five minutes from RAF Bentwaters. We enjoyed living away from the base and, although our neighbors were few and far between, we both had a soft spot for the village.

As moving day approached, I began to consider how I might deliver a small farewell tribute to our home and our village. You won't be surprised to learn that accolade involved a couple of airplanes and a bright sunny day. There was only one minor drawback: in order to do it right, I would be forced to slightly bend the regulations covering low flying. Ashbocking was relatively remote, with no major population centers or built-up areas nearby, but it was outside the designated low-flying areas and therefore subject to a 500ft minimum altitude restriction. In my humble opinion, overflying our house at 500ft would not only be underwhelming, it would hardly constitute a proper mark of respect.

I don't recall who was on my wing that day, but I did ensure he was one of the good guys who wouldn't come running back after the flight trumpeting my transgression for all to hear. We flew a solid training sortie and then on the way home, I brought him into close formation and set up for a straight-in pass over the homestead. We dropped down to slightly less than 500ft (that's my story and I'm sticking to it) and performed a flawless Warthog pass directly over the house, pulling up smartly after we had passed clear.

Elaine had a pretty good idea I'd be by to say hello that day, but she didn't know exactly when. Unlike the Phantom and most other fighters, the 'Hog was relatively quiet, sometimes referred to only half sarcastically as the Whisper Jet. She caught a glimpse of us coming in from the kitchen window and caught the virile WHOOSH as we passed over, but she was ready for the second pass she knew was coming. As we pulled up into our wingover and set up for another run, I couldn't help but laugh; there she was jumping up and down and frantically waving a pair of orange rubber gloves in the middle of the back garden, accompanied by Mr Sidney Smith, our ancient but magnificent gardener (an RAF veteran) and Jimpy, our trusty Golden Retriever. The second run (including wing waggle) was even more majestic than the first and perhaps even slightly lower. We headed for home base knowing we had at least made Elaine's day.

Many months later, long after moving to Germany, a large envelope arrived in the Deutsche Bundespost. Inside were some excellent photographs of two A-10s, arguably a tad below 500ft, beginning to pull up from a Showtime pass. There was also a brief note from the gentleman who lived in a large Tudor manor house, set well back from the road opposite our former home in Ashbocking. He had, he said, noticed two airplanes bearing down on the village at low altitude and had grabbed his camera to record the event. He assumed at the time that his American neighbor had taken the opportunity to bid farewell to the village in the most dramatic way available and complimented the pilots on the tight formation and the exceptional navigation required to find the target house and overfly it, twice!

I've no idea how he managed to track us down in Germany, but I'm awfully glad he did. The much simpler alternative would have been to send the photos to the commander at RAF Bentwaters (for whom I still worked as a detachment operations officer) and request they be forwarded. This option would undoubtedly have resulted in Major Ladd receiving, at very least, the mother of all reprimands and potentially far more severe penalties. Our neighbor's diligence in locating us in Germany thus saved my bacon and I remain grateful to this day.

Chapter Eleven

Dritte Staffel (Third Squadron)

I n the meantime, I had forgotten all about my air show and was deep into the process of establishing a small but perfectly formed American flying operation on German soil.

We were fortunate in many respects: the aforementioned personnel effort had apparently been well-conceived for a small, comparatively self-contained operation because they earmarked some truly outstanding technicians to form the nucleus of our hardy little band. People like Master Sergeant Bucky Pope, Technical Sergeant Joe McGinnis and Technical Sergeant Walt Myers proved absolutely invaluable as we started the wheels turning and I had a small command and control contingent led by Technical Sergeant Ben Davis that served equally well in setting up our miniscule command post.

There was another small USAF unit stationed at Nörvenich: the 7502nd Munitions Support Squadron (or MUNSS) who were the US custodians for the nuclear weapons Uncle Sam would release to the Luftwaffe in case the balloon went up in Central Europe. These folks knew the local area and had excellent contacts on the German support side of the house. This served us well when we started the long and stressful process of acquiring local housing for all our people and their families; something that, for sure, wasn't in a fighter pilot's job description. Setting up the detachment was one of the greatest challenges of my career, and one of the most satisfying chapters. We would be manned by seventy NCOs and enlisted personnel. Most of these were bringing families with them and many of them had never been overseas; talk about group culture shock. Although the Air Force prides itself on taking care of its own, in this instance the support we received from Uncle Sam hovered right around the zero mark.

As our personnel started to trickle in, the Germans joined us in finding them places to live in the surrounding area. Our five officers

(John Casper, myself, a US Army ground liaison captain, an aircraft maintenance captain and a first lieutenant admin officer) mastered a couple of hundred German words and phrases between us. Clearly, our solo attempts to converse with German rental agents and landlords would have been, at very best, gross buffoonery. The US Air Force failed to provide the administrative and linguistic expertise required for the bed-down, but the Germans bailed us out – big time – and we were eternally indebted.

I will no longer accept criticism about my multi-tasking deficiencies after this ground-breaking experience. In addition to the obvious housing issues, there were kids to educate, temporary furniture and fittings to obtain while waiting for the shipments to arrive, and oh, by the way, a fairly complex flying and maintenance organization to assemble from scratch. Our folks were temporarily living in hotels and *Gasthauses* in a number of nearby towns and villages and their children were rounded up daily to be bussed to school; well over an hour each way for the older ones. Before long, the strain of balancing an exasperating lifestyle with a demanding mission task began to show among the troops and we looked urgently for a way to boost morale. John Casper came up with the answer and it paid major dividends.

Our sister USAF unit, the MUNSS, had a small club in its compound, complete with bar, dance floor and a number of seats. It was nothing elaborate, but a bit of Americana on foreign soil. We were always welcome there, but in the early days many of our troops were saddled with children who they had no place to park and couldn't partake. The MUNSS occasionally hired a band for an evening of dancing and it was this opportunity we seized upon. John called the troops together a week or so before the event and announced that they would all be going to the dance and they were all going to enjoy it because we, the Officer Corps, were going to look after their rug rats for the evening. This may not have been a major production, you might think, except for the fact that none of *our* wives had arrived in the area yet and the formidable task of shepherding forty-odd kids for an entire evening would fall to two childless fighter pilots, a maintainer, an Army captain and a single lieutenant on his first assignment. What could possibly go wrong?

As it turned out, this experiment was a massive success. We commandeered a large hall in the MUNSS HQ Building, then barricaded ourselves and the kids in with enough toys, snacks and soda pop to enthrall everyone under 10 in a medium-sized Midwestern state. We then learned to appreciate the meaning of 'herding cats' for four hours or so.

Meanwhile, in the MUNSS Club, our harassed NCOs and their wives and partners had a marvelous time, dancing the night away and NOT worrying about their offspring for a change. Their appreciation for this small gesture created a bond with their officers that endured for years. Result!

The biggest unknown factor became the most gratifying success story of all. Here we were, descending upon a respected Luftwaffe fighter-bomber wing, *JaboGeschwader* 31, with a contingent of Americans who were going to appropriate a significant chunk of their real estate. Then we would build a command center, aircraft shelters and revetments to house probably the ugliest flying machine on the planet. Finally, we would expect to share their runways, taxiways, air traffic control functions and numerous other undertakings that previously were under complete control of the Germans. Although the bed-down of our detachment had been thoroughly negotiated and formally accepted by our hosts, we would not have been the least surprised to encounter some measure of resistance, resentment and wariness as we steadily encroached upon their turf.

In fact, we were welcomed with the exact opposite reaction from the German wing commander (or *Kommodore*, as he was commonly referred to), who bore a marked resemblance to Sean Connery and went by the remarkably Teutonic moniker of *Oberst* Gert Overhoff. The *Kommodore* appointed a project officer, Major Ritz, who devoted his entire working existence to ensuring that our transition went smoothly. Ritz was a great guy and tireless in his support. Every day, he opened doors that eased our difficult transition and hastened our assimilation into the wing.

Day by day, week by week, we grew in strength and our brand-new corps of maintainers started laying the foundation for aircraft operations. Our enlisted contingent carried on the grand old traditions of military men everywhere. They established contact with their German counterparts, rapidly developed a thriving underground economy and very soon, logistical bits and pieces we badly needed to operate but couldn't source quickly through US channels were coming our way. In return, American cigarettes and bottles of Jack Daniels were being enjoyed by German logistics and maintenance NCOs. We officers (and our German counterparts) enthusiastically found other things to worry about and the net result was progress for the detachment.

So positive was our budding relationship with the German wing that they invited us to become their third squadron (or *Dritte Staffel*). As each of the A-10 FOLs had its own unique uniform patch, I set out to design Detachment 4's version. It was shamelessly copied from the German wing's emblem with a couple of subtle changes. An oncoming Warthog replaced the superimposed red wings, and banners top and bottom proclaimed that we were the 3rd Squadron *JaboG31* (in Germanic font) and Detachment 4 of the 81st TFW (in Olde English).

Shit hot! We liked it a lot! We ordered and distributed hundreds of patches and a few plaques (one of which proudly adorns my study wall), and I was feeling mighty pleased with my design abilities until, after a few beers, one of my German fighter pilot friends politely pointed out that the Luftwaffe abbreviation for *Staffel* is *Stff* and the 'l' I had deposited on the end was quite absurd. I felt badly about this, although not too badly as I had also had a few beers and by the following morning, I had forgotten all about it. It subsequently came back to me a week or so later, but I decided to keep it to myself, so except for all my German friends, who graciously didn't harass me about it, you readers are the very first to know.

Living and working among German military folks, especially fighter pilots, was a genuine treat. My wife, daughter of a lady who built Halifax bombers for the RAF and niece of a wartime air-raid warden, wasn't particularly keen to reside among the old enemy, but even she accepted rather early on that these were good people and Nörvenich grew on us in a very positive way.

Our relationship with our hosts was near seamless and we rarely ended up in any kind of incongruous situation as Luftwaffe tenants. We shared the Cold War mission: stepping up to the Russian bear and, to our mutual benefit, we scratched their back and you know the rest.

On one occasion my nemesis 'The Politician', who had somehow managed to fool some of the people all of the time at Bentwaters and be anointed as a squadron commander, brought his eighteen-aircraft contingent to Nörvenich for a couple weeks' training. While most squadron bosses were primarily concerned with ensuring his pilots were the best they could be, the warped little gears in his head were always turning in a way that would result in his looking good. He decided that he had a reasonable shot at getting his face on the cover of *Rolling Stone* or at very least the European edition of *Stars & Stripes* by staging a Warthog extravaganza consisting of all eighteen of his aircraft taking the runway simultaneously and then departing as a squadron. John Casper and I attempted to diplomatically advise him that eighteen Warthogs on a runway constituted a pretty lucrative target – not a million miles away from eighteen fish in a barrel – and perhaps did not fall into the realm of tactically sound training activities. As was his wont, he ignored us and, with visions of glittering awards and promotions dancing in his head, set out to orchestrate the fandango. This included locating a couple of German photographers who would no doubt help him on his way to fame and fortune through colorful portrayals of his mighty armada, ready to roll.

My boss rolled his eyes, shook his head and shrugged his shoulders, but I had other ideas and ventured forth to set them in motion. It was easy, really. I called *Oberst* Boettcher, German deputy commander for operations, a big bear of a man with a gruff presence but an ever-present twinkle in his eye, and suggested we meet for a beer. While we set the world to rights, I casually mentioned that our deployed squadron commander had big plans for assembling a gaggle of 'Hogs on *his* runway the following morning and that Casper and I had tried to talk him out of it to no avail. I ended the conversation by giving my German friend a USAFE salute. You remember, don't you? Upturned palms, an exaggerated shrug of the shoulders and an expression of utter exasperation. I walked out of the *Offiziersheim* bar secure in the knowledge that something most enjoyable was going to happen on the morn.

Dawn broke, as it often does, and 'The Politician's' airborne flotilla was scheduled to congregate on the runway at 0900 sharp. Nothing dramatic was occurring, but I did notice unusually active German F-104 activity at around 0830. Their normal launch pattern, in twos and fours, commenced around 0930–1000 and rarely exceeded eight or ten aircraft. On this occasion, there were more launches, twenty or so, and I suppressed a wry smile of anticipation as I went about my mundane chores.

At 0840, the flock of Warthogs started engines and called the tower to taxi about fifteen minutes later. By 0855 they were queued up on the taxiway like Londoners waiting for a bus and 'The Politician' in his lead aircraft called ready for take-off: 'Snake [his squadron's call sign] Zero One is number one with eighteen of the world's finest,' he said in his best impression of John Wayne. 'Snake Zero One, you are cleared onto the runway to hold,' replied the German tower controller and the great behemoth lumbered onto the active runway and squatted there as four flights of four with a trailing twosome. Once in position, they accomplished their preflight checks and waited for tower clearance to take off.

John Casper and I, anticipating what was to come, had gathered as many of our troops as could be spared from their duties and took up a peerless observation position on an embankment overlooking the runway. The only thing we forgot was the popcorn.

If you've ever been to a military air show, you'll recall that the fighter demonstration teams enjoy making their astounding entrance low and fast from behind the crowd. The German F-104s achieved this element of surprise in spades with the first four coming in over us in a spread formation perpendicular to the runway. They were simulating a low-level napalm delivery against – you guessed it – 'The Politician's' Flying Circus. This pass in itself would surely have taken out most of the assembled Warthogs, but they hadn't even started the show at this point. Two F-104s followed within a few seconds straight up the runway simulating low-angle strafe passes and then two more did the same from the opposite direction. With no clearance to take off, 'The Politician' and his pilots had no alternative but to sit in their cockpits and soak up the colossal simulated drubbing they were taking. Had we been a bit closer, I suspect we might have seen the steam emanating from 'The Politician's' cockpit while he endured the humiliation of having his squadron's collective lunch eaten by *JaboGeschwader* 31's F-104 pilots who later, in the bar, referred to them as *leichte Beute* (sitting ducks) and the overall scenario as *kinderleicht sein* (child's play).

The Greatest Show in Nordrhein-Westfalen lasted another five minutes or so, featuring precision sequenced attacks simulating delivery of all manner of munitions from low-angle bombs to high-angle strafe. Had the ordnance been authentic, 'The Politician's' fighter squadron would have been reduced to small heaps of burning scrap metal.

When the Luftwaffe grew weary of kicking the Snakes around, they departed the traffic pattern and 'The Politician's Folly', as it came to be known, was provided clearance by a slightly derisive German tower controller: 'World's Finest, you're now cleared for take-off.' What he had hoped would resemble a departing phalanx of Centurions, complete with blaring trumpets, however, more closely resembled a pack of whipped puppies; you could almost sense them drooping as they got airborne.

When they straggled back an hour or so later, John Casper and I were waiting by the operations desk. 'The Politician' was the first to emerge and, because he was at least as fond of me as I was of him, he fixed me with a steely glare that clearly said 'I dare you to say anything.' Flashing my most endearing smile, I accommodated him: 'Well that went well, didn't it?'

The German intelligence network was active that day because 'The Politician' hadn't taken three steps into the building when the phone rang. Casper answered, handed it to him and said: 'It's the *Kommodore* for you.' We couldn't hear the conversation, but it was extremely brief and unidirectional. The now somewhat contrite recipient uttered 'Yes, sir' a number of times and skulked off to hang up his flying gear. We later learned the gist of the *Kommodore*'s terse message: 'If you ever try to do anything as tactically absurd as that on my airfield again, your feet won't touch the ground on your way back to Bentwaters.'

As much as I disliked 'The Politician', I felt extremely sorry for his pilots, who were subjected to this level of humiliation simply because their boss was obsessed with his own image and forging another step up the ladder. I met up with most of them for a beer later in the afternoon and although I won't divulge exactly what they had to say about their leader, I couldn't honestly disagree with any of it.

Survival *auf Deutsche*

Germans, in my opinion, often get bad press and are stereotyped as dour, over-regimented and inflexible. There is something in this, of course, just as we Americans are sometimes branded as insular, loud and ill-informed about anything outside our borders. Nevertheless, we found our counterparts in the Luftwaffe to be gregarious, good-natured and welcoming and not at all tentative about making the best of any situation.

February, in the areas surrounding Cologne, Düsseldorf and Mainz, is *Karneval* time, and this mammoth celebration begins on *Rosenmontag* (Rose Monday) and runs on for nearly a month. In the midst of the festivities – the Thursday prior to Shrove Tuesday – is arguably the most festive night of them all: *Weiberfastnacht* or Women's Carnival Day, the day the ladies take charge. Partying is widespread and traditionally starts at 11.11 am after which the ladies, all in fancy dress, run riot for the rest of the day and evening, cutting off men's ties (a terrifying symbolism) and generally creating havoc. As you might expect, the following day brings with it the mother of all hangovers for many and consequently, most businesses don't bother to open.

JaboGeschwader 31 [the German Wing] annually made a valiant effort to emulate local traditions by taking the day off, but the Luftwaffe High Command wasn't having any of it and decreed that, hangover or not, the special Friday was to be a work day. The *Kommodore* saluted smartly, as he was forced to do annually, and set out to make the compulsory working day something special.

This took the form of a mandatory full-day survival exercise and, as the only assigned *Dritte Staffel* aviators, John Casper and I were cordially invited to attend. On the previous evening, we had managed to locate a local *Gasthaus* while our wives enjoyed the *Weiberfastnacht* evening in the center of Cologne. We had solved many of the world's pressing problems over a few foamy glasses of *kölsch*, the local brew, and arrived for the morning exercise with requisite hangovers where we were welcomed accordingly.

We were bussed westward into the dense forest of the Eifel National Park and deposited in a small clearing; thirty-odd fighter pilots in flying suits and jackets thirsting for knowledge. This was provided by one of the German wing pilots whose additional duty was survival equipment and training. He had assembled various equipment demonstrations and gave us a brief talk on constructing shelter, making fires, nibbling on roots and twigs and generally staying alive. Casper and I looked at each other, wondering what the hell we were going to do for the *rest* of the day. We didn't have to wait long for the answer: we were split into groups of four or five and our leader was Major Peter Bündgen, Second Squadron commander and all-round good guy. Each group was briefed individually and presented with a large-scale map with a triangle drawn on it. For a fighter pilot, a triangle on a map denotes a target and finding that target was to be step one in the day's activities. Successfully pinpointing the target would, disappointingly, result only in finding another map with another triangle and so it would go on. Casper and I shared another surreptitious glance. It was bitterly cold and snowing in the German forest and this sequence of events didn't point to a particularly enjoyable day being had by all. We began our forced march under a cloud of minor gloom and with precious little enthusiasm.

We had been dolefully tramping through the forest for about twenty minutes when we came upon another small clearing and a single-track road. There, waiting for us, was a Luftwaffe ambulance and two or three of the other groups who had arrived via slightly different routes. The ambulance was manned by the German flight doctor and one of his orderlies and the rear doors were open to reveal a couple kegs of *kölsch*, numerous bottles of schnapps and brandy and an impressive array of rollmops, sausages and other Germanic culinary delights. Peter Bündgen, who had been quietly enjoying our simmering melancholy, sidled over and remarked that the ambulances were always provided to ensure the health and wellbeing of the participants throughout the exercise. He flashed a smile, poured a couple of glasses of *kölsch* and the whole complexion of the day's events suddenly became much brighter.

Refreshed and significantly more motivated, we pressed on to locate the first target. This sequence of events was repeated three or four times and as dusk began to fall, we were feeling supremely mellow. The last leg of the survival course looked like a lengthy one and although we were well-oiled by this time, we were also getting a bit tired. We were straggling along a minor road when a vehicle approached from behind us. Time for a brief digression. In peacetime, the Germans wear flying suits of bright international orange to enable easy recognition by search parties in the event that they are forced down. This attire came in particularly handy when Peter realized that the vehicle advancing towards us was a school bus.

He stepped into the middle of the road, held up his hands and when the bus had stopped looked up at the driver and, in an authoritative voice that would have done Starsky or Hutch proud, proclaimed: 'German Air Force, I am commandeering your vehicle.'

These were gentler days, free from Jihadi suicide bombers and similar acts of mass barbarism, so the bus driver, recognizing the uniform, acquiesced and we all trooped aboard and mingled with some very curious and excited children on their way home from lessons. Peter was just about coherent enough to explain to a very good-natured bus driver where we were bound and he proceeded to chauffeur us to our final 'target': a *Gasthaus* on the edge of the forest, very close to civilization.

During the next hour or so, we were joined by the other teams, who obviously had not been quite as creative in their mode of conveyance and had actually walked the final leg of the journey. As we had obviously not had enough beer, brandy, bratwurst, rollmops and other diverse accouterments to survive during the afternoon trek, we re-energized at the *Gasthaus*. The remainder of the day blurred into something approaching oblivion. I hasten to add here that at no time did I lose consciousness, really. I do recall lots more *kölsch*, a number of juvenile competitions and a rousing chorus of bilingual fighter pilot songs which simultaneously amused and appalled the locals who had made the mistake of dropping by on that particular afternoon for a peaceful drink.

Grand Theft – Warthog

Military units are constantly drilled in contingency plans: responses to virtually every imaginable occurrence. This enhances the organization's readiness and trains the troops in both the specific scenario being trialed and the ability to react to similar occurrences. As the 'Third Squadron' of the Luftwaffe's Boelcke Wing, we were occasionally asked to participate in contingency training for our German hosts.

When I was invited to meet with the German *Kommodore* and his director of operations for a coffee in mid-1982, I could not have imagined how much fun I was about to have. The Germans wanted to test security in two different areas: theft of an aircraft and the unannounced arrival of a defector. It didn't take long to determine we could kill both these birds with a single Warthog. We settled on a plan, known only to the three of us and my boss, John Casper and a date the following weekend.

Like many European military air bases, Nörvenich was designed to confuse potential attackers, heavily landscaped to reduce visual target acquisition from the air. Some of our aircraft were parked along taxi routes hidden deep in forestry and I chose one of these as my loot-to-be. There was some element of risk in what I was about to do and we had chosen a time when no other aircraft would likely be taxiing, taking off or landing. Early on a Sunday morning (well, it worked at Pearl Harbor) I briefed one of my most trusted crew chiefs and we drove over to the aircraft. The Warthog is extremely easy to start and launch and the two of us had me up, running and out of the chocks in three minutes flat. I had the radios set to Nörvenich ground control with Emergency Guard, but I wasn't talking to anyone. Somewhere in the forest, a German security policeman watched what was going on and, as he anticipated no activity that morning, raised the alarm.

The ground controller transmitted: 'A-10 aircraft proceeding eastbound on north taxiway; identify yourself.' I ignored him and continued swiftly towards an intersection of Runway 25 (as the aircraft wasn't heavily laden I didn't need the whole runway and planned a short take-off). The next transmission from ground control was the same, but this time on Guard frequency and at least an octave higher. I could see blue flashing lights converging on my position, but none were close enough to intercept me. As I approached the runway, I had a good look left and right, then in the rearview mirrors where I saw three vehicles arriving much too late to the party. I'd already completed the preflight checklists so when there appeared to be no conflicts, I rolled onto the runway, firewalled the engines and, laughing heartily to myself, broke ground and headed towards the green and pleasant rural countryside to the south-west.

The next twenty minutes or so were delightful. I amused myself by wandering around local farms and woodland at *very* low level (to thwart air traffic control radar), and listening to the pandemonium I had caused on the radio. In keeping with their ops plans, the Germans had scrambled two of their Tornados to hunt me down like a dog and force me to bring the Americans' airplane back. They had taxied but were stood down before launch by the *Kommodore* for reasons only he (and his DO and John Casper and I) were aware of.

It was time for Act Two. I made a couple of surreptitious passes at low level and again determined that there was no conflicting traffic. Due to the prevailing wind, the active runway was 07 (to the north-east), but I'd already broken so many rules I figured one more couldn't hurt. It's customary (nay, mandatory) to announce your arrival and intention to land to ATC and/or the tower prior to entering the airfield's restricted airspace, but that would have taken all the enjoyment out of it. Instead, I set up on a 2-mile final approach at 100ft or so above ground level. Still refusing to chat with the tower, just inside a mile out, I pitched up abruptly to 500ft or so, pulled the throttles to idle and extended the speed brakes. I dropped the landing gear and flaps and touched down on south-east Runway 25 about fifteen seconds later. As if by magic, the bedlam resumed: blue lights started flashing again and the tower frequencies became flooded with panicky (and often contradictory) directions. The thief had morphed into a potential defector and all the rules of engagement instantly changed.

This time the Germans were ahead of me. They blocked my path and I rolled to a stop on the runway. They then proceeded to box me in on all sides and I looked down from my cockpit at about a dozen frustrated and obviously angry young men with automatic weapons pointed at me. They'd all been running around for the last half-hour or so taking vast amounts of ridicule and abuse from their bosses for letting me steal an airplane in the first place and they now appeared to be keen to get even. A few of them had brought their pets along: great snarling Rottweilers and Belgian Malinois attack dogs. Not a single tail was wagging and for the first time I began to wish I was home reading the Sunday papers.

Never mind; might as well play this one to the hilt. The engines were still running and my canopy was down and locked. The senior security type directed me to shut down with a slashing motion to his throat. I stared at him and slowly shook my head, which he obviously didn't appreciate. We went back and forth on this issue a few times and finally I relented and shut down the engines. We conducted a similar charade with the canopy and again, after a few jabs and deflections I conceded, opened the canopy, unstrapped and put my hands in the air. There was slight confusion as my 'captors' didn't know where the internal ladder button was. I wasn't going to help so they finally brought a step ladder. The first man to reach me pulled a canvas bag over my head and he and his buddies hauled me out of the cockpit. I was a bit concerned because it's a long way down from an A–10 cockpit, but they were efficient, if not at all gentle.

I then enjoyed a blind ride in the back of a panel truck, destination unknown. When we arrived, I was hustled out of the van and into a cold room that smelled like concrete. My captors finally pulled off the bag and I looked at a half-dozen senior NCOs who were literally rubbing their hands together in anticipation of a vigorous interrogation. They were obviously a bit apprehensive because they were now custodians of a pilot in an American flight suit with an ID card in Cyrillic text around his neck (this had been donated by the German Wing Intelligence section). Nevertheless, they appeared to be perfectly willing to give me a few hearty whacks in search of information to determine just what the hell I was up to. I was spared significant pain and suffering by the timely arrival of the *Kommodore*, who finally let the proverbial cat out of the bag, briefing his troops on the day's entertainment and scheduling a 'lessons learned' session for later that afternoon.

Then he took me to the Officers' Mess for a beer and a bratwurst. A perfect end to a perfect day!

Chapter Twelve

Berlin: Cold War Personified

I'm going to briefly digress from aviation-related topics and relate an experience made possible by my profession but not directly associated with it. There was never a more powerful illustration of the high-tension Cold War confrontation between East and West than the divided city of Berlin. Jointly occupied by the four major victors of the Second World War – the US, Great Britain, France and the Soviet Union – Berlin for many years represented the powder keg that constantly teetered on the edge of conflict between 1945 and 1990. Anyone of a certain age will recall photographs of American and Russian tanks facing off over Checkpoint Charlie and sporadic reports of East Germans being shot by their own countrymen as they audaciously sought to gain freedom by crossing over to the West.

As hazardous as Berlin appeared to be, it was readily accessible to military personnel from all the aforementioned victorious nations and, improbably, their families as well. Indeed, travel to Berlin was encouraged by the US government and as Elaine and I were young and fearless, we decided to embark on the adventure and experience history in progress. Preparing for such a foray was administration gone mad. As Elaine is British, she needed clearance from her Embassy and I was required to fill all the squares thrown at me by the US bureaucracy. This took weeks to complete, but we were too excited by the prospect of visiting the world's most precarious city to become discouraged by it.

Berlin was situated approximately 100 miles inside Soviet-controlled East Germany and there were, in essence, three ways to reach the city during the occupation:

- The Allied Powers had flight access to the city via three air corridors which terminated in airports in the US, British and French sectors
- Both the US and UK military operated 'troop trains' to the city via specified railways. Trains were sealed for the duration of the East

German leg and no stops were allowed. As an aside, the British troop train was rumored to be superior in terms of comfort and ambience
- Finally, it was possible to drive a private vehicle on the Autobahn from Helmstedt in West Germany to Berlin. As we felt it would provide additional flexibility in Berlin, we opted for this mode, despite the additional administrivia required to make it happen.

When departure day arrived, we pitched up at Helmstedt at the appointed hour. This provided a tantalizing prelude to the drive we were about to take and it bore no resemblance whatsoever to any pleasure trip I'd ever taken before. Our first stop was at Checkpoint Alpha in Helmstedt. Here a US military policeman looked over our special travel orders which also included a Russian translation. Here, too, we were briefed on the coming trip. We were reminded that the US did not recognize the sovereignty of East Germany, and that we should have nothing to do with any German official of the East Zone. We were also advised that the only people on the other side with whom we may deal were uniformed Soviet military personnel.

Our car was checked to make sure we had enough gas to make the trip and all the necessary equipment for changing tires or performing other emergency repair work. The speed limit on the road was set at 50 mph and we were given between two and three and a half hours to make the trip. Our mileage was checked and noted, as was our time of departure. This was relayed to Checkpoint Bravo on the outskirts of Berlin. If we arrived significantly early we faced a slap on the wrist for speeding, and if we failed to appear by the appointed hour, somewhat disgruntled US military personnel would be backtracking from Berlin to locate us. We were years away from the magic of mobile telecommunications and the civilians we were likely to encounter en route were not particularly disposed to assist us, so a failure to arrive on time would be a cause for concern. We also could not exit, so there was no chance of a 'potty break' en route; this was emphasized to my bride. If the car broke down, we had been given two accident report forms. The drill was to complete them and hand one each to an Allied or West German driver going in opposite directions. Having handed in those accident report forms, we were to sit tight until help arrived.

We were advised that, at any time, we were liable to be harassed by East German police. They had a habit of stopping Allied drivers to ask for papers, to claim we were speeding, to hitch a ride or to ask for a visa or an Autobahn road tax. As they weren't 'recognized', the guidance was to ignore them. We were not to engage in any conversation with them, except to ask for a Soviet officer who in turn should contact American officials. If we did anything else, even show our documents, it would be considered as recognizing East German authority and we would be liable to prosecution by US authorities. Ironically, our briefer followed this low-level threat with 'Have a nice trip.'

Having been suitably intimidated, we hacked the clock and pressed eastwards from Helmstedt. We had recently bought a new car. It was nothing particularly sensational, just a Mitsubishi Galant four-door sedan, but it was a striking metallic blue in color and, being Japanese, relatively new to the German market. This becomes mildly interesting as the story continues.

After leaving the checkpoint we moved about 150 yards to an East German customs police barrier. Here a Russian soldier met us, directed us through the barrier and led us to the Soviet checkpoint 50 yards inside of East Germany. I parked the car in the center strip behind a low wooden building and the Soviet soldier checked my documents and motioned towards the building. My wife remained in the car and I told her to lock the doors. This was just a bit paranoid, but it was a slightly surreal situation and we were both on edge, face-to-face with the enemy for the first time.

Inside the darkened room, which I shared only with portraits of Lenin and Marx, there was a tiny slit window with the glass painted white. I tapped it lightly and stood before it. The window opened quickly and a hand reached out to take my documents. I was supposed to confirm that the hand belonged to a Russian military official in uniform, but failed miserably; he was a bit too quick for me, but I did wonder exactly what I was supposed to do if the hand had belonged to, say, an orangutan.

Whoever had snatched my papers had them now, so I waited for about a half-hour. I was prepared for this; just a little game the Russians played because they could. Finally, I got my papers, now stamped by Soviet authorities and including a barrier pass, back from what appeared to be the same hand that took them in the first place, and stepped out into the rain. I showed them to the Russian soldier again and got into the car.

We drove about another half-mile where there was an East German policeman. I handed the pass to him, but did not show him any other documents. He raised the barrier and we were on our own. I regaled my wife with the exciting tale of how I twiddled my thumbs as Marx and Lenin looked down on me disapprovingly and she reciprocated by telling me how much she had enjoyed being leered at by an 18-year-old Russian soldier with pimples and metal teeth in a soggy, ill-fitting wool uniform. We briefly considered why we were doing this.

As we approached Berlin there were other potential hazards. There are three exits (*Ausfahrt* in German. Oh, how I enjoyed that expression!) to West Berlin and had we taken the wrong one we could have ended up in East Germany. We were briefed on these turn-offs before we left the Allied checkpoint and given a map which we had to return at the end of the trip.

We went through the same process in reverse at Checkpoint Bravo entering Berlin, but having completed it unscathed, we were ready to enjoy the world's most enigmatic city for the next ten days. Arrival in Berlin was no more relaxing than getting there in the first place. We faced another briefing from the US Security Service. This one was a bit more intriguing as it also included a bit of cloak-and-dagger lore reflecting relations between the Allies and the Russians that were not at a high ebb in the mid-'80s. Firstly, there was the awkward relationship with the East Germans. Again, we did not recognize them as the sovereign authority in the Soviet sector so we were advised to ignore them. Any difficulties we faced while in the Soviet sector had to be referred to a Soviet officer and, of course, the likelihood of them being particularly obliging was very slim indeed.

One of the requirements of visiting East Berlin was that I had to wear my Class 'A' blue uniform any time we crossed the border. I'm sure I bitched moderately about this as I was always far more comfortable in a flight suit. Nevertheless, this was our declaration of our entitlement to enter Soviet-occupied East Berlin as a member of the Western occupying powers and it also applied to British and French military personnel. The same dress code applied to the Russians visiting West Berlin but we didn't see many of them in the Western sectors as there was always the possibility they might like to stay for a while. The Russians were very, very selective about who among them could enjoy the freedom of West Berlin.

Even though we were all sympathetic to their plight, we were cautioned to be extremely vigilant as the East Germans had become very adept at finding their way westward. We were advised to check the trunk of the car prior to heading back through Checkpoint Charlie to the West and to pay a great deal of attention to any attempts to engage us made by East Germans. There was nothing wrong with innocent interaction, but the penalties for assisting escape attempts were harsh. Very occasionally, an American (or British or French) serviceman or woman had to be extricated from the clutches of the Russians by military and diplomatic action because of innocent attempts to show friendliness. Any contact initiated by an East German citizen had to be reported and debriefed on return to the West.

Finally, we were carefully briefed on shopping in the East. I use the term 'carefully' because the most fascinating aspect of the shopping briefing was a brief but most useful reference to the currency exchange rate. Officially, East and West German Deutschmarks were pegged equally against each other, but the lieutenant who was briefing us, after glancing furtively about the room, came forth with the following: 'You can only spend East Marks in the Soviet Sector. You can, of course, exchange West Marks for them at any bank here in the West, but we recommend you use "X", "Y" or "Z" banks,' and he winked at us, he really did. We found out why later that day when we visited 'X' bank to exchange 1,000 West Marks. The cashier took our money and returned an envelope which contained just over 4,000 of East Germany's finest. I looked at him quizzically, but he just nodded and we went on our way. Later in the Officers' Club bar, I got into a conversation with a fellow Air Force officer stationed in Berlin and asked him what was going on. He figured out pretty quickly that I was a dumb fighter pilot and knew absolutely nothing about the murky world of international politics and finance. He patiently explained that taking our 1:4 ratio East Marks shopping was, in our very small way, a patriotic contribution towards destabilizing the East German economy. We drank to that and I can tell you I felt just a little bit prouder.

Before we ventured into East Berlin on our own, we took a tour conducted by the US forces and American Embassy. This helped us get our bearings and gave us access to some interesting points we probably wouldn't have visited otherwise. The first thing that struck us was the dilapidated condition of the East German infrastructure. Many buildings were crumbling and there was ample evidence of the fighting that had gone on in 1945 with many structures still displaying bullet holes. We passed a number of poorly-maintained buildings which served as Russian officers' quarters. They were decidedly neglected with tatters of dirty curtains on the windows. In contrast, we were staying in the Officers' Mess quarters at the former Templehof Airport in the US Sector. Upgraded by the Nazis, Templehof is an enormous structure, now inactive, and served as the main terminal for American military transport aircraft which, along with our British and French Allies, thwarted the Soviet blockade of the city during the Cold War. We took a fascinating tour of the facility, a step back into the 1940s. Our quarters there were not plush but certainly well-appointed and very comfortable; we felt very fortunate not to have been born Russian.

On the other hand, we were taken to the Russian Military Museum where we learned, much to our surprise, that the Soviets had triumphed in the Second World War all by themselves and really needed no assistance at all from the rest of us. The star attraction at the museum was a life-sized photo of the 'authentic' corpse of Joseph Goebbels, Nazi Minister of Propaganda. This impressive exhibit was an awkwardly-arranged crispy critter, unrecognizable in any way, and our Russian guide explained that Soviet Forces had found it in Hitler's bunker and now displayed it as a trophy of their great victory over Nazism. OK Boris, if you say so…

Returning from the tour, we stopped at the Soviet War Memorial, an enormous (8-meter) bronze statue of a Russian soldier, constructed after the war. The sheer size of this edifice was quite incredible, but the short story surrounding it was even better. Apparently, within hours of its inauguration, the East Germans, exhibiting the sardonic sense of humor for which they are renowned, had christened the effigy 'The Tomb of the Unknown Looter'.

Having now taken the approved tourist expedition, we took advantage of having brought the car to Berlin. We could, at our leisure, drive through Checkpoint Charlie into the East and, within broad geographic constraints, wander at will through this Communist wonderland. The standard harassment games were in force and I found myself facing an East German policeman every time I attempted to park, shaking his head and motioning for me to leave. I was getting somewhat agitated at this when Elaine, always the pragmatist, reminded me that East German authorities didn't really count and said 'What's he going to do, give you a ticket?' At this point, I stopped worrying about the traffic cops and no, never got a ticket.

Bargain-hunting was high on Elaine's list, as it was for most spouses and families visiting East Berlin. As the Soviets had worked hard to establish East Berlin as a sort of Communist showcase, there were a number of opportunities to obtain goods produced behind the Iron Curtain. These items were far out of reach for the average East German citizen and, if you looked a little further than the window displays, you realized that stocks were not plentiful. Nevertheless, there were specialty items such as cameras, binoculars, lush goose down duvets and beautiful Meissen china, along with crystal and porcelain manufactured in Poland, Czechoslovakia and other Soviet satellite states. There was some clothing, especially the excellent Salamander shoes, produced in the West but sold much more cheaply in East Berlin. All these goodies were available in very limited quantities but the accomplished shopper (such as my wife) could, with some effort, root them out. Wherever we found somewhere to shop, I ignored the East German cops and parked the metallic blue Mitsubishi. Invariably, when we returned with our loot, the car was surrounded by curious East Germans having a look at a Japanese automobile they hadn't seen before. This was all good-natured but clearly punctuated the differences between East and West.

Finally, not wishing to miss any of the opportunities available in the divided city, I researched East Berlin's nightlife and we decided we would take advantage of Communism's European showcase. Restaurants and nightclubs did not abound in the same way they flourished in West Berlin, but the presence of droves of Soviet military officers, politicians and their East German minions meant that a certain level of ambience existed for the entitled pleasure-seeker in the Soviet Sector.

There was no limitation on our visiting the East after hours as, once again, we were exercising our right to free movement within the city. Wearing of the uniform was still mandatory and I'll address that shortly. Given the fact that our selfless and patriotic employment of the exchange rate would provide a 75 per cent discount on meals, booze and entertainment over our Communist brethren made the prospect of a night or two on the town even more attractive. We identified a few venues to sample. There weren't many as the spoils were there primarily for the Russians and East German military and bureaucrats, but as we were to discover, the few that existed were very good.

Our first foray into tripping the light fantastic, Communist-style, was dinner on the rotating viewing level of the *Fernsehturm* (television tower) above the Alexanderplatz. Construction of this edifice was completed in 1969 by the administration of the German Democratic Republic (GDR). It was clearly intended as a symbol of East Berlin and a testimonial to Communist creativity and is easily visible throughout the central and some suburban districts of Berlin. With its height of 368 meters (including antenna), it is still the tallest structure in Germany and the third tallest structure in the European Union. The rotating restaurant is at the 200-meter level and in the '80s it was clearly the place to be seen in East Berlin. I had reserved a table, but we felt slightly out of our comfort zone as we were surrounded by high-ranking Russian and East German military officers and civilian officials of elevated status. Nevertheless, Major (USAF) Ladd avoided spilling the soup down the front of his Dress Blues and Elaine was IMHO clearly the most glamorous lady in attendance.

As I recall, the meal was very good and the ambience within the restaurant top-notch, but one aspect will stay with me forever: the restaurant rotated 360 degrees every hour and we were stunned by the stark contrasts that revolution revealed. As we looked towards West Berlin, we were treated to the kind of lively, vibrant panorama you would expect to behold from any major city at play. There was an impressive light show virtually all the way to the horizon: streets, buildings, billboards, all illuminated and brimming with energy and life. As the rotation carried us around to the East, however, an almost surreal transformation occurred. Along a slightly irregular but unbroken line which defined the

Wall, the carnival atmosphere abruptly ended and morphed into an eerie, depressing gloom with only the occasional glimmer of light to break the darkness. This murkiness, too, extended as far as we could see and we commented that this was not the sort of image the East Germans would wish to convey to the outside world. Nevertheless, it is difficult to imagine the stark disparity between East and West was not playing on the minds of those Russians and Eastern Bloc dignitaries viewing the same dramatic dissimilarity.

The contrasts between East and West Berlin were abundant and well-defined, but I am convinced that nowhere were those disparities more powerfully displayed than they were that night in the rotating *Fernsehturm* restaurant. A chilling, compelling glimpse of two conflicting ideologies exhibited side by side for comparison.

I couldn't very well leave the paradox that was Cold War Berlin without a very small touch of intrigue. Not exactly John le Carré stuff, but a tiny taste of the shadowy atmosphere and how it affected some very ordinary people. Our last night in Berlin and once again, we ventured into the Soviet Sector for some night life. We had booked a table at a legendary Berlin restaurant called Ganymed on the River Spree. Built in the 1880s and established in 1931, Ganymed was the Cold War favorite of many of East Germany's artists and literary types as well as the usual crowd of Soviet and Eastern Bloc military and bureaucrats. It still exists as a restaurant (although its current TripAdvisor rating doesn't elevate the pulse). There was no way of visually detecting the 'opposition' but they had no trouble at all in pinpointing me. On the evening we visited I was, not surprisingly, the sole customer sporting a set of USAF Class A Blues complete with senior pilot wings and, if anyone was looking hard, a Distinguished Flying Cross, Air Medal with oak leaf clusters, and a Vietnam service ribbon. I won't say I felt conspicuous; after all, the uniform was mandatory and not totally uncommon in the East. Nevertheless, I had visions of what it must feel like to be a fox in the midst of a pack of hunting dogs. Elaine was, as always, looking good and this had a calming effect.

We enjoyed a very good meal (and forgive me for mentioning, yet again, our 'patriotic discount') and as we lingered over drinks, a small jazz combo supplied the music; very pleasant when you consider we were in enemy territory. We had a couple of dances and were enjoying the ambience when a young German approached the table. He clicked his heels (really!) and asked in quite good English if he could dance with my wife. A few unobtrusive alarm bells went off in my head; not jealousy, mind you, but very clear paranoia. Nevertheless, he was very pleasant; I looked at Elaine and she nodded, so as graciously as I could, I agreed and off they went to the dance floor. I looked over at the table he had vacated and his partner, a very pretty girl, smiled at me. Ding Dong! The bells returned and got a bit louder and I did what I do very well: absolutely nothing. When Elaine returned, she said: 'You really ought to have danced with his girlfriend.' I agreed, but pointed out to her that grainy photos of Major Ladd, renowned fighter pilot, doing the fandango in his Dress Blues with East Germany's version of Mata Hari would not look good in my personnel records and we settled back to enjoy the music.

Shortly thereafter, Elaine took the obligatory stroll to the ladies' room and I noticed the girlfriend got up and followed her down the stairs. Ding Dong! I impatiently awaited her return, but on arrival she told me they had chatted (imagine that). She seemed like a lovely girl and they were just interested in talking about the weather and art exhibits and our metallic blue Mitsubishi and the price of asparagus and couldn't we just sit with them for a few minutes? I looked over at their table where they were both smiling broadly and, against my better judgment, asked the waiter if they could join us at the table for a drink. He fetched the maître d' who patiently explained that, no, that would not be possible. As master of negotiations, I then asked if we could join them at *their* table for a drink. No, that was too difficult to arrange as well; however, there was an empty table of exactly the same proportions in a quiet corner of the room and we could all congregate there. DING DONG! DING DONG!

At Elaine's urging and against my better judgment I agreed, confident that I could keep my mouth shut about the NATO Air Order of Battle and our pre-planned armor kill zones for a few minutes. This self-assurance didn't stop me from running my hands all over (and under) the table looking for wires and peering at the ceiling to identify the location of the cameras I just knew were there. We spent an hour or so with the young, curious couple which would have been far more enjoyable had I not been analyzing every question and comment, looking for the tell-tale signs of low-level espionage. As it turned out, nothing appeared to be the least bit sinister, with much discussion of riveting topics like our metallic blue Mitsubishi and the price of asparagus.

When we finally decided it was time to go, they asked for our address, which we politely declined to provide. Written evidence was a small bridge too far. We asked for our bill, which the young man caught sight of on arrival. I know because his eyes widened appreciably. We had, during the course of the evening, ordered the very best of everything on the menu and wine list and the grand total reflected this. Later, Elaine and I agreed that our perceived splurge had been somewhat excessive, but my conscience rapidly cleared when I reminded myself that this was our little part in the Cold War propaganda exercise: a shameless demonstration of how much better off we in the West are (and wouldn't you be a lot happier on our side?).

We said our goodbyes, suggesting that someday we might be able to meet in London (where we had hinted we lived), and drove the short distance to Checkpoint Charlie where, as always, the car was thoroughly searched on both sides of the border. On arrival in the American sector, I went in search of the Officer of the Day, who turned out to be an Army lieutenant. As we'd been briefed to do, I reported that we had been approached by East Germans and related everything I could recall about our encounter. He took it all in, smiled and nodded and told us that what we had experienced was an unexceptional occurrence and should be of no real cause for concern. I felt slightly less like a paranoid fifth-grader when he confirmed that yes, the table was almost certainly bugged but from my account of the conversation, we'd just provided a bit of boring dialogue for some lowly East German analyst to catnap over.

We've talked about this incident many times and I'm practically convinced that they were, as they appeared to be, an intelligent young couple who were simply curious about the stark differences between their world and ours, a few hundred meters to the west. Nevertheless, we'd been briefed about East Germans attempting to bribe Allied military personnel for a westbound ride in the trunk of the car through Checkpoint Charlie and unrelated scams to put us in compromising positions. We were frustrated not to be able to talk to them more freely and felt a twinge of remorse for refusing their request for contact details when we departed, but the alarm bells were simply too persistent and the stakes were too high. Based on my performance that night, my potential as a secret agent was very limited indeed.

As a footnote, we went back to Berlin a few years ago (well after the demise of the Wall), and as you might expect the transformation was dramatic. The only clear reminder of that monstrous Wall is a trail of contrasting bricks laid in the pavement and an occasional sign or monument denoting an unsuccessful escape attempt. Young people you encounter are unlikely to remember the Wall and many have little appreciation of the extraordinary role their city played in history. The city is now lively and colorful but to me lacks the menacing edge I recall from the early '80s. Consequently, I found it somewhat less interesting. My warped perspective, I suppose, but I guess you had to be there to experience the atmosphere.

Chapter Thirteen

The Eureka Moment

In the years to come, I would be fortunate enough to progress into positions that were undoubtedly more prestigious and carried with them far more responsibility and authority than Detachment 4 Operations Officer. Nevertheless, I can honestly say that my tour at Nörvenich was a genuine highlight, so much so that I opted to extend the assignment for a further year, despite advice from others that doing so would hinder my developing career prospects.

This is probably a most appropriate time to discuss ambition among fighter pilots. You've probably gathered by now that we are a diverse lot and this characteristic applies equally to aspiration. As in any profession, there are goal-oriented fighter pilots whose every waking hour is devoted to moving up the ladder to the land of shiny stars and staff cars. 'The Politician' comes to mind here, but I see no reason to elaborate on this aspect of an Air Force career other than to point out that many of those in this category spent so much time playing career chess and planning three assignments ahead that they never smelled any of the roses on the way up. Just saying...

I can only speak with total authority on my own perspective on career progression. As a lieutenant and later a captain, I was totally focused on the reason I joined the Air Force in the first place: flying fighters. After a few beers at the bar, I could often be heard making eloquent, insightful statements like 'I don't give a shit if I ever get promoted, I just want to keep flying jets.' I wasn't alone in holding this sentiment; lots of young fighter pilots in my day would have been perfectly happy to remain at a certain level of advancement as long as we could grab hold of a stick and throttles a few times a week and burn up the skies.

Most of us at some point had a Eureka moment, albeit often a subtle one, and decided that some level of progression would not only enhance our careers, but would also provide significant personal fulfillment for a number of reasons. As a group, fighter pilots are vocal and vigorous critics of our own hierarchy and culture; in other words, we tended to bitch a great deal about the shoddy way 'our Air Force' was being managed. This characteristic comes with the inherent arrogance that defines most capable fighter jocks, but when the light finally dawned for me, at least, with it came the realization that I wasn't going to exert any great influence on these management deficiencies as a captain or major. My Eureka moment crept in near the end of my tour at Nörvenich, when I was promoted to lieutenant colonel, and it was very, very subtle. I never experienced a bout of 'stars in my eyes' or had visions of striding purposefully through the corridors of the Pentagon with legions of minions padding along behind me, notebooks in hand. Indeed, although I knew there was rank and progression, if not fame and fortune to be achieved there, throughout my career I had a pathological fear of being assigned to the Pentagon and becoming, even for two or three years, a 'Staff Puke' in the infamous Fort Fumble.

Chapter Fourteen

Paradise Regained:
Back to the Weapons School

Consequently, as my idyllic tenure at Nörvenich drew to an end, I was pleased, nay ecstatic, to be offered the opportunity to interview for command of the Fighter Weapons Instructor Course A-10 Division. You may recall I recounted some of my experiences as a student at the Weapons School as an F-4 pilot in earlier days. I won't apologize for reiterating that this course was the most demanding, stressful and humbling training experience of my life. Nevertheless, completing it successfully was the most gratifying and fulfilling achievement of my career. Now, having nearly concluded an assignment at a small USAF detachment at a Luftwaffe fighter base, someone in high places thought enough of my talents to give me a crack at leading the team of instructors who were conveying this world-class tuition to the cream of the A-10 crop.

During the 1980s, the Weapons School comprised four separate but closely aligned divisions: A-10, F-4, F-15 and F-16. It has expanded briskly since then, rightly adding F-22 and F-35 fighter weapons courses. Unfortunately, in my cynical opinion, it has also apparently multiplied like a colony of rabbits, adding bomber, drone, helicopter, C-130, ICBM, Weapons Director, Space/Cyber and operational support (!) courses. Today, there are now nineteen squadrons (not divisions any more) spread all over the United States and I assume graduates are all entitled to wear a graduate patch, which no longer reads <u>Fighter</u> Weapons School. Progress, I suppose, but again, IMHO, not for the best.

FWIC division command positions don't just land in your lap. There was competition to be had and there were others who would be just as delighted to grab this opportunity as I was. Full of anticipation and enthusiasm, I flew out to Nellis AFB – 'the Home of the Fighter Pilot' in Las Vegas – for an interview with the commander of the 57th Fighter Weapons Wing, Brigadier General Mike Kerby. I'd never met General

Kerby, but I had a day or so to gather intelligence from some of the instructor pilots I was hoping to command. He was considered to be one of the good guys as general officers went and the leaks suggested I was, apparently, the front runner for the job. I reported to his office in my Class A Blues and was encouraged to find him seated behind his desk in a flight suit. He motioned me to a chair, pulled out a drawer and plopped a boot on it. Shades of my pilot training hero, Tony Chace, but the general's boots were shinier.

We talked informally about the expected issues. Why did I think I was right for the job? How would I handle this situation or that one? What did I think of the current direction the Weapons School was taking and the quality of the graduates it was producing? All very casual and agreeable and after the better part of an hour, I sensed the interview was almost over. My sources had alerted me that he also had a pet question for interviews so when he finally sprung it, I was ready. He pulled his foot off the drawer, leaned forward, gazed at me intently and said 'Steve, are you lucky?' Many years later, I learned that he'd 'borrowed' this zinger from none other than Napoleon, but to this day, I consider it a great interview question. I only hoped my answer would be adequate:

> 'Well, Sir, I'm sitting here with you interviewing for the best job in the Air Force. If I'm successful, I'll be commanding the *crème de la crème* of the A-10 community, teaching the best pilots in the world at the most advanced training facility there is. I've got a wife who supports me and I'll renew my license to strap a Warthog to my butt a few times a week as a bonus. Yes, Sir, I'd say I'm very, very lucky.'

He must have liked it, because the following morning I got a call advising me the job was mine and I needed to hotfoot it back to Germany, get packed and prepare for the next adventure. Yep, I was lucky.

Normally a new flying assignment requires requalification in the specific aircraft to be flown. Since I was already current in the A-10 no basic flying conversion training was necessary. What *was* crucial was dramatically upgrading my proficiency level and this will take a bit of explaining.

I flew regularly as the Detachment 4 Ops Officer and I was qualified as an instructor during that tour, but the single-mission emphasis at the

Detachment meant the requirements were clear-cut and the complexity of our normal flying was relatively predictable. I was about to assume command of an organization providing cutting-edge training to hand-picked pilots in every possible aspect of the mission. In terms of instructing, I had done precious little at Nörvenich, but as the Weapons School Division Commander, I would be expected to brief, lead, instruct and debrief at a lofty standard I had not attained for quite a few years. I wouldn't actually be competing with the guys I commanded and as professionals there was no doubt they would follow my lead, but I was damned if I wasn't going to earn their respect. This was a daunting proposition because, if you recall my previous dissertation regarding my student days at the Weapons School, my flock of instructors would include the very best in the A-10 Close Air Support business.

For a fighter pilot, taking command at any level is an exhilarating experience, but the opportunity to lead a small, elite group of hand-picked professional fighter pilots, all distinguished graduates of the curriculum we would be providing was heady stuff indeed. Did I mention I was lucky?

Immediately after I assumed command, my guys began to shepherd me through an extremely accelerated mini-course designed to get me up to speed with the syllabus and the flying environment at Nellis AFB and its extraordinary training facilities. This was an 'interesting' experience, both for me and my new cadre of instructors. Despite the fact that there was a normal student class in progress when I took over, we crammed a taster version of a six-month course into two or three weeks. I had to up my game appreciably in terms of mission preparation and delivering a crisp, thorough, informative training flight briefing. I also needed to progress from wingman to flight leader and instructor in virtually all the disciplines and mission types the course comprised. I was the new Boss and, politically, there was no way I was going to fail any of these increasingly demanding sorties but, in my mind, that wasn't the point. I needed to prove to each and every one of them that I had the judgment, skill and situational awareness to lead the pros professionally.

If all that activity wasn't enough, I took command just prior to the class detachment. Each A-10 course syllabus included a week's deployment to experience working with a US Army unit on their home turf. We went to varying locations and trained extensively with the kinds of regular Army organizations we were likely to support in wartime. On this occasion, we took our eight students and all our instructors to Fort Carson in Colorado Springs. Accompanying our little band was the FWS Commandant, Colonel Don Logeman (who I suspect was tagging along at least partly to keep an eye on the greenest division commander). I don't think he was disappointed, but he was certainly entertained.

Mike the Knife

Colorado Springs in February is predictably wintery. So it was when we began our deployment. Because Fort Carson had limited aviation facilities our A-10s staged from nearby Peterson Field. The detachment went well for a couple of days with our students and the Army sharing some world-class close air support training in their training areas. On the afternoon of the third day, Colorado turned white and we battened down for a day or two due to the forecast of heavy snow. We canceled flying in late afternoon and, as fighter pilots are prone to do, my students and instructors headed for the Officers' Club for a beverage or two. As the snow fell and the welcoming fire in the 'O' Club worked its magic, the initial drinks continued on into the evening. Colonel Logeman wasn't much of a drinker, so he had one with the boys and excused himself. I hung around a bit longer, but there was a reasonable shot at flying on the following day and as I would be leading a student flight (in apprentice status), I wanted to prepare properly. I made my excuses (soaking up a few catcalls), and trudged back to our quarters through the drifting snow. My first test as a commander was about to begin, big time.

About an hour later, there was a knock on the door and one of my IPs and Mike, one of my students, stood there. The IP looked angry; the student very, very uncomfortable. Mike, the student, was a talented flyer and a gregarious officer, always good company. My assessment was that he had far-reaching potential as an officer and aviator but this clearly now hung in the balance. At this moment, however, it was obvious he'd had more than a few toddies and was more than a little bewildered.

'What's going on?' I asked, and my IP began, carefully, to fill in the blanks. As the snow continued to fall heavily, the Officers' Club manager, a captain, had decided to close the facility and send his staff home for the night. This decision was greeted with a fair amount of mostly good-natured bitching and moaning from our contingent, virtually the only patrons left in the bar. Mike, however, had apparently mislaid his senses, whipped out the survival knife he had in a sheath sewn to his boot (not uncommon among A-10 pilots) and waved it around, shouting something about his inalienable right to drink in an Officers' Club whenever he wanted to and similar gibberish. This lasted only a few seconds because one of his fellow students, a very large young man, backed him into a corner, disarmed him and threatened to abruptly switch his lights out if he didn't pipe down. Unfortunately, the episode lasted just long enough for the Club Manager to realize he was the target of the tantrum, catch sight of Mike's flashing blade and become very, very irate.

He was on his way to phone the Military Police when a few of our more rational aviators convinced him that their boss (me) would undoubtedly handle the situation to his satisfaction and would be in touch with him. I immediately called the club, spoke to the manager, apologized profusely and confirmed that I would, indeed, 'handle the situation to his satisfaction' not later than the following morning.

I asked Mike for his version of the story, but he was by this time unintelligible. It was clear, however, that he was now aware that he was in the deepest of shit. The Air Force frowns profoundly on thugs, above all in its officer ranks, and unless there was one helluva justification, not only would his participation in the most prestigious flying training in the Air Force be abruptly terminated, his career as a pilot was likely to follow.

I wanted to get my head straight before taking that step, so I summoned everyone who had been present in the bar and, one at a time, interrogated them. The stories were all consistent. 'Did he mean business with the knife?' I asked each one. 'No sir,' came the unanimous response. 'He was drunk and incredibly stupid, but he's not a violent guy and would never have done anything other than posturing.'

Satisfied with the reported course of events, I headed for Colonel Logeman's room, knocked on the door, gratefully accepted the offered scotch and began to talk. Fortunately, there had been no leaks, so he was hearing the saga for the first time from me. He was a pretty straight arrow, so I was expecting to hear 'Off with his head' from the outset, but he listened patiently to the tale of woe and my proposed resolution, thought about it for a couple minutes, nodded to me and said: 'You're the boss, take care of it.'

Instantly motivated, I returned to my quarters where Mike was slowly recovering. Wrong time for the lecture, so I glared at him: 'Here, 0800, shiny boots, clean flight suit, ready to grovel.' 'Yes, Sir,' he said; he knew what was coming, but not completely. To his waiting classmate: 'Make damn sure he's here.'

The next morning, Mike appeared at 0800 on the dot, apparently recuperated from the previous night's excesses and wearing an expression of extreme humiliation. We had an hour, so I sat him down and advised him that I wasn't going to put words in his mouth, but he needed to understand that his career was completely in the hands of the guy he'd brandished a blade at the night before.

We walked to the club through the snow that was still falling and made the 0900 meeting I'd arranged with the Club Manager. 'Captain Mike has something to say to you,' I told him, then settled back to watch. The apology was articulate and, above all, clearly sincere. They shook hands and Mike's career was technically salvaged, but I wasn't quite through driving the lesson home. I'd called a meeting of all hands at 1000 (it was obvious we wouldn't be flying that day) and Colonel Logeman joined us as well. 'We had an incident last night that reflects badly on us all,' I began. 'Mike has done the right thing by the Club Manager, but that's not quite the end of it.' Mike looked suddenly dispirited. 'Since we can't seem to keep our act together in public, the "O" Club is off limits for the rest of the deployment.' The brute force of peer pressure thus energized, I waited for the response. Resigned silence all round, but Mike suddenly became the least popular man on the planet. He took the opportunity to apologize again – just as eloquently but this time to his classmates and instructors – and when I caught Logeman nodding his head, I finally felt I'd passed my first commander test.

The weather front passed through Colorado Springs and the snow stopped falling later that afternoon. By the following morning, we were back in the air training our students in the violent art of close air support. I got a call from the Officers' Club Manager later that day lamenting the loss of bar receipts since my social ban was imposed, and 'just wondering if your guys might be able to come back for the last couple days of your deployment.' I asked if that meant Mike as well. He allowed that an apology accepted wiped the slate clean as far as he was concerned. I relented without much of a fight and gathered the boys up to give them the good news. The deal was simple: 'O' Club bar privileges were restored, but a single incident, no matter how small, would result in confinement to quarters when not flying and nothing but pizza deliveries and soft drinks for the duration. The last few nights were comparatively tame, but still preferable to a steady diet of Domino's and Dr Pepper.

Mike the Knife completed the A-10 Weapons School Course, proudly wore the prized graduate patch and flourished in fighter aviation. He rose through the ranks to full colonel and, though he later 'downgraded' from the 'Hog to the F-16 (the healthy rivalry between fighter types never ends), his Air Force career was clearly a success. The last I heard he was chief executive of his own business in the civilian sector. From my own perspective, this incident was corroboration of the Eureka moment I had a couple of years earlier. I'd attained a position with a modest measure of influence and consequently had an opportunity to either arbitrarily send a talented young man down the proverbial tubes or follow my instincts and provide him a bit of top cover along with a moderate kick in the ass. Reflecting on the bosses I most respected throughout my career, I have no doubt I made the right choice and to this day, I feel pretty damned good whenever I think about Mike the Knife.

Commanding the Weapons School Division was undeniably challenging for two reasons, first the requirement to rebuild and maintain my proficiency to fly and instruct at the PhD level requisite at the school. Simultaneously, I had to participate in the obligatory politics and administrivia that command carries with it. The former was exciting and fulfilling; the latter much less so and I won't belabor that aspect of the job in general terms.

On the other hand, being the boss of a small cadre of fighter pilots at the top of their game was by far the easiest role I ever had. That's entirely because of who and what these guys were. As fighter pilots, they were the crème de la crème. The job was challenging: they had to teach a complex and demanding academic curriculum, instruct an equally taxing flying syllabus and, finally, in their spare time, take care of all the mundane administrative functions that are part and parcel of being in the military. They were by far the most enthusiastic and motivated group I ever encountered and when they were griping (which, as fighter pilots, they didn't shy away from), it was invariably about something that richly deserved being bitched about.

I never considered myself an 'ideas guy' but my troops were absolutely full of them. It was my prerogative to provide a helpful vector from time to time, but rarely did a day pass when one of my boys didn't come up with a better way to approach this or an improved technique for achieving that. When there was tedious work to be done (usually supporting the obligatory politics and administrivia mentioned above) for reasons I never quite understood, the eagerness endured. Consequently, it was necessary only to point out what needed doing and designate the appropriate personality and *voila!* positive things happened. Often, it was best for me to simply get the hell out of the way. It was enough to spoil me as a boss, but even so, there were a few events during my tenure that slightly dulled the luster.

The Incredible Shrinking Class

Attending the Weapons School was an honor and a privilege for virtually everyone who had the opportunity. I expounded earlier about my own experience vying for a student slot when I was a captain flying F-4s and the process of earning a class placement was, for those in the regular Air Force, fiercely competitive. I specify the regular Air Force because Weapons School attendance is also available to pilots in the Air Force Reserve (AFRES) and the Air National Guard (ANG), as long as they meet the same entry-level criteria.

Without getting too technical, both the Reserve and Guard provide an extension of the Regular Air Force. The ANG is, in effect, a State militia component whereas the AFRES is Federally-operated and administered. Both organizations operate front-line equipment such as A-10s, F-15s and F-16s in the fighter specialties as well as a myriad of supporting assets: cargo and tankers, helicopters, early-warning aircraft, for example. The preponderance of aircrew are part-timers or respectfully known as 'Weekend Warriors', most of whom have full-time careers, mainly as airline pilots.

They are an extremely valuable addition to the regular component, augmenting when required and responding when necessary. For example, the response of ANG and AFRES units during and after the 9/11 terrorist attacks was extraordinary. As you can probably tell, I'm a fan of our Weekend Warriors, and the story I'm about to tell in no way reflects on the vast majority of ANG/AFRES aviators.

Whereas the active duty pilot has no additional professional responsibilities other than to his unit, the Weekend Warrior normally has to juggle his airline job (there were other careers, but we'll stick with the most common one for now) with his commitment to maintaining proficiency and combat-ready capability in his military aircraft. Consequently, there was always a risk that the Guard jock or Reservist selected for advanced training such as the Weapons School was an individual who could somehow afford to put his civilian career on hold for the six months required. This led to a further possibility that he might not necessarily be of the caliber or possess the motivation that his active duty counterpart had to demonstrate to even *compete* for the opportunity to attend the course.

The likelihood of running into difficulties as a result of this element of the Guard/Reserve environment was very low due to the accepted maturity and professionalism of the typical Weekend Warrior. Nevertheless, in the class that began in the winter of 1984 we were bitten by this particular snake, twice.

This class was slightly unusual as we had six students representing the active duty Air Force and two from the ranks of the ANG and Reserves. One of the Weekend Warriors was a lieutenant colonel and therefore automatically the class commander; the senior student and class liaison with me and my instructors for any difficulties that might arise. The second, from a different unit, was a major who would have been the class commander had he not been outranked by his colleague. The class commander role is semi-formal but important nevertheless as he was the guy with the experience and hopefully the leadership skills that would provide moral support and mature encouragement to the junior students who in this case were all captains.

As was normally the case, the students arrived the week before the class start date to get bedded in and, as fighter pilots the world over tend to do, gravitate to the 'O' Club bar for the sacred tradition known as Happy Hour on Friday afternoon.

Weapons School students-to-be were almost always pumped up to near fever pitch as the class start date approached and I talked to a number of the eager captains in the bar that Friday. They were focused and couldn't wait for the starting gun, much as I expected. What I didn't anticipate was the conversation I had with Gary, the Weekend Warrior lieutenant colonel. Granted, he was mature and had a lot more experience under his belt than the others. Unfortunately, his approach to the course was patently cavalier and I got the impression he was looking forward to a tranquil and amusing diversion from his airline job. Additionally, there was a hint of Second Lieutenant Ladd in pilot training: he was having visions of debauchery and uninterrupted hell-raising in Las Vegas. I made a mental note to have a serious chat with him in less boisterous surroundings but, as you shall see, this was not to be.

As was often the case, my wife joined me at the bar for Happy Hour and we planned to have dinner in the club later. While I was conversing with Gary and some of my other young students-in-waiting, she ended up at the bar with Dick, the other AFRES pilot waiting to join the class and they conducted an animated conversation. Elaine is a very perceptive lady and when we rejoined I asked her what she thought of Dick. She rolled her eyes towards the heavens and said softly: 'He just spent forty minutes talking about Cabbage Patch Dolls.' I took another mental note: keep a close eye on both these guys. There's something a little out of kilter here.

Monday rolled around and the serious course induction process began. Participation in this PhD for fighter pilots carries with it a number of prerequisite requirements: total flying hours; total *fighter* hours; age and rated pilot time limits (both of which our Weekend Warriors were exempt from meeting) and, most importantly, minimum currency requirements. The latter meant that a student must have flown at least ten bona fide training sorties within the previous thirty days. This provision was devised to ensure that our students were not only capable but up to speed in terms of proficiency and ready to begin a program that was fast-paced from Day One.

It was on the Monday afternoon when Jim Rose, one of my cadre of remarkable young instructors, knocked on my office door and said:

'Boss, you need to see this.' Jim's additional duty as my standardization/evaluation officer involved verifying all the prerequisites listed above to ensure all our students had ticked the appropriate boxes prior to course entry. He dropped a computer printout in front of me which belonged to Gary, our lieutenant colonel Reservist and class commander (the guy we hoped would serve as role model for the younger troops in the class).

'Check the last month's sortie record,' he said, and I could only shake my head while doing so. Gary had theoretically achieved his required sorties, but they consisted of taking off, one circuit of the traffic pattern, landing, allowing the brakes to cool and doing it all over again, times ten. This performance violated both the letter of the law (bona fide sorties) and most certainly the justifiable intent of the requirement: a current, proficient student from Day One.

My mind went back to my brief encounter with him on Friday and I told Jim 'That's why we pay you the big bucks', before scooping up the computer printout and steaming down the hall to my boss's office. Colonel Joe Merrick was the Fighter Weapons School commandant and the one-man Supreme Court for legal/ethical situations like this. Our conversation lasted less than a minute. He told me to locate Gary and bring him back to discuss the situation. On arrival, Little Joe (as we called Colonel Merrick very carefully behind his back) wasted no time at all. The dressing-down took less time than my earlier discussion with him, punctuated by a brief reference to the computer printout and a few invectives Michael Landon would never have used on *Bonanza*. It ended abruptly and simply: 'Pack your bags; you won't be participating in the Fighter Weapons School.'

The last I saw of Gary was a slightly dazed man in a flying suit heading for the officers' quarters, presumably to pack his bag as directed, call the family (somewhere in the Mid-West, as I recall) and announce he would be home in time for dinner. There were a couple of distinctly pithy phone calls from Little Joe to Gary's parent unit, announcing his premature departure from the program and undoubtedly discussing the quality of their selection criteria, but other than that, he simply vanished. The whole episode had lasted less than an hour and I inserted Little Joe Merrick under the 'respected' category in my mental filing system.

The dust had barely settled from Gary's abrupt departure when I called Dick, the second Reservist, into the office for a little chat. I explained, very briefly and without the details that Gary was no longer with us and as he was now the senior-ranking student, he now had the distinct honor of becoming the class commander. His eyes rolled, he flushed and he emphatically declined. I was, at very least, disappointed with his response. Hopefully I've conveyed enough about the fighter pilot psyche to reveal that most relished assumption of a challenge and a chance to lead. Had he been a regular Air Force officer, I clearly would have had the authority to order him to assume the role. As a Reservist, the lines were somewhat blurred, and for a fleeting moment I considered ignoring his refusal and forcing the responsibility on him. Fortunately, a little voice in the back of my head nagged: 'Do you really want a man who has an apparent preoccupation with Cabbage Patch Dolls and clearly doesn't want to lead to act as role model for the younger troops?' I may have been slightly brusque when I dismissed him, but as he hurried out the door I remember thinking that my Weekend Warrior problems were not over quite yet.

As the course proceeded through its gradual stepping-stone approach, it quickly became obvious that Dick was an incongruity; a barely competent pilot in the midst of younger, far more gifted and motivated aviators. This wasn't his fault, of course, but in a group of pilots who had won their chance to compete in this demanding course through sustained achievement, not effortless availability, he struggled mightily to keep up. As the academics and training missions evolved into more complex scenarios, his shortcomings became more pronounced.

Elimination from the course was a genuine rarity; the stringent selection process was very effective in preventing those not technically up to the standard from gaining entry, but of course Dick hadn't participated in that process and in a very real sense, this was to his disadvantage. Whereas the prospective students needed to meet a lofty benchmark to qualify for the course, it was my job to ensure our output did not fall below a far higher bar. This progression would guarantee that the man wearing the graduate patch was adept at talking the talk *and* walking the walk. His job, from graduation forward, would be to return to his operational unit, advise his commanders on tactical training, weapons employment and tactics and act as that all-important mentor and role model for all things involving weaponry and how to use it.

To say Dick didn't grasp this concept would be an understatement. He didn't have the motor skills of his classmates, but even more concerning was the fact that he didn't think like a leader or instructor. In his mind, if he led a flight in a tactical scenario and got everyone home in one piece, he felt he had succeeded. He could simply not fathom why my IPs probed his vague briefings, erratic flight leadership techniques, ill-defined tactics and inability to reconstruct the mission during an instructional debrief, the very core of what we were trying to teach him. My instructors went well beyond the call of duty to give him a fighting chance in the program. They came in early, stayed late and provided a level of personalized instruction that his classmates didn't require because they started the process at a significantly higher level. Nevertheless, I couldn't help thinking that all the attention he was getting must have had some impact on the training his six colleagues were soaking up. Characteristically, my instructors made sure the others were kept ahead of the power curve and the students seemed to take it in their stride because they knew Dick was in trouble and empathized.

Elimination was a rarely-enforced 'three strikes and you're out' process; in other words, three failures on the same mission would mark the end of the trail. As the commander, I would be the final arbiter if we reached that stage. I told my scheduler early on not to program me to fly with Dick as I felt it likely that situation would arrive sooner or later. He went to the brink at least three times, failing a flight and then, with the benefit of lots of TLC, managing to pass it at the second attempt.

In the midst of this dilemma, my wife and I took a few days off to visit San Francisco. The sky wasn't going to fall in my absence and I truly needed the break. I mention this only in the context of the job, because what I hadn't anticipated was the fact that I had become so immersed in Dick's drama that in spirit, he came along with us. When we had dinner, there he was, seated in between us. Strolling through Fisherman's Wharf, there he was among the red snappers, salmon and lobsters on display and it wasn't long until most of our conversations turned to Dick and his issues. A student in difficulty shouldn't have bothered me at this stage; I'd instructed for many years and busted more than a few along the way, but somehow this was different. In a normal flying training program, the occasional failure was commonplace and no stigma was attached. In the

Weapons School, the sheer talent and motivational level of our students meant that one busted ride was worth a sleepless night, two was cause for weighty concern and, to be honest, one of our apprentices arriving on the precipice of an elimination ride was traumatic for us all.

When I returned from San Francisco, it was obvious the boys weren't going to let the Old Man continue to relax. Dick had flown independent basic fighter maneuver (BFM) sorties with two of my best and most experienced IPs and they had both failed him for inadequacies in leadership and performance. There was no question of malice here; my instructors had busted their asses to try and instill the drive and attitude that Dick was lacking and it was obvious that they felt his failure was partially their own. Nevertheless, he was now established at the fabled last chance saloon and it was my responsibility to pass judgment.

The mission facing Dick was far from the most complex in the syllabus. It was a two–ship instructional ride which he was tasked to brief, lead and debrief. The emphasis at this stage in the program was on his ability to take a 'student', demonstrate a number of basic drills and maneuvers, then require the student to replicate his demos and critique the student's performance in the air. On the ground, he should be able to reconstruct the maneuvers flown and again, point out the good, the bad and the ugly of the student's performance. Considering he had flown the exact same profile twice in the previous week, he should have been able to put together a performance that would dazzle me to distraction and re-establish him firmly on course for graduation.

We met up for the briefing at a very civilized hour and I donned my 'student' persona, listening intently, occasionally asking basic questions to draw out the trainer in Dick. This gave him an opportunity to elaborate and demonstrate his grasp of the instructional techniques he was supposed to be learning. To my astonishment, he ignored the desired 'teacher/student' scenario and briefed me like one of his buddies back in the Midwest, from whence he had come. The briefing was tolerable in that he covered all the formally required items (there was always a checklist for briefings). Unfortunately, it was woefully inadequate for what he was aspiring to do: provide expertise, motivation and incentive to a trainee who was working his way up a building-block approach to proficiency. The allotted briefing time was an hour, the standard. Dick raced through it in twenty minutes. Although there was no firm obligation to fill the duration square, it occurred to me that, had I been dangling by a thread in a program, I'd have found a way to fill every minute with rich dialogue, vivid, enthralling examples and the occasional attempt at humor. There was none of that, thank you, and when he asked if I had any questions, I could only shake my head.

Most of my team were hanging around when we headed for the airplanes. None of them looked me in the eye, but I'll die believing they were all participating in a wager on whether or not the Old Man would actually lay the hammer down if it were necessary to do so.

After a few years in a fighter cockpit, you get a feel for how things are going to go from the mission briefing. This is not infallible, but the likelihood is viable and Dick's BFM flight was no exception. Like the briefing, in my most charitable disposition, the best I could do was mediocre. There's no need to bore you with detail here, but Dick's performance as a pilot was competent at best; as an instructor and potential Weapons School Graduate it was hopeless. In keeping with what was apparently his definition of success, he had managed to lead us around the skies for an hour or so without a mid-air collision or similar calamity and we had both landed and climbed down from our cockpits without suffering bodily harm.

Clearly, in his eyes, this constituted a triumph of sorts and he prefaced his debriefing with a concise synopsis of how well he had done. His summation of the mission was at least as lackluster as the briefing had been. There was no reference to specific drills, maneuvers or situations and not a word of assessment of his 'student's' performance, the clear objective of the exercise. I timed the debrief at twelve minutes and Dick was obviously ready for a celebratory beer. This was not going to be easy. 'Dick,' I said, 'you're not dangerous and you're not incapable as an aviator, but neither are you Weapons School Graduate material and I'm afraid this is the end of the road.'

He blinked rapidly as though he had been pole-axed and then almost immediately, the tears rolled down his cheeks as my brief précis and resulting verdict struck home. There was literally nothing more I could or wanted to say, but I had harbored a theory that the course was too much for him from early days and this dismissal was in fact a desired outcome. His response didn't support this premise and I was left with a nagging incredulity. How could a man go through nearly four months of an extremely demanding syllabus ignoring what all his instructors were constantly trying to instill in him about his flawed approach to the basic objectives of the program and then be astonished when told he hadn't measured up?

He turned and departed without a word. The paperwork would follow in the morning. I headed back to 'The Trough', as our Warthog Division ready room was aptly named and virtually all the instructors were there, awaiting the outcome. I shook my head and continued on into my office. The mood was subdued. To a man, everyone agreed that Dick should not have graduated, but no one wanted to see a student fail and despite the best efforts my troops could muster to keep him afloat, the inevitable outcome troubled us all.

The End of an Era: Phantom Pharewell

Every now and then, something exceptional happens that pulls your thoughts back into the past to events that transpired long before. Such an occurrence cropped up near the end of my command tour at the A-10 Division and I was fortunate enough to take part…and remember.

In 1985, ten years after I completed the FWIC and twenty years after the F-4 Weapons School first opened its doors, progress caught up with the mighty Phantom, at least within the Fighter Weapons School. Newer fighter aircraft with more sophisticated weaponry and avionics, the A-10, F-15 and F-16, began to adopt the roles the F-4 had handled for years. The time had come to begin the lengthy process of leading the old warhorse out to pasture. Don't get me wrong, Phantoms continued to fly for many years to come. As recently as 2018, the Air Forces of Greece, Turkey, Iran, South Korea and Japan were still burning up the skies with McDonnell Douglas's most versatile warplane. Nevertheless, USAF technology dictated that the new kids on the block were taking over and the Weapons School needed to cater for them.

In the fighter world, there's no time for remorse and dirges. Although to those who flew her she was an old friend whose days were numbered, there were only two appropriate reactions: a 'Nickel on the Grass' and one helluva wake.

The wake was the Weapons School's 'Phantom Pharewell', a fitting remembrance of twenty years of world-class training and the instructors, students and supporting personnel that made it all happen. It took place in the Nellis Officers' Club and every F-4 graduate and instructor was invited to attend. Attend we did: more than 800 fighter pilots, wives and girlfriends pitched up to raise a glass (or many) to memories, friends and colleagues, triumphs and failures, but most of all to the guest of honor, a spit-shined F-4E from the FWIC inventory. We couldn't get her through the door, but she had been towed through the streets overnight and reigned over the parking lot where she had her photo taken with dozens of those who had flown her over the years. A proper salute to a venerable lady and a noteworthy era.

Chapter Fifteen

The Staff Job: Fighter Pilot Purgatory

There's no doubt about it, when I think about my twenty-eight-year Air Force career, I was a very, *very* lucky man. Through very little skill and cunning on my part, I managed to repeatedly turn up at the right place at the right time and, unlike the vast majority of my colleagues, was able to cling on to a cockpit job for nearly all those years. The norm was for the fighter pilot to be pulled, kicking and screaming, out of his natural habitat and placed behind a BGD (Big Gray Desk) at around the twelve-year career point. Many of them never managed to scramble back into active flying and spent the rest of their careers frantically pushing pencils and forwarding reports, dissertations and recommendations upstream. These were often reviewed by other frustrated aviators who wielded their own red pencils and sent it all back down to be revised and otherwise adjusted, resulting in repetitive frustration all round.

My string of good fortune came to an abrupt halt when I relinquished command of the Fighter Weapons School A-10 Division in 1985, eighteen years after Mom pinned the gold bars on my shoulders. Despite my best attempts to find another airplane-flying position, my bosses made it abundantly clear that my time had run out. I was going to have to do my penance in a tiny cubicle at some headquarters far away from runways, the smell of jet fuel and the sight and throbbing sound of turbine engines. I had recurring nightmares of being chained on a galley boat bench next to a near-naked Charlton Heston while some full colonel beat a monotonous cadence to keep us all scribbling in unison.

As was the custom in those days (and probably still is today), when assignment time loomed the hapless officer touched base with the MPC (Military Personnel Center) in San Antonio Texas and laid out a comprehensive request for his or her next assignment, known in the trade as a 'Dream Sheet'. The MPC is manned by shoe clerks, known as

'Flesh Peddlers' due to their special mission. In the interest of fair play, I'll emphasize that the Flesh Peddlers who stage-manage assignments for rated officers (pilots, navigators and other aircrew) were predominantly unfortunate aviators, plucked from their comfortable cockpits to 'manage' the careers of those of us who were trying to avoid a similar fate.

I recognized that a BGD was waiting for me somewhere. My bosses lobbied hard for me to grovel and scrape to get a position in the Pentagon (not so affectionately known as the Puzzle Palace, Fort Fumble or the five-sided Wind Tunnel). I was told Air Staff jobs (as these Washington D.C. plums were known) were great career-enhancers and 'really looked great on the résumé'. Obstinate bastard that I was, I would rather have put a campfire out with my face and I decided to look further afield for my inevitable stint in perdition. I made a number of calls to my friendly Flesh Peddler in San Antonio, always prefaced with 'How about a cockpit job?' and always answered with 'In your dreams'. The personnel system was far-reaching and those officers ripe for reassignment often surfaced on 'hit lists' perused by unit commanders, flying or otherwise, throughout the Air Force.

So it came to pass that one of my previous flying Operations Officers (Major Larry Keith), formerly of MiG 'Project Have Idea' renown and now a brigadier general, spotted my name on such a list and called the Flesh Peddlers expressing an interest in bringing me to work for him in his own BGD empire. General Keith was reigning as Deputy Chief of Staff for Operations of the North Atlantic Treaty Organization's 2nd Allied Tactical Air Force (2 ATAF) based at Rheindahlen, Germany.

My Flesh Peddler buddy called me at Nellis one afternoon and asked me how I'd like to go to 2 ATAF. Flaunting my familiarity with the Air Force's far-flung outposts, I said: 'What the hell is that?' He went on to explain what and where it was, but most importantly, that Larry Keith had asked for me. I promised to get back to him in a couple of days and headed off to investigate. Joint Headquarters (JHQ) Rheindahlen turned out to be the primary British Forces Germany Headquarters, home not only to NATO components 2 ATAF and the Northern Army Group, (NORTHAG) but also Brit-specific elements Royal Air Force Germany (RAFG) and the British Army of the Rhine (BAOR). That's enough jargon for now, I think.

To a man, my buddies and bosses regaled me with predictions of impending career suicide. I *really* needed to fight for a Pentagon or at very least a major command staff assignment, they said. Wandering off into the wilderness of a NATO backwater would surely be the end of me and my career would come to a screeching halt. In the end, my pigheadedness overcame whatever motivation for future fame and glory the boys were trying to instill in me and I went with my heart, certainly not my head. I was looking at three years in a British-dominated headquarters near the Dutch and Belgian borders shuffling paper at the behest of a general I respected. I like the Brits – hell, I married one – and I liked the idea of working, as I would, in a NATO environment broadly populated by shanghaied British, German, Dutch, Belgian and American pilots exiled to serve their administrative stretch. The fact that I prefer European beer also factored into my decision. I got back to the Flesh Peddler and symbolically held out my hands for him to put the cuffs on. I then started trying to get psyched up about thirty-six months of impending shoe clerkdom.

Tales of the Big House

Transitioning from a Weapons School Command at Nellis to HQ 2 ATAF was about as close to a rapid deceleration as I have ever experienced. Nellis was fast-paced and high maintenance, with a buzz that was undeniable and constant pressures to plan, execute and deliver, right now. Twelve-hour workdays were the norm and, when the chips were down for some important project or mission planning requirements, that could rapidly expand. No one begrudged this rapid pace; the flying and the mission were the best and most fascinating on the planet and rarely did we forget that we were very lucky to be a part of it.

Rheindahlen (and NATO, as I was to learn very quickly) was the other extreme. I hasten to add this was not necessarily a bad thing – just different – and oh, was it different. Almost 6,000 of us toiled in and around the center of activity, the Big House. Those of us in the NATO components (review the jargon above; I'm not going to repeat it) were an intriguing federation of varying personalities and work ethic. The Dutch were a jovial bunch and took nothing too seriously; they were, in a nutshell, excellent company. The Belgians were more serious-minded, but certainly not more motivated and always seemed to be on holiday (more about that later). The Germans were an enigma: despite the fact that they were, like me, displaced aviators, very few of them exhibited the enthusiasm or the spirit that I had been impressed with when serving with the fighter pilots at Nörvenich. Perhaps they were even more frustrated with being shoved behind a BGD than I was. The Brits were very similar to the Yanks in most respects, but it pains me slightly to note that, by and large, the Brits seemed to populate 2 ATAF with more capable people than we did. Yeah, I know; what does that say about me?

The operational tempo at Rheindahlen (if you could actually call it a tempo), was undeniably sluggish, but in some ways very relaxing. The Brit Security Police opened the Big House doors at 8.30 am and locked them promptly at 5.00 pm. There was no burning of the midnight oil, no face time and the overall philosophy seemed to be 'this is NATO and absolutely nothing is so important it can't be finished tomorrow morning.'

Working with our NATO allies was a never-ending source of fascinating occurrences and observations. As mentioned earlier, the place was teeming with Brits and the most intriguing of these were British Army officers, part of the British Army of the Rhine and NORTHAG. Although I'd enjoyed some wonderful times with British fighter pilots, I had never crossed paths with their ground-pounding officer corps. The British Army is known for its resplendent uniforms and numerous traditions. (We'd probably still be part of the Empire if they hadn't worn bright red coats and marched into battle in tight formations.) A couple of these observations invite brief discussion. Somewhere in the distant past, British Army officers developed an affinity for hunting dogs, not just to hunt with, but also to take to work to languish under the BGD all day as a kind of panting, yawning, farting office ornament. Most of the Army personnel (British and otherwise) worked in an area of the Big House distant from our own Air Force digs. Since arrival times at work were apparently inconsequential, I would occasionally stroll around the building to enjoy the daily parade of Golden Retrievers, black, chocolate and yellow Labradors and various models of working spaniel that sashayed into the building with their masters each morning.

The canine companions had to be left at home when we participated in war-game drills, but the British Army found a suitable substitute. Two or three times a year, we would deploy to the field to take part in massive NATO exercises. Joint maneuvers such as the REFORGER (Return of Forces to Germany) series and ABLE ARCHER combined the forces of NATO allies in a relatively realistic escalating wartime scenario. This tested our ability not only to deploy and fight, but to control the battle from austere locations. To give an example of the scope of these frolics, ABLE ARCHER in November 1983 was acted out by some 40,000 troops Europe-wide. Army and Air Force components participated in these actual maneuvers and had all the fun, driving their tanks through farmers' crops and carrying out the kind of illicit aerial battles I described earlier. We shoe clerks hunkered down in tents, froze our goolies off and bitched quite a bit. The Brits, bless 'em, made the best of a truly wretched situation. They had tents, just like the rest of us, but in a tradition that dated back to pre-Wellington times, each mealtime was celebrated by breaking out the regimental silver, and the glistening array of tableware and cutlery was truly inspiring. Never mind that they were dining on the same revolting Meals, Ready to Eat (MREs) as the rest of us; they were doing it in style from solid silver plates and washing it all down with whatever liquid refreshment they could find from silver goblets, then finishing it off with – what else? – tea, brewed in china teapots and served in gleaming china cups. They never invited us plebeians to join them, but taking full advantage of the pageantry taking place in our midst, we peasants invariably gathered to launch a round of good-natured taunts and catcalls, which the Brits ignored, flaunting their stiff upper lips most impressively.

All the participating nations were known for various characteristics and idiosyncrasies. Taken as a group, we were a sociologist's dream and of course, we capitalized on the contributions of the others. Take holidays, for example, which we certainly did. One of the truly gratifying aspects of NATO service was the fact that we all enjoyed each other's holidays. The Belgians were the uncontested champs in this department, celebrating no fewer than twenty festive days during the year. Some of these were only intended for certain subdivisions of the population (Day of the Flemish Community, French Community Holiday, Day of the

Walloon Region, for example) but since there were members of each of these communities serving, they unashamedly took them all (and so did the rest of us). Add the usual time off for Christmas, New Year's Day and Easter, not to mention the unique breaks of other countries (Washington and Lincoln's birthdays, Thanksgiving, UK bank holidays, the Day of German Unity and Labor Day, the Dutch king's birthday and Dutch Liberation Day) and it becomes obvious we had a whole lot of time off.

Organizationally, we were just as chaotic. I was Chief of Fighter Operations in the Offensive Ops Division. I reported to my immediate boss, a Belgian full colonel, who was an extremely cultured man with some very good ideas, but slightly challenged in the charisma department. He, in turn, reported to Brigadier General Larry Keith for the first year of my tour and later, one of my all-time Air Force heroes, Brigadier General Billy McCoy, both US fighter pilots who had abundant talent and magnetism to drive the Operations Directorate very skillfully from the top.

I had two Germans working for me, one a lieutenant colonel who was a rated pilot but hadn't flown for years. He had been christened Hertwig, but went by the nickname 'Hardy'. Hardy? Hardly. He was a bit too fond of his schnapps and somewhat erratic in his social behavior. A firm believer in the status quo, any new idea or concept that may have caused him to exert a bit of additional effort was met with sucking of teeth and a skeptical 'I don't know about that.' Hard(l)y had been appointed as my sponsor on arrival. Military sponsors, if competent, are invaluable for introducing you to new colleagues, the modus operandi of the organization and, perhaps most urgently, getting established in terms of accommodation. This element was particularly critical in Germany, because the sponsor's linguistic assistance in finding a suitable place to live for the individual and family was very near the top of the priority list. In this role, Hardy was about as useful as tits on a boar hog. He took my wife and I to a couple of semi-slum dwellings and when we didn't react with great enthusiasm, he had a tantrum. I told him thanks, but we'd manage nicely on our own, thanks. We did, I will add, and rapidly found a beautiful home to rent in nearby Mönchengladbach. His attitude on the job wasn't much better and I spent most of my tour covering his tasks rather than relying on him for any quality work.

My other German officer was far more competent: a major who flew F-4s and was actually pretty bright. Unfortunately, he was also a bit of a narcissist and permanently alienated himself from Elaine and I one night when we invited him for dinner. While I was out brewing the coffee he announced to her that she could do a lot better than me and perhaps they should come to some arrangement. She didn't embarrass him by mentioning this to me over the petit fours, but we had a good laugh about it afterwards and subsequently, as if by magic he managed to soak up the most onerous chores I could think of for some considerable time ('Never get mad; get even.').

I bring these two up because they were the notable exceptions and I simply had the ill fortune to have them on my small team. My other guys, a Dutchman and a Brit, were good troops and a pleasure to work with, as were most of the other captive aviators in the organization.

Lest I give the impression I'm picking on our NATO allies, I hasten to point out that we Yanks had our faults as well. Most of us were reasonably gracious guests in this multinational environment but sadly our culture gives rise to some embarrassing traits and we had a few that flaunted these peculiarities for all to see. Take the language, for example; we and the Brits have often been described as 'two nations separated by a common language'. There were a few in our midst who insisted on leaning on Yankee colloquialisms to publicly pronounce that they 'spoke 'Merican'. Sorry, Billy Bob, there's no such animal (so to speak).

There aren't many prouder of their country than yours truly, but it genuinely galled me when our handful of 'ugly' Americans steadfastly refused to accept that they were guests of another nation and might just want to participate rather than resist. I had a major who worked for me who would not wear a tie to social functions because he was ''Merican' and didn't have to put up with that nonsense. He was an authentic shoe clerk, but unusually dim. Shortly after my arrival, when specifically asked about the dress code, he advised his brand new boss (me) to attend my first officers' drinks gathering in shirtsleeves and open collar. On the night, he and I did our impression of the Beverly Hillbillies all evening amid a sea of professional-looking gentlemen in jackets and ties. Fortunately, Elaine looked the part as always, and diverted a bit of the humiliation.

Don't get me wrong; folks like this were in the minority among the American contingent but there were enough of them to sour the overall experience slightly. The mostly-gentle clash of cultures occasionally influenced some of the best aspects of a NATO assignment. For example, the main venue for the numerous social gatherings that bound the five nations together was the British Officers' Mess, an impressive edifice spacious enough to accommodate large groups. Now, at the time, British military tradition reigned and officers' ladies were not welcomed in the Mess unless specifically invited. This prohibition did not apply to the aforementioned retrievers and spaniels, however. We actually had a couple of vocal ''Mericans' who often and stridently proclaimed they wouldn't frequent a club where they could take their dogs but not their wives (I will diplomatically refrain from making any comparisons here).

The phrase 'cutting off one's nose to spite one's face' comes to mind as the 1980s' NATO social life was fully subsidized and events were not only plentiful and enjoyable but the ladies were nearly always specifically invited. Our little band of malcontents presumably stayed at home wolfing grits and gravy for supper and watching the *Dukes of Hazzard* on the video player rather than joining in with what was invariably great food and drink, stimulating company and usually some pretty special entertainment. This was provided for the price of Mess membership at $20-$30 per month as I recall and I always regarded that attitude as a special kind of stupidity.

I can't move on without providing a couple of examples to illustrate the comments above. Spread throughout the year were parties organized by each of the five nations and again, heavily subsidized by NATO. Generally, these were planned loosely around our own cultures. I was tagged to run the American effort during my second year, so Elaine and I went in search of something not quite as corny as some of the previous Yank barn dances had been, but a touch of Americana just the same. We found it in some rather unusual places. We had been very partial to margaritas at a particular Mexican restaurant in Las Vegas and they were kind enough to provide us with the recipe. We tried in vain to locate a slushy machine to manufacture the frozen variety but finally settled for our 'gritas on the rocks. We took a field trip to the large US military facility at Ramstein AFB and, aided and abetted by the Brits who negotiated a suspension of our booze ration allowance for an 'official' function, purchased enough Jose Cuervo tequila to float an aircraft carrier and vast quantities of lime juice, triple sec and typically mediocre American beer to supplement the margaritas. It couldn't be an American event without steaks, baked potatoes and corn on the cob, so we stocked up on dozens of extra-thick T-bones as well.

Having negotiated the repast and laid plans for filling the watering hole, we turned to entertainment. This was not quite so easy but we were running out of time, and I took an enormous gamble and settled on a recommended band out of the nearby Netherlands. I say gamble because there was no opportunity to audition these guys; we had to go with their reputation.

These events were very well attended and we were expecting hundreds of Germans, Belgians, Dutch and Brits (with their ladies!) along with the majority of Yanks who didn't shoot themselves in the foot socially. The Brits donated the services of their large kitchen staff and on the day we showed up to give them a tutorial on the gentle art of margarita-mixing which they were going to accomplish in enormous zinc bathtubs (I didn't ask where they found them). We also provided Elaine's acclaimed marinade recipe for the steaks and, when we were happy they had their act together, we left them to work their culinary magic.

When we pitched up a few hours later, it was abundantly clear that the Mess kitchen staff, most of whom had probably never sampled a margarita, had shamelessly mixed business with pleasure and were about as jolly as a bunch of cooks could be. This was not an issue, as there was plenty to go around – or so we thought – and we laughed along with them as they fumbled their way through the preparation of the evening's feast.

Having been prepared by a number of seriously alcohol-impaired cooks, dinner turned out surprisingly well. The T-bones went down a treat (American steaks being the pinnacle of beefy repast in those days), and the spuds and corn did a superb job of accompanying. Nevertheless, there was only one genuine star of the show: those marvelous (and potent) margaritas. I can't recall exactly how much was blended in those zinc bathtubs, but it was in the tens of gallons, and it wasn't nearly enough.

Less than two hours into the event, an awful lot of NATO's finest were showing signs of advanced euphoria, but the bathtubs were draining fast.

The good news at that point was there was plenty of beer on hand to supplement; the bad news was it was mainly American beer (by design as we Yanks had sponsored the event and I wanted my European colleagues to taste what they wouldn't mind missing). Fortunately, after priming the pump with Jose Cuervo and friends, most couldn't have cared less whether the beer was palatable or not.

It was at this point that our band made their appearance. I was filled with trepidation. True, I had hired a Dutch band unseen, but these guys were a scruffy-looking collection of Filipinos and Dutch Guineans that piled out of an ancient VW camper like jesters from a clown car. They meandered onto the stage, set up some antiquated sound equipment and I prepared to be run out of town on a rail. The drummer kicked off with four quick rim shots and…magic happened. They played Creedence Clearwater better than Creedence, Beatles and Stones damn near as good as the originals and a whole lot of other great stuff that had dozens of mostly-sozzled desk warriors on their feet pretending they could dance.

It turned out to be arguably the best party Elaine and I ever attended, but to be fair, most of the social events at Rheindahlen were of a similar caliber.

One more quick case in point and I'll move on. The Brits arranged an annual fancy dress party that was always top-notch. During the third year of my staff officer sentence I had pretty much run out of ideas so I cut the sleeves off an old camouflage fatigue uniform, found a black fright wig and a toy assault rifle and went as Rambo. Elaine wore the royal blue party suit preserved from my combat tour at Ubon, sporting my pilot wings and a Thai translation of my name (or not; it could very well have said 'Denny Dumbshit' or similar). It was also festooned with patches such as 'Yankee Air Pirate' and 'Participant, South-East Asia War Games' as well as the 435th Squadron badge, a Disney-designed Eagle brandishing a machine gun. This flight suit had been an essential part of our drunken brawls at Ubon, but I have to admit it looked a lot better on her.

As always, the party was well-attended, food, drink and entertainment were exceptionally good and we spent the evening enjoying all of it while a few of the ladies decided it would be fun to tug on Rambo's chest hair just to confirm it wasn't a merkin. Painful but amusing, I guess.

As the evening drew to a close the winners of the fancy dress competition were announced. To my surprise, Rambo took the honors in the male division and another young American lady, who had gone to far more trouble than Rambo, was crowned for her very impressive hand-made Cinderella ball gown. As tradition had it, the winners Rambo and Cinderella had the last dance. I noticed that Cindy appeared to be a few sheets to the wind and propped her up rather than dancing with her for the most part.

One of the most valuable services provided by NATO was the post-party taxi service home which kept us all from a) being arrested, or b) running into a tree which had unexpectedly vaulted onto the road. This convenience was provided by the German Army motor pool free of charge and today would be vigorously attacked as a waste of taxpayers' money.

Elaine and I ended up in the same mini-van as Cinderella and her husband and two other couples as we were headed in generally the same direction. Our chauffer was named Udo, an unfortunate young German conscript detailed to get us safely home, but he was cheerful and polite and we set sail at around 1.00 am. About fifteen minutes out, Cindy was showing signs of urgent digestive upset and without further warning, deposited her dinner (and possibly all of her intake for the last couple of days) unceremoniously in her lap and on the seat and floor beside her. With virtually no urging at all, Udo pulled over and the other two men and I helped her out of the van. Bizarrely, her Prince Charming wasn't that at all and remained rooted to the spot, providing virtually no assistance or support. We never quite figured that out, but we were finally able to get Cinderella sorted out and safely home. Alas, her ball gown was rendered fit only for waxing the car and we suspected Prince Charmless might wake the next morning to find a single glass slipper inserted in a very inconvenient orifice. As a positive footnote, we helped Udo rinse out his vehicle on arrival at our home and he was suitably grateful.

Aside from the buzzing social life at Rheindahlen, there were other benefits to a NATO tour. With lots of time off, little stress and a very convenient central European location, there was scope for some very pleasant trips and we took advantage of this. We often drove the twenty minutes to the Dutch town of Maastricht for dinner and into Belgium where we discovered about 1,000 different beers and the wonderful world of mussels. During a three-year tour, thanks to the NATO holiday calendar, we also enjoyed outings abroad including Egypt and Africa, a couple of cruises, and extended motoring visits to France, Spain, Italy, Switzerland, Austria and numerous forays into other regions of Germany.

There was a final silver lining to the NATO staff assignment cloud. It was more work than fun, but in the long run carried far more benefit. Every profession has its somewhat paradoxical requirements. In the world of US Air Force officership, one of these was the implicit necessity to have a Master's Degree tattooed in your personnel records if you were to have any chance of achieving promotion to full colonel. Virtually all Air Force officers are educated to Bachelor degree level, thus putting us on equal educational footing for promotion. That'll do, as they say, up to lieutenant colonel, but that difficult single step further up the ladder (only one in twelve AF officers ever pins on the Eagles) requires an additional tick in the box. I know one or two that made it without a Master's Degree but they are very scarce indeed. I was unconvinced, maintaining that I could get promoted on the strength of my stellar performance in the air and my boyish good looks. Indeed, I had once considered a concept that surfaced one evening during a lengthy session at the bar. Officers are considered for promotion via a review of their personnel record and within that folder is an official photo (my last one is on the inside flap of this book, all steely-eyed and determined). Those of us imbibing on this particular evening came up with the perfect plan based on the rising tide of affirmative action within the Air Force. The solution was simple: we would have our official photos taken in blackface, wearing a sombrero and a brassiere. Promotion would surely follow. In those days we weren't incarcerated for such irreverent thoughts and the plan evaporated quicker than our hangovers. Back to the drawing board.

For some considerable time, my wife, who is a far more strategic thinker than I am, 'robustly encouraged' me to add the 'M-word' to my curriculum vitae and my USAF profile. This would give me a fighting chance in the Full Colonel Selection Derby when my number came up. The curriculum was of no importance: the Masters could be in any field of learning from Cannabis Cultivation or Puppetry (I promise I am not making this up; thanks, Dave Barry) to Astro Physics. As long as it was permanently embossed in the 'Civilian Education' section of DD Form 214, it was a valid ticket to enter the Colonel Sweepstakes.

I had a number of exceptional reasons for not pursuing this option. I was far too busy; I couldn't possibly divert my mind from my demanding NATO duties to academic quests; I had to wash my hair every weekend; and finally (this was my zinger), where the hell am I going to get a US Master's Degree in Northern Germany?

Well, Elaine saw through the first two in a nanosecond or so and laughingly dismissed the third, but I was right on target with the geographic sidestep. Unfortunately (or fortunately, as it turned out), the same convenient Central European location that had enabled us to see the sights provided the solution that ultimately trashed my resistance.

The US military has always had a world-class system of educational opportunities for the benefit of personnel worldwide. Supported by a number of distinguished American universities, campuses are set up at hundreds of military installations. Courses are regularly taught on weekends and evenings by certified faculty members in a number of disciplines (Cannabis Cultivation and Puppetry are not among them). The cost to the service member is minimal, being facilitated by the GI Bill and active duty educational benefits. One of these far-flung campuses was situated at Soesterberg Royal Dutch Air Force Base, home of the American 32nd Tactical Fighter Squadron and a mere 106 miles from Rheindahlen. The curriculum was run by Embry Riddle Aeronautical University, a respected Daytona Beach, Florida aviation specialist institution, and they offered a Master's degree in Aeronautical Science and Management spread over roughly two years.

So it came to pass that Lieutenant Colonel Ladd enrolled in the Master's course and we sat down to work out the logistics. Classes were taught at Soesterberg all day Saturday and Sunday, every other weekend. The Big House doors were locked and latched all weekend so there was never any danger of NATO duties getting in the way. Elaine and I decided to depart after work on Fridays, drive the hour and forty-five minutes to Zeist or Utrecht, the closest towns to Soesterberg, check into a reasonable hotel and have a nice meal before turning in. On Saturday mornings, our paths diverged: I went to Soesterberg, sat in a classroom for eight hours and then returned to the hotel. Elaine awoke to breakfast in bed served by a blond Dutchman she described as 'dishy'. She then got up at her leisure and sashayed into Zeist/Utrecht for an arduous day of shopping, lunching and sightseeing. We rendezvoused in the evening for a meal in a restaurant she had pinpointed during her challenging day out. We repeated most of this sequence on Sunday, heading back to Rheindahlen after my class finished.

This routine recurred on alternate weekends for eighteen months and, although it became extremely repetitive, I'll have to admit it was not nearly as unpleasant as it might have been. At the end of it all, I got the Masters (and ultimately the promotion), but there's very little doubt who had the most fun.

Back to the 'Real' Air Force

My three years' 'punishment' as a staff officer was rapidly drawing to a close. As a 'brevet' full colonel (I had been selected but had not yet 'pinned on' the silver Eagles) my career destiny was now controlled by a small but perfectly formed cadre of Flesh Peddlers in San Antonio known as the Colonels' Group. I anticipated this would mean a more sophisticated and sympathetic approach to my next assignment, but discovered very quickly they were simply more cunning and smoother in sticking it to you.

So I waited confidently for the triumphant return to the cockpit and flying command position I clearly merited. When I got a note to call my Flesh Peddler, I was already organizing the party in my head. Imagine my astonishment when he calmly announced that I had been 'hand-picked' to head 250 miles south from Rheindahlen where I would be welcomed with open arms to the US European Command (EUCOM) in Stuttgart. There I would be treated to another three years of working NATO issues from behind what was possibly a slightly bigger gray desk. Translation: there was a leaky bucket in Stuttgart and since I was ripe for assignment, I was as good as anyone to plug the leak.

I was almost a colonel now, so sobbing, throwing my stapler and in-basket across the room and holding my breath until I turned blue were not considered appropriate. Nevertheless, I was able to convey to this glorified shoe clerk in San Antonio that I would be most grateful if he'd try again, harder. He promised to do so, but if we had not been on the phone, I'm sure I would have seen him rubbing his hands with glee, eyes rolling and his lips moving.

I went home and talked at length to Elaine and the conversation drifted to a deed I'd never had to resort to in an airplane: bailing out. Discussions of the next step dominated the next few days while I waited for the slave masters to get back to me. When they finally did, the verdict was predictable but no more acceptable than it had been the first time. The flesh-peddling major's argument revolved around the dubious assertion that I was the 'only man on the planet' who could do justice to this designated staff slot. As much as he wanted to blend my objectives with the requirements of the Air Force, it simply couldn't be done... etcetera, etcetera. I managed to bid him goodbye without referring to his questionable parentage or bizarre sexual proclivities and went home to formulate the plan. I had about six weeks to plot my evasion (or pull the figurative ejection handles).

Elaine and I had been mulling over the options for this unhappy outcome and the next step was a chat with a man who had the wherewithal to make better things happen, if I could convince him to do so.

Brigadier General Dale Tabor had been my boss at RAF Bentwaters in 1982 when he was the 81st TFW Wing Commander and I was the Detachment Operations Officer at Nörvenich. I didn't know him well, but I did know he was one of the good guys: apolitical, reasonable and a fighter pilot at heart. He was now Assistant Deputy Chief of Staff for Operations at the Air Force's Major Command Headquarters, Ramstein (home of the fabled USAFE salute). His responsibilities included oversight of officer assignments within Europe and as such he was, quite literally, my one-man assignment supreme court.

We packed up the car and headed south to Ramstein. I had secured an appointment with General Tabor the following day and had to make it count. Elaine and I talked tactics into the night and I felt I had a pretty good game plan when I headed over to his office.

He greeted me warmly, we chatted about Bentwaters and how much we both missed driving Warthogs and finally, he said: 'I understand you want to talk about your assignment.' I was out of the chocks like a (slightly overweight) sprinter. I explained that I respected the requirement to recruit good people for NATO staff jobs and (crossing my fingers behind my back) I appreciated the opportunity to take on this important challenge. I reminded him I was just completing a similar NATO staff job and while I reveled in the diversity of multinational cooperation and planning (fingers remaining crossed), I strongly felt it was time I came home to the US Air Force after three years in a joint staff position. My patriotism and reverence for the American way literally gushed across the table. Had there been iPods in those days, I'd have had one in my pocket, looping the Air Force song (*Off We Go Into the Wild Blue Yonder*) and Kate Smith's *God Bless America*. I acknowledged that a flying job wasn't in the offing, but that was my objective and I would be working hard to achieve it, but I wanted sincerely to do so in an all-American environment.

I took a moment to catch my breath, ready to continue the onslaught, but he looked at me with a mixed expression of bemusement and sensitivity. 'I knew you weren't very happy with the EUCOM posting, but I never expected you to come in here with your dagger drawn. Let me see what I can do.' He smiled, sincerely; I saluted and left my fate in his hands.

A few days later, I got another message to call my Flesh Peddler in San Antonio. He sounded somewhat annoyed when he answered the phone and I hoped against hope it was because someone more important had been tampering with his empire. Indeed, he said curtly, he had managed to find another 'only man on the planet' to take the staff slot at Stuttgart and I would soon be reporting to my new boss in DCS Operations at HQ USAFE Ramstein, one Brigadier General Dale Tabor.

Regrettably, I never had an opportunity to work directly for General Tabor. He pinned on another star and headed off to bigger and better things just as we were moving to Ramstein. There was one fleeting opportunity: the Air Force organized an excellent Indoctrination Program for recently-promoted full colonels (and importantly, their wives) at Ramstein but I only had time to thank him briefly for his intervention. If you read this, Boss, I'm grateful to this day.

Despite the fact that no one was going to let me get anywhere near an airplane, I looked forward to working at Ramstein. As the European Headquarters, it was a major hub: a huge base with superb facilities and a crossroads for Air Force personnel. Dropping by the shiny new Officers' Club for a drink more often than not led to a chance reunion with a buddy or two you hadn't seen for years and a chance to tell a few war stories and reminisce about the 'good old days'.

Although my new USAFE position, Assistant Deputy Director of Operations, was yet another big gray desk job, it was directly involved with US operational issues and was a potential springboard back into a cockpit somewhere. I couldn't dwell on this because a) it was truly a long shot, and b) it would only happen if I excelled behind the BGD. I worked for another colonel, Eddie Pickrel, all-round good guy and, I always thought, general-to-be. He, in turn, reported to the two-star Director of Operations who worked directly for the four-star USAFE Commander.

One of the redeeming features of working in a US senior staff position was the return to an American work ethic and culture. Yes, the hours were longer and the tempo was far more accelerated than NATO had been, but on the up side, working relationships were more congenial; in the NATO environment, there was always an overtone of political correctness. You always had to watch your step for fear of offending a German, Brit, Dutchman or Belgian. Most were amenable to a bit of banter, but the threat was always there. In a US-only headquarters, particularly one staffed by operational types – aircrew and flying support people – the gloves were pretty much off. Practical jokes and verbal jousting were common and, as long as reasonable taste was adhered to, appreciated by (nearly) all.

Pulling the Boss's chain was high on the list of hobbies for the exuberant, temporarily-grounded fighter pilots on the staff. A couple of dozen worked for me and they didn't wait long to test-drive my sense of humor. One Sunday afternoon, Elaine and I were moving into the house we had rented off-base. Among the activities I hate most in this world is moving house and, as usual, our tempers were short. We were walking a fine line between affectionate cooperation and open warfare. Suddenly there was a knock on the door and I stood face-to-face with a German delivery boy in whose arms was a stack of pizzas, a dozen or more in total. In my fractured German, I explained to him that there was obviously a mistake and he was at the wrong place. He replied in equally broken English that 'No, *ze* address is *klar* and *zese* are *ze* pizzas you ordered.'

We were inching towards Armageddon when, from behind the bushes in the yard, nearly all my new workforce emerged, enjoying my elevated blood pressure immensely and laden with beer, wine and goodwill. The ringleaders, Eddie Pickrel and Major Danny Clifton, stepped up with an open beer for me and a big glass of chilled *halbtrocken* for Elaine, smiled broadly and said simply 'Gotcha!' They had, of course, and we enjoyed the pizzas, beer, wine and camaraderie far into the night. What a great introduction to the organization, but in the back of my mind I had already started thinking about how I was going to pick up the gauntlet that had been thrown down.

The opportunity to do so surfaced sooner than I had hoped. One of my Divisions, Operational Training (DOOT) was the focal point for all the issues that kept our aircrew honed and ready to go. Some of these issues were extremely contentious and low-level flying training was at the top of this list. Navigating 250ft over the ground at between 300 and 500 knots (depending on the aircraft) using 1980s' technology is not an undemanding task. Given the challenges, the only way to gain and maintain proficiency is through practice, lots of it. This is easily undertaken over the Nevada desert, for example, as it is difficult to annoy the inhabitants when there are very few of them. Such is not the case over Western Europe: Germany, France, Belgium, the Netherlands and the UK. As the Cold War was drawing down and human nature began to rapidly relegate the importance of the military to the back burner, there was more and more popular hue and cry to cease and desist the noisy, unnerving practice of fast jets terrifying horses and chickens and infuriating the friendly natives on the ground.

Our job in the headquarters was to champion our ability to train realistically in the face of growing opposition. Without the ability to effectively operate at low level, we would be hard pressed to defend the folks who were calling for our training to cease. The DOOT guys were right in the middle of this fracas, because the interest level had soared and the requirement to massage the sensitivities of the general public through reason and savoir-faire had increased. These young men had become our chief diplomats and not a week passed that didn't involve them speaking to local civic groups (often through translators) and hosting visiting VIPs: US Congressmen, European politicians, NATO military brass, the media, the list goes on and on. Many of these presentations were at very short notice and required hurried preparation to cover the pertinent points.

As inconsiderate as it sounds, it was this situation that provided my opportunity to get even for the Great Pizza Hospitality Check. Because of the hard work and flexibility these guys demonstrated every day, the Boss and I ensured that at least quarterly, we gave them all a full afternoon off for what had become a cherished tradition: the DOOT Golf Tournament. Danny Clifton and his merry men planned this event meticulously and looked forward to the event as a fitting chance to blow off steam generated by their high-profile efforts on behalf of Western Europe and we supported them to the hilt (well, usually).

The day of the tournament dawned and the boys readied themselves to escape from the headquarters promptly at 12.30 pm for opening 1.00 pm tee times. I had gained the confidence of the Boss's secretary Dianne (who was undeniably the light of all our lives between 8:00 and 5:00 Monday through Friday) and at precisely 11.55 am she dropped a telex message in to Danny Clifton. It read:

To: HQ USAFE/DOO/DOOT
Subj: VIP Visit
Dr. William B. Hogan and the Rt. Honorable S. Jackson Snead will be visiting the Commander, HQ USAFE this morning from the Department of Defense, Washington D.C. They have requested a briefing on low level training issues commencing at 1400 hrs. DOOT should be prepared for a Q&A session following the briefing.

From my concealed vantage point, I could hardly contain myself as I watched the blood drain from Danny's face as he read the de facto obliteration of the long-awaited DOOT Golf Tournament. He gathered his troops around him and passed on the devastating news; they looked like a litter of whipped puppies and I could barely resist a compulsion to punch the air and shout 'Yes!' Nevertheless, as I knew they would, my little band of pros sucked it up, concealed their deep frustration, and set about feverishly preparing what would undoubtedly be a sterling, in-depth presentation for these D.C. bigwigs.

At 12:25, Diane went back to DOOT. The office was a beehive of activity, officers hurriedly assembling briefing slides and background papers. She found Danny Clifton, looked at him with a wonderful air of urgency and said, solemnly: 'I think you'll want to read this.'

To: HQ USAFE/DOO/DOOT
Subj: VIP Visit For the Attention of Major D. Clifton
Dear Major Clifton
It is with regret that we will have to forego your presentation this afternoon due to other pressing business. Your Commander, General Kirk, has advised that we really should check out the excellent Ramstein Golf Course while we're here and we've decided to take his advice. He also mentioned that you and some of your colleagues may be taking part in a tournament today as well. We hope you enjoy it and we may even see you at the 19th hole.
Regards
Ben Hogan and Slammin' Sammy Snead

P.S. GOTCHA

As the boys shuffled past me on their way to their golf tournament, I took the only suitable action under the circumstances: gloating enthusiastically. My 'Gotcha' clearly trumped the pizza wind-up and unmistakably established me as a boss not to be trifled with. Even my co-conspirator Dianne, standing beside me as they traipsed past, furtively commenting on my parentage, seemed to enjoy their humiliation, despite her undying protective affection for each and every one of them.

As it turned out, the tournament was a great success, even though Ben and Slammin' Sammy never turned up. Not only did the victims not hold a grudge, I learned from various sources later that the exasperation at being duped in the first place was overwhelmingly eclipsed by the elation of being liberated at the last minute. There was never going to be a different outcome: everyone triumphed and morale took a leap forward.

As much as I appreciated the opportunity to return to my USAF roots rather than toiling in another NATO Headquarters, there is no denying that the Ramstein DOOT assignment was still being tethered to a Big

242 From F-4 Phantom to A-10 Warthog

Gray Desk, far away from the aroma of jet fuel and 'Jet Noise, the Sound of Freedom', as seen on many Stateside bumper stickers. There were, of course, high points such as the pizza prank vs. golf hoax above and my wife Elaine pinning on my colonel's eagles at a modest ceremony in the headquarters, but this digest is designed to focus on fighter pilots. Although there were many of them in the headquarters, they were all trapped in a parallel universe where airplanes were just out of reach and they were condemned to toil at their gray desks (big and small) until something magical happened and they found themselves back in a cockpit.

That magical something materialized for me only a few months after we settled in Ramstein when my Big Boss, Major General Jim Jamerson, sent word that he wanted to see me in his office. General 'J' was genuinely one of the good guys; nevertheless, a summons could only mean one of two things: something was satisfactory (or maybe even better), or I was in trouble. On the way to the office, I reviewed my recent activities. To the best of my knowledge, I hadn't made or generated any major blunders and this should have comforted me, but human nature being what it is, it didn't and I waited apprehensively outside the door.

I walked in, saluted and he motioned me towards a chair. 'I can't imagine why,' he said, 'but someone in the Personnel Center wants to stick you back in an airplane and go to the 81st Wing at Bentwaters as Director of Operations.' I stifled the urge to do a cartwheel right there and, in as measured a voice as I could muster, I said: 'That's great news, Sir. Are you going to let me go?' 'Can't wait to get rid of you, but keep it to yourself for a week or two until the paperwork catches up,' he retorted, then grinned at me and offered his hand in congratulations. I did the cartwheel later; enthusiastically, but admittedly not very well.

The last part of that announcement led into my introduction to the delightful world of senior officer politics. Only a few days after my delightful meeting with General Jamerson, General Bill Kirk, the four-star commander of US Air Forces Europe, relinquished his command and retired from the Air Force. He was honored with a gala farewell evening at the shiny new Ramstein Officers' Club which would be attended by unit commanders throughout Europe, including my Boss-to-be at the 81st Wing, Colonel Tad Oelstrom. Although the paperwork hadn't caught up and we still couldn't openly discuss my upcoming assignment, Elaine and I thought this would be an excellent opportunity to break the ice with Oelstrom and his wife, neither of whom we had ever met. Conscious of the requirement for discretion, we introduced ourselves and attempted to start a convivial conversation. Their response was decidedly frosty at best and, after a very few awkward moments, we excused ourselves and readily found some more agreeable companions. As was to become painfully obvious over the next couple of years, Oelstrom had the personality of a beached cod, but there was more to the attitude he displayed than simple dullness. It was only after a great deal of deliberation we figured out that I was not his preferred candidate for Director of Operations and he was still stealthily trying to get my assignment overturned. Years later, he ended up with stars on his shoulder, which I suspect is what he wanted, but at that moment in time I had been selected for the DO job and he failed to get me jettisoned, which is for sure what he wanted. Gotcha, Tad.

When the assignment was officially confirmed by the Flesh Peddlers at Randolph a few days later, a number of friends and colleagues called or wrote (no email in those days) with congratulations. Conspicuously missing was a greeting from my new boss, who I suspect was probably pouting. Never mind, I was seriously excited. For a fighter pilot, Deputy Commander for Operations (or DO) of a fighter wing was the pinnacle of any career because it was the last bastion of leadership directly involving men who fly jets in anger. Unlike my somewhat chilly new chief, my job wouldn't heavily involve infrastructure, logistics, budgeting and all those other peripheral activities that supported the flying operation; those were *his* problems. Mine, as far as I was concerned, were far more stimulating: making sure the tip of the sword was sharp – weapons and tactics, training, command and control, flying safety – in short, those functions that directly (or very nearly so) resulted in getting bombs and bullets on target. Oh yeah, there was one more thing: not only was I accountable for these sweeping functions, a big part of the job involved climbing into an A-10 cockpit regularly as a hands-on leader, to keep an eye on my troops – their training, morale and motivation – and how effectively my plans and programs were being employed.

As soon as my assignment was definite, my administrative duties at the headquarters were curtailed and I was quickly funneled into preparing for my new role. The best part of this process by a long shot was what was commonly known as the 'Senior Officer's checkout', which was to a 40-something fighter pilot what an extended trip to Disney World is to a 10-year-old. Since I hadn't flown for three years or so, it was necessary to get me spooled up again as an A-10 driver before I took over the Wing DO position at Bentwaters. As the assignment was imminent, there was no waiting for a scheduled flight training class and an absolute minimum of administrivia in processing the training. I was on my way to Davis-Monthan AFB (D-M) in Tucson within a week of assignment confirmation and eager to get back in 'the game'.

True, I had been out of the cockpit for some considerable time, but I had already amassed over 1,000 hours of flying time in the bird, much of that in the graduate level training environment of the Weapons School. Although I can't honestly say getting back up to speed was like re-learning to ride a bike, it would certainly be less challenging than learning to fly a brand-new jet from scratch.

The sabbatical to D-M was scheduled for a month or, as one of my instructors sarcastically put it, three days of training crammed into a four-week course. This was no exaggeration as there were no formal academics (I was given a dozen cassette tapes covering aircraft systems, performance and operating limitations) and no stipulated flying curriculum. I would progress at my own rate and indeed I had regained a level of reasonable competence after the first three or four rides. The good news was that D-M's training budget was obviously not under threat, there was no shortage of instructor pilots and virtually all of them were more than happy to take the 'old man' out and give him a pasting on the gunnery range. I'm delighted to report that it didn't always turn out that way and I took a respectable bounty of quarters and nickels from my much younger and more current mentors a fair amount of the time. I flew once and sometimes twice a day during the full four weeks and tuned up my proficiency to pre-Big Gray Desk levels. Although I should probably have felt repentant, I will now confess that there was never a single twinge of guilt while I was having the time of my life at the taxpayers' expense. My rationale was that the sharper I was at driving my Warthog, the safer America would be overall. Just sayin'...

Alas, all good things must come to an end, but I headed back to Europe to undertake even better things. I stopped by Ramstein where my long-suffering but always supportive bride – bless her – had prepared for our move to England. We said our goodbyes to the folks in the headquarters and headed across the Channel to take the operational reins of the biggest, most complex Fighter Wing in the Air Force; in my mind, the *best* job in the Air Force.

My new adventure meant project management on a massive scale: the 81st Tactical Fighter Wing comprised 6 A-10 Squadrons, 18 aircraft each for a total of 108 plus a squadron of 18 Aggressor F-16s. These replicated Soviet aircraft performance and tactics to provide realistic combat training for Allied fighter units throughout Europe. My A-10s, as previously noted, established a presence from far north to deep south at our four forward operating locations spread the length of Germany, and all seven squadron commanders (lieutenant colonels with the *second*-best job in the Air Force) reported directly to me. Not wishing to be coarse, but this whole scenario rendered me happier than a pig in shit.

Chapter Sixteen

The Overseas Fighter Wing

The military organizational set-up is certainly as complex as but radically different from a similar medium-sized company. The 81st Wing, for example, had a 'workforce' of approximately 5,000 to 6,000 if you count the wing's personnel at the German detachments. Add to that the families ('dependants' in military jargon) and local civilian employees and presto! You have a rather substantial 'company' and town. (Please don't hold me to these numbers; happily, meticulous human resource bean-counting was among Commander Tad's responsibilities.) Every Air Force unit completely recycles all its personnel – from the commander to the most junior Airman Basic – over a two- to three-year period due to the Air Force's rotational assignment structure. Consequently, the concept of long-term continuity is virtually nonexistent. There is good news and bad news about this phenomenon. The good news is that there is a continuing process of injecting fresh ideas and concepts as decision-makers rotate in and out of the unit; the bad news is that the refreshed ideas and concepts are not always better than the ones they replaced and a fair amount of 'reinventing the wheel' is inevitable. Nevertheless, the military has been operating this revolving door system of leadership and management for many, many years and the units mostly keep delivering the goods. From a personal point of view, consider this: if you end up working for a tyrant or a clown, either you or he/she will be gone in, at most, a couple of years. Hell, most of us can manage that with our eyes closed.

There's a lot more to a fighter wing than you'll see in the movies. The tip of the sword is undeniably the Operations Directorate (mine, he said proudly), which encompasses the squadrons, pilots and their administrative roles. Additionally, Operations includes those functions which *directly* support the flying program: Command and Control, Operational Training, Intelligence, Plans and Programs, Personal Equipment (the technicians who maintain aviators' life-support gear of helmets and 'G'-suits). These direct support functions are many and varied.

Outside the flying operation, supplying and maintaining three or four (or in our case, seven) squadrons' aircraft is a herculean task in itself. This requires large numbers of personnel, the majority of whom are specialists: aircraft maintenance mechanics, propulsion specialists, armorers and munitions technicians, fuel and hydraulic experts, electricians, avionics technicians (who service the communications and specific weapons systems within the aircraft), egress technicians (who maintain ejection seats and equipment), and a separate group that maintains all the aviation ground equipment required by everyone listed above.

In addition to maintainers, as you might expect, a unit of this size supports an enormous supply and logistics organization and a small army of administrators, security police and the flying operation wouldn't get off the ground without air traffic controllers.

I'll apologize in advance because I'm sure I've neglected to mention a few key players (and I'll no doubt hear about it), but the intent is to illustrate, in a few broad paragraphs, the sheer size and scope of a modern fighter wing.

I should take a moment to recognize the challenge of bedding down all these people. The Air Force has long maintained a reputation for taking care of its folks. This is particularly important for an overseas unit where personnel and their families may find themselves in an unfamiliar environment including a language barrier (not strictly true in the UK, although deciphering a deep Suffolk twang could be considered a challenge).

The Air Force is renowned (and sometimes criticized) for 'taking America' to foreign shores. This aspect of Air Force life is expensive, complex and sometimes unappreciated by its beneficiaries but from a morale perspective is spectacularly successful. Large installations such as Ramstein and medium units like Bentwaters all share in offering a measure of home to personnel and their families stationed abroad. There are similar facilities on Stateside bases but to me these never had the impact of overseas locations in terms of providing a welcoming environment to those stationed abroad, so I'll limit this brief discussion to foreign installations.

Virtually every Air Force base will have a Base Exchange (department store) and a Commissary (supermarket). Large installations will have facilities of a size and scope rivaling commercial Stateside retail services, but small outposts may have little more than a convenience store that supplies a minimum measure of Americana and a taste of home. Resupply is facilitated by the Air Force's logistics machine and, in this age of the internet, goods can be ordered and delivered to even the most remote installations. Movie theaters, gymnasiums, bowling alleys, rod and gun clubs and even golf courses are not uncommon at substantial installations. All provide American-style recreation and entertainment for personnel and families. An important sidelight to the domestic facilities is the fact that they are usually staffed by local civilians, providing employment opportunities for the native population.

As time has gone by, commercial organizations have been brought on board by the military to provide even more touches of home. Despite the presence of excellent dining halls for the troops, there is no US military facility of any reasonable size today that doesn't have a contingent of fast food outlets: burger, chicken, pizza and taco joints to provide that extra little touch of Americana.

Large units will normally have comprehensive medical facilities: first-rate hospitals, dental care, and family health services and schools, from kindergarten through high school, administered by contracted American faculty. Years ago, education of dependants revolved around hub schools in certain countries. For example, when my Dad was first stationed in England, at RAF Alconbury in Huntingdonshire, there was only one American high school in the UK: Central High School, Bushy Park, London. Those of us from the provinces climbed on a bus every Sunday and made the trip to London where we boarded in converted open bay barracks, slept in bunk beds, studied very little, and managed to spend most of our time causing various levels of trouble. We came home on Friday for the weekend and the cycle started again on Sunday afternoon. In 1961, a brand-new American high school was opened at RAF Lakenheath, near Cambridge and as Alconbury was fairly close, I transferred there for my junior year. Despite a quantum leap in creature comforts, the weekly trek remained the same. As we were still youthful, under-supervised and over-enthusiastic, the borderline delinquency continued unabated. Nevertheless, the vast majority of us completed our encounter with the Department of Defense school system with a better-than-average learning experience and without acquiring criminal records. I attended five high schools in four years; a true test of flexibility. Nevertheless, to this day I'll defend the experience as a positive one overall.

The point of the last few pages was a brief excursion into the family environment the Air Force fighter pilot normally inhabits during peacetime. Naval aviators spend lengthy tours away from the nest on carriers in far-flung waters which has both positive and negative aspects. While they are able to focus entirely on the job without distractions of domestic complications, the comforts of home and the warmth and closeness of the family unit are completely out of reach. Today, the internet, Skype and other social media have taken some of the edge off this issue, but the military is, as always, a challenge for all its families.

Chapter Seventeen

Command and Senior Rank:
Good News and Bad News

M y new job as Director of Operations was, quite honestly, further up the food chain than I ever expected to be. In my younger days, I watched a number of colleagues whose obsessions with promotion and advancement resulted in clear confirmation of the old proverb 'All work and no play makes Jack a dull boy.' In essence, some of my fellow fighter pilots lost the facility to 'smell the roses' as they progressed and became somewhat obsessive about chasing assignments that would look good on their promotion records. Dumb fighter pilot that I was, I was just as obsessive about avoiding the Pentagon and Major Command staff jobs that were touted as 'career broadening steps', and energetically pursued positions that kept me in fighter cockpits far away from Big Gray Desks. Despite not being able to demonstrate a propensity for shifting from one high-profile staff job to another, I continued to be pleasantly surprised when my name appeared on promotion lists for major, then lieutenant colonel.

When I found myself promoted to full colonel, I noticed that some contemporaries who had been among the good guys as captains and majors had developed a disturbing condition known as 'stars in their eyes' when promoted to positions of leadership. Their aggressive pursuit of general's stars somehow robbed them of flexibility, a sense of humor and the ability to empathize with those junior to them who still retained those traits. This affliction didn't affect all of my associates by any stretch of the imagination, but it was common enough that I began to see disappointing characteristics emerging in some of my old buddies. In some cases, this forced me to be very wary in my relationships with them for fear of political repercussions. This depressing state of events is not, of course, limited to the domain of the Air Force officer (or certainly not that of the senior fighter pilot). Indeed, it is found in industry, in government, and even in charities, hospitals and church groups, but that doesn't make it any more palatable.

The other (and most disappointing) aspect of leadership was loss of the coveted status known as being 'one of the boys'. Rank may have its privileges, but it also sports a few detriments, one of which is a subtle but very noticeable loss of trust among the brethren. This phenomenon, like the politicization mentioned above, exists in virtually every walk of life where there are bosses and work forces but I would submit it is more upsetting in a military environment due to the closeness of the relationship, on and off the job, between war-fighters.

The cooling of relationships between line pilots (lieutenants, captains and majors) and their commanders and supervisors (lieutenant colonels and above) may well have a linkage with the 'stars in their eyes' syndrome. Rightly or wrongly, the bosses may be perceived as selling out the troops through decisions that they probably wouldn't have made in years gone by; decisions which may have, or could appear to be made, to enhance the Boss's standing and/or gain favor with the Boss's superiors. Undeniably there is some of this – perhaps more than I'd like to admit – but I'd like to think that, in vastly more cases, the culprit in these situations is an imbalance of information. The Boss normally has more of this at his disposal than the irate lieutenant/captain/major and the decision often must be made without the Boss being able to share this excess information with those ultimately affected.

The only way for the Boss to combat this insidious loss of trust was, in many ways, out of his hands. As mentioned many pages ago, the secret ingredient is to provide 'leadership so powerful as to earn unconditional loyalty'. In the world of fighter pilots, considerable skill in the cockpit was a pre-requisite for establishing respect. The colonel who couldn't hold his own in the air was at a serious disadvantage in establishing credibility among his group.

I once had a deputy who really didn't like to fly, probably because he wasn't very good at it. The troops picked this up immediately and behind his back he was known as the Seagull (because he was interfering and annoying and you had to throw rocks at him to make him fly). I couldn't openly support this abuse of my number two, of course, but I cannot in all good faith say I disagreed with the evaluation. The Seagull finally extinguished himself in my eyes when he came into my office one afternoon, threw a tantrum because I wouldn't authorize his leave when he wanted to take it, and told me he was quitting. I suspect it astonished him when my response was 'OK, great; clear out your office before you leave today.'

I called my Boss, Roger Carleton, the wing commander (Oelstrom's successor and one of the good guys), told him what had happened and that I had no problem soldiering on without the Seagull (who had, in all fairness, become an albatross around my neck). We agreed that I would immediately begin recruiting a new deputy. That recruitment was well under way when I got a call from Carleton advising that politics had reared its ugly head and *his* Boss, a two-star general, was displeased that his fair-haired boy was getting the heave-ho and wanted the decision reversed. Despite my protests the reversal occurred, of course, and I was stuck with the Seagull, but he was relegated to a role slightly less influential than the office furniture.

Apologies for that brief diversion. Even more important than stick-and-rudder expertise was the ability to empathize and to listen. I learned far more from troops with a few beers under their belts at the 'O' Club Happy Hour on Friday evenings than I ever picked up in the numerous staff meetings I attended on a regular basis. Human nature dictated that most of the pilots under my command wouldn't approach me with anything contentious or negative, even at the bar, but there were always a few who dared to speak up when they perceived something was unfair or inappropriate or downright senseless. Some of this was simply idle bitching about how the imagined 'they' were running the Air Force, and of course I had precious little influence on these high-level mismanagement issues. On the other hand, there were one or two of my squadron commanders and ops officers who risked their Officer Efficiency Report (OER) ratings to graphically (but always diplomatically) point out issues that were clearly within my purview or those that I was personally screwing up. These were the guys I learned the most from and whose counsel often resulted in improvements in how we did the job. Believe me, their efficiency evaluations only improved as a result of their willingness to be candid.

Chapter Eighteen

Flying Safety is Paramount

robably the most common thread of Happy Hour counsel was firmly focused on safety. The Air Force takes flying safety *very* seriously. Not only are many millions of dollars invested in aircraft and associated hardware, but those of us lucky enough to operate this equipment constitute an even greater investment. This includes funding the best training in the world and also in a more personal sense: the fighter pilot fraternity comprises the warrior cadre and you cannot put a price on a deceased member of this corps.

Incidents and accidents at all levels are vigorously investigated and a minor aircraft mishap that might be classed as a fender-bender in a road haulage firm will be pursued relentlessly; not intentionally to assess individual blame but to determine if there is a 'fixable' cause that could preclude recurrence.

Bumper 'Hogs

Once again, I'm digressing to discuss an incident that occurred some years earlier to set the stage for the flying safety discussion to follow. One of my instructors at the Weapons School had an accident which for a while looked like it might bring a promising career to an end. Doc Pentland was returning from a mission and, as he taxied into his parking bay in the midst of a long line of parked A-10s, his nose wheel abruptly deflected and despite immediately braking, he was unable to avoid colliding with the aircraft to his left. The damage was more than superficial, less than colossal, but represented a substantial repair effort and two A-10s that would not be available to fly for some time.

To a pilot, any accident is anathema, but a *taxi* accident is the most loathsome of all because the vast majority of these fall into the category that spreads icy fingers of terror over your heart: the dreaded 'pilot error'.

As the incident involved one of my troops and two of my airplanes, I had been scrambled to the scene and met Doc as he came down the ladder. Employing my best investigative approach, I posed the astute analytical question: 'What the hell happened?' Doc shook his head, gave me a dejected USAFE salute and replied: 'I don't know, Boss, the nose wheel snapped left without warning. I hit the brakes but the next thing I knew it was sideswipe time.'

Nose gear steering (NGS) on most fighters is electrically activated by a button on the control stick. Once activated, pushing the rudder pedals right or left swivels the nose gear hydraulically and the aircraft turns gently. Once a straight path lies ahead (such as taxiing into a parking bay), NGS is deselected, the nose gear centers and the aircraft continues straight ahead. This delicate end of the mission is performed at less than a man's walking speed. Nevertheless, a 28,000lb A-10 veering as a result of a hard–over nose gear will be difficult or impossible to stop within a very few feet. Mass times acceleration; thank you, Isaac Newton.

Aircraft accidents and incidents have a way of drawing very senior people to the scene. If the 'fixable' cause involves failures in command and/or control, the ramifications can escalate to much higher levels very quickly. Indeed, it is possible for heads to roll if the investigation reveals a serious lapse in leadership or management. This explains why, very shortly after my arrival on scene, the two-star commander of the Tactical Fighter Weapons Center at Nellis pulled up in his very shiny staff car. He took one brief look at two scraped and dented A-10s and immediately determined that Doc was the guilty bastard and should be, at the very least, summarily executed. Sometimes the objective of the AF Accident program 'not intentionally to assess individual blame' gets forgotten in the heat of the moment.

I accept this would not be an unreasonable knee-jerk conclusion to draw, but knowing my instructor as I did, I was not quite so quick to arrive at the same conclusion. I had to ground Doc temporarily (this is common practice for anyone involved in an accident or incident), but I remained unconvinced and enlisted the aid of a friend in the Test and Evaluation Squadron who had very close ties with the maintenance side of the house.

It wasn't quick and it wasn't easy, but we persuaded the maintainers to run some very exhaustive tests on the NGS electrical and hydraulic systems, above and beyond the routine checks that normally would have been made following an incident of this magnitude. Long story short, it was one of these additional assessments that exposed a chain of events resulting in a rogue electron causing precisely the hard-over nose gear situation that had bitten Doc. Gremlins like this are not uncommon in aircraft and some, like this one, go undiscovered for years. The point is that isolating the fault enabled the maintainers to eliminate it for future flyers and oh, by the way, deftly removed the albatross from Doc's neck. Win-win.

Doc's incident, albeit personally traumatic for him, was at the bottom of the safety totem pole. No one was injured and damage was comparatively light. At the other end of the spectrum comes the fatal accident. The loss of an aircrew member and his aircraft sits right at the top of priorities. Entire fleets are grounded if maintenance or aircraft performance is suspected and no human factor's stone is left unturned in investigating every possible aspect of a fatality. The following is an example of the process as I lived it and a return to the chronological flow.

Major Aircraft Accident Investigation: The Air Force Way

As Director of Operations at Bentwaters, I was in the enviable position of being able to cherry-pick the missions I flew. I simply dropped a hint to Jackie, my favorite (and the world's finest) secretary and she made it happen, every time.

So there I was, on a crisp, cold February morning, leading a flight of four A-10s to the gunnery range at Wainfleet in the Wash area in south-eastern England. We'd been airborne for less than a half hour when very faintly we picked up the most chilling transmission there is: 'Mayday, Mayday', followed by a garbled message that was incomprehensible due to the fact that we were at low level and apparently some distance from the transmitting aircraft. I advised Air Traffic Control (ATC) we were climbing and took the flight up to a medium altitude where we would be more likely to hear further transmissions and lend any assistance. Nothing was heard and we continued towards the gunnery range.

About ten minutes later we got a call from ATC: 'Hog 01, you're directed to RTB (Return to Base) immediately.' I responded: 'Is that order for the flight or just Hog 01?' 'Just you, Sir,' she replied. I handed control of the flight over to my deputy lead and broke away to head for home. I remember thinking 'I don't know what this is about, but I'm pretty sure it's not going to be pleasant.' This was to be one of the great understatements of my career.

I landed uneventfully at Bentwaters a few minutes later and was met by the Wing Flying Safety Officer, who plugged a headset into the aircraft and briefed me on the situation (not something you want to discuss on an open radio frequency). An A-10 from the 10th Tac Fighter Wing, our sister wing at RAF Alconbury, near Cambridge, had crashed while doing low-level training in South Wales. There was precious little information available but the pilot, Captain Rob Burrowes (better known by his nickname, Brad), was dead and it was his wingman who had made the initial Mayday call.

The reason for my summons? The wheels were already turning to assemble an Accident Investigation Board and the president of that board had to be a full colonel, currently qualified in the accident aircraft type, but assigned to a unit other than the accident wing. I furtively looked around and didn't see anyone else in the vicinity that met those requirements. Despite the fact that I was just getting my feet under the Ops Director desk and Elaine and I were up to our ears in moving into our new home, there was no question of quibbling here. I was 'It' and this was an entirely new challenge.

The fact that the board president had been selected before the smoke had even cleared from the wreckage indicated that assembly of the investigation team was a smooth and practiced process. Within hours the team structure began to fall into place. I would be commanding a group of officers and senior NCOs whose specialties covered every conceivable aspect of a major aircraft accident. My investigating officer was named as Captain Glen 'Sammy' Samels, a graduate of the Flying Safety Course I would have attended had I not been selected for the Fighter Weapons Instructor Course years before. He turned out to be a font of all knowledge in terms of investigative issues. I was assigned a maintenance officer, Captain Troy Childs, a tall, lanky and very talented young officer unceremoniously plucked from his flight line supervisory duties in one of our Aircraft Maintenance Squadrons. I also had a flight surgeon, Major John Mayer, whose responsibility would be forensic investigation of the remains and contributing physiological and psychological factors. There was an NCO from the Contracting Squadron, the man I went to for acquisitions and expenditures, a communications specialist, plus a number of administrators to handle the inevitable comprehensive and lengthy reports that would be generated as the investigation progressed.

In addition to the key players noted above, I was going to need significant extra people power for the most distressing element of the investigation, evidence collection. Aside from substantial pieces of the aircraft which would be retrieved by Air Force salvage teams equipped with heavy equipment, my team would have to identify and document smaller items of evidence, including lesser aircraft fragments and, unnervingly, body parts. More about that to come, but my organization provided me with thirty to forty junior enlisted troops to round out the investigation team. I can't speak highly enough about these young people; their task was about the least gratifying I can think of, yet they approached it with a dedication that impressed me greatly. Perhaps this was because the assignment was a bit out of the ordinary and therefore something of an adventure, but I like to think that in some way they wanted to show their respect to a departed flyer.

The next few days were a blur. To ensure transparency and eliminate any hint of partiality, a major accident investigation is always carried out by a unit not involved in the mishap. Nevertheless, I was going to be leaning on the 10th TFW for much of the initial evidence we would have to gather. Just as I had been plucked out of the sky to direct the process, I was immediately assigned a 10th TFW pilot to represent the wing's leadership and also to provide a vital link with the squadron members and other locals who would contribute to the effort. In this respect I was, once again, very, very lucky. My pilot officer, as he was officially known under the terms of the investigation, was Captain John 'Conley' Condon. I knew him socially and liked him very much, and as the investigation progressed, he was to become my right-hand man.

As some evidence is extremely perishable, the 10th Wing was responsible for collecting some of the vital human evidence we would rely on. The day after the 10th Wing commander, chaplain and medical representative had taken their stressful Blue Sedan journey to the home of the deceased pilot, another equally disturbing visit took place. This one was led by the wing's flying safety officer, accompanied by a medical representative (psychologist), the chaplain (who had been requested), and a fellow squadron pilot and close friend of the deceased and his family. This was perhaps even more challenging than the initial notification as it required a diplomatic but thorough conversation with the widow and family members to establish a history of the deceased in the day or days leading up to the accident. What had the officer been doing in the seventy-two hours prior? Was he physically well? Had he self-medicated for any minor illnesses? This was extremely important. Within the letter of the law an aviator was forbidden to take any form of medication that hadn't been prescribed by the flight surgeon. There isn't a man among us who hasn't popped a cold tablet or snorted an antihistamine to maintain our precious flying status when we felt slightly under the weather. Nevertheless, the question had to be asked and answered.

What had Brad eaten and drunk? Was he under any obvious stress? Had there been any family disagreements or arguments that might have affected his frame of mind? Had he slept well? You get the picture. It was a very intrusive but necessary interrogation conducted by supportive professionals for the purpose of collecting vital evidence. Although traumatic in every respect, the visit produced numerous pieces of the puzzle.

The next step was a reconstruction of the fatal flight. John Condon and I held extensive interviews with the surviving wingman, Greg Johnson, a young lieutenant, new to the squadron. Our discussions covered everything we could think of, from Brad Burrowes' frame of mind on the morning to the thoroughness of his briefing and his performance as the flight leader up until the accident occurred. We also went through every element of the flight from start/taxi/take-off. We learned a great deal from this interview. There had been clear blue sky above 2,000 or 3,000ft but the low-level weather had deteriorated gradually as the flight proceeded westbound towards the designated low flying area in south Wales. Typically the low-lying clouds had obscured the valleys and hilltops in the area known as the Black Mountains.

Armed with the data captured in our discussion with the wingman, John and I briefed to fly the exact same profile in order to re-enact the events of a few days previously right up to the moment of impact. Hopefully, we would gain valuable insight into the anatomy of the accident.

The weather for our reconstruction was forecast to be much better than it had been on the day of the accident. We departed RAF Alconbury and headed west at medium altitude with Conley in the lead, assuming the role of Brad Burrowes. I maintained a loose, comfortable route formation until we approached the let-down point into the published UK Low Flying system. We advised Air Traffic Control we were transitioning to VFR (Visual Flight Rules; with no ATC control or monitoring service) and I dropped into a 'Fighting Wing' formation, a flexible, maneuverable position behind and offset from my leader. This formation was the same as Lieutenant Johnson had flown on the day of the accident. This allowed me to keep Conley in sight, maneuvering as necessary to maintain spacing and visually cover the flight's '6 o'clock' (rear quadrant).

South Wales' LFA (Low Flying Area) 7 was a popular destination for Warthog drivers seeking the delights of ultra-low-level flight for very good reason. Even in February, its rolling hills and narrow valleys were covered in a lush green carpet and presented a stimulating challenge to pilots at a legal 250ft AGL (Above Ground Level).

On the day of the accident, Lieutenant Johnson had followed procedures to the letter. He followed Brad down to low altitude in his fighting wing position, but lost visual contact because Brad had entered thick but intermittent clouds in the descent. He made a radio call: 'Skull Two is lost wingman' alerting his leader that he was no longer in formation. He then pulled up and away from Brad Burrowes' flight path and began a slow orbit above the clouds waiting for him to reappear. Instead, he observed a thick column of black smoke rising up through the cloud cover and made the unsettling distress call on the emergency UHF frequency: 'Mayday, Mayday. Salty 01 is down 9 miles north-north-west of Abergavenny. Salty 02 is squawking Emergency for location.' (He switched his transponder beacon to code 7700 to aid air traffic control in triangulating the position.)

Within a very short period of time, the area was swarming with police, fire crews, ambulances and the RAF's Mountain Rescue Team.

Air Rescue forces had arrived from RAF St Athan near Cardiff by Sea King helicopter within minutes of the accident. After hovering for some time waiting for the clouds to clear sufficiently, they located the aircraft wreckage and determined the pilot had not survived. As the actual crash location was uninhabited, police were dispatched to secure the area and preserve the wreckage and all potential evidence. All these actions were completed within three hours of impact and, due to the predictable arrival of the media, even the local red telephone box was designated off limits to the public with a policeman stationed outside.

On the day of our reconstruction, the weather was superb with unrestricted visibility and we began the same low-level route that ended in tragedy only a few days earlier. Following a script derived from our discussions with Brad's wingman, Conley continued his descent into a series of parallel valleys. At a pre-briefed point I replicated losing sight of him as he continued his course at 250ft. I called 'Salty Two, simulated lost wingman' and started a loose orbit. I watched as Conley continued his flight path and we were both horrified to see that the charred point of impact was only a few feet below the crest of a relatively steep incline at the far end of a gently rising valley. The crash site was so close to the summit that both engines had torn away from their fuselage mounts on impact and continued their trajectory for hundreds of meters straight ahead on to the meadow at the end of the valley.

There would be far more analysis to be done in the days ahead, but Conley and I had no doubt that we had lost a talented young man by a matter of a few vertical feet.

Our investigation was comprehensive and time-consuming. We rented an entire hotel in nearby Abergavenny to house and feed a large team. Except for the hardiest of walkers, Abergavenny in February is not a thriving hub for tourists. Consequently, we had little difficulty getting all our people settled together and the hotelier was delighted to accommodate us. The locals treated us wonderfully and living among them for what would turn out to be more than six weeks was a great experience.

It was only 8 miles as the crow (or 'Hog) flies from our hotel to the crash site, but each day's journey was an adventure taking between forty-five minutes and an hour plus on the narrow, twisting roads of the Black Mountains. This commute was complicated periodically by snowfall and driving rain. We'd set up a headquarters (military jargon for a tent) at the base of the valley, and established communications links; remember, this was pre-mobile phone era and our internal comms were based on walkie-talkies. We had dozens of them along with the cumbersome chargers to go with them and generators to power the chargers. Air Force communications teams quickly set up a rudimentary telephone exchange to keep us in contact with the outside world. Our HQ looked like a Second World War movie bunker.

Although virtually all my troops had already brought government-issue cold weather gear with them, there was one item the Air Force doesn't provide as standard issue: Wellington boots (or 'Wellies' in the British vernacular) for working in cold wet weather. I sent my contracting guy out to source some suitable footwear and he came back with the kind of one-size-fits-all rubber galoshes your kid would wear going out to play in the snow. He'd barely started talking about the good deal he could get when I spun him around and pointed at one of the local farmers who had been helping us set up. This old fellow was wearing an ancient pair of Aigle Wellies that had obviously weathered the Welsh climate for more years than my contracting NCO had been alive. I told my guy to get a list of sizes from the troops and go find a pair for every member of the team. The good deal evaporated as he located a source for just over $100 a pair (this is 1990, remember), but I was confident we wouldn't be looking at frostbite or trench foot in the weeks ahead.

I organized our teams into sections and we started the arduous task of identifying evidence. We climbed to the point of impact (a minor ordeal in itself) and started combing the area near the flight path for anything metallic, plastic, glass or indeed human remains, much like a police force beating the bushes for evidence one step at a time. When such material was discovered, a flag (yellow for aircraft; red for tissue or body parts) was planted so the appropriate specialists could collect the evidence. The pilot's body had been located strapped in his ejection seat, but less than completely intact, so when one of my young searchers asked for me on the walkie-talkie I was crestfallen but not completely surprised to be shown a flying boot which still contained a foot.

As time went on, we had hundreds of flags to attend to, and within a few days the forensic techies had arrived. These experts were civilian contractors who specialized in evaluating evidence from major accidents (aircraft and otherwise), and drawing some very compelling conclusions from tiny fragments to major parts. Some examples:

- The engine and instrument specialists looked at the turbine blades (found a few hundred meters beyond the point of impact), throttle positions and the point at which the instrument needles smacked against the glass at impact to determine both engines were running properly and at full power when the aircraft hit the ground
- Flight control experts examined the rudder, ailerons, elevators and stick positions and movements to conclude that the pilot had, at the very last instant, pulled the stick abruptly aft in a futile attempt to climb, implying he had seen or sensed his impending collision with the ground
- Human factors forensic specialists combined data from the post-mortem and evaluation of evidence found at the site to establish that the pilot had been looking straight ahead with his feet on the rudder pedals, left hand on the throttles (which were full forward) and right hand on the stick at impact.

Don't ask me how they came up with their conclusions, but they were sound and rational and had the clear support of the senior staff who would be making the final judgment on the outcome of our investigation. Suffice to say, I was dazzled by their skill and proficiency.

It took most of the month for my team to complete their gloomy task and I can't praise them enough; day after day spent foraging for aircraft parts and human tissue up a steep slope in bitter cold, snow and rain. This was not a pleasant experience, but there was one incident that I will remember fondly for the rest of my days.

We were about three weeks into the task and the day was, as most of them were, bitterly cold with freezing fog and drizzle. I'd just finished my gourmet lunch compliments of the Air Force, a spaghetti MRE (Meal, Ready to Eat), I think it was, when a call came over the walkie-talkie: 'Sir, we've detained a civilian in the restricted area. Can you come and deal with it, please?'

My transportation guys had come up with a couple of 4-wheel-drive all-terrain vehicles (ATV) for those instances when walking up the hill for an hour wasn't practical. I climbed aboard and headed for the scene of the incursion. When I arrived, I found a Security Policeman (SP) with an M16 weapon which, to his credit, he wasn't pointing at a tiny Welsh lady, obviously in her 80s, and a small boy of 9 or 10 who was carrying a bunch of flowers. Somehow they had eluded the numerous British and USAF security types who were maintaining a cordon around the site.

'Can I help you, Ma'am?' I said. She was obviously distressed at being apprehended by a young military policeman with a weapon and said, very quietly: 'We're all aware of the accident in the village. We know the young man who died was here to defend us and my grandson and I just wanted to pay our respects.'

I thought, very briefly, about sternly advising her of the vast importance of site security and preserving vital evidence for the very significant investigation we were conducting, but somehow, when I started talking, it came out as

'Ma'am, I'm very proud to meet both you and your grandson and we are most grateful for your condolences. This Security Policeman is going to drive you both to the crash site. Take as much time as you like and, when you are ready, he's going to drive you home. Thank you and the boy for coming here today.'

I gave the keys to the SP (who saluted smartly), and started the long walk back to our HQ tent, suddenly feeling very good about the events of the day. The young lad's flowers were still in evidence at the crash site when we packed up and terminated the on-site investigation a week or so later.

The culmination of any accident investigation is generating a report based on all the evidence collected and briefing this report at Major Command Headquarters. In my case, this was HQ United States Air Forces Europe (USAFE) at Ramstein, Germany. There is nothing that commands the attention of senior officers more than a fatal aircraft accident and our report and my briefing would be scrutinized by every general officer in the operational arm of the headquarters from the four-star commander on down. Consequently, my ability to draft a comprehensive chronicle of the events of 7 February and present it convincingly was likely to seal my professional fate for the foreseeable future.

I gave my senior team a week to get the report together. We convened at Ramstein, commandeered an empty office and got to work. Joining me on this project were John Condon, my pilot officer, and Sammy Samels, flying safety officer, along with my maintenance officer, Troy Childs, and flight surgeon, John Mayer.

We had all been coordinating throughout the investigation and our conclusions were very solid: Brad Burrowes was a talented and capable young fighter pilot who, on the day, made a monumental and fatal error in judgment and flew up a valley he had not intended to take into the top of a steeply-inclined hill. He failed to maintain visual references that would have saved him and the aircraft he was flying. The autopsy showed that he had a 'therapeutic' level of an over-the-counter cold medication in his bloodstream. This meant the drug was doing what it was supposed to do and had not been taken to excess. Nevertheless, self-medication was against the rules and this was technically a minor black mark against him.

My briefing added great volumes of documentation based on our findings and the evidence presented from numerous sources. I wanted very much to try to accentuate the positive, if that was possible. This was, after all, a skillful and proficient young man who made a mammoth mistake which cost him his life.

I'd lost a fair amount of sleep worrying about the final report and presentation, but fortunately the generals readily agreed with our assessment and signed off the report with little additional comment. I breathed a sigh of relief and happily went back to my day job at Bentwaters.

Chapter Nineteen

The Idyllic Cruise that Wasn't

In late July of 1990, following the accident investigation, Elaine and I decided it was time for a break so we embarked on a fifteen-day cruise on the Baltic to wind down and blow away some cobwebs. I won't belabor the itinerary, but we were able to visit Copenhagen, Gdańsk in Poland, Tallinn in Estonia, Riga in Latvia and St Petersburg in Russia, returning to Stockholm en route home to the UK. The Berlin Wall had tumbled, the winds of change were gusting and the decline of the Soviet Union was apparent wherever we disembarked. We saw a recently-toppled statue of Lenin in Tallinn and a small flotilla of tethered, neglected Russian submarines in St Petersburg. It was fascinating to meet people who were obviously itching to celebrate getting rid of the Soviet yoke but were slightly hesitant to talk about it publicly.

Despite this sluggish decay in Russia's neighborhood, other parts of the world were threatening to ignite. On 2 August, Iraq invaded Kuwait and the US rushed to assemble a coalition to counter the incursion. We were lounging on the deck of the good ship *Victoria*, blissfully unaware of all this frantic activity (no cell phones, no English language news and certainly no onboard internet). I remember picking up a discarded newspaper whose headline trumpeted the rapid build-up of allied forces, and involuntarily blurted out the fighter pilot catchphrase: 'Shit!' I left Elaine soaking up the sun and headed for the bridge, where I hoped to find some world-class communications equipment and tell my boss I was on the way back. I had distressing visions of my legions of Warthogs launching to join the burgeoning coalition while I was sipping a cold beer on the *Victoria*'s poop deck. This was not the kind of leadership I wanted to provide. My fighter pilot ego kicked in and there was absolutely no doubt in my mind that the wing's participation in Operation DESERT STORM would fail miserably without me at the helm.

The *Victoria* had spacious, comfortable staterooms, sparkling entertainment, good food and a seemingly inexhaustible stock of booze, but her communications capability sucked. I spent the entire day trying to establish a ship-to-shore link with my command post at Bentwaters without success and Elaine had to put up with one seriously ill-tempered travelling companion.

It was another day before we docked in Stockholm and I was able to get through to the 81st Wing command post. The conversation left me even more exasperated than my previous inability to establish contact. During the past forty-eight hours, the bright sparks in the Pentagon had decided to ignore the substantial Air Forces stationed in Europe, a stone's throw from the impending action. Instead, they would deploy a massive armada of US-based aircraft thousands of miles to the Gulf while combat-ready units like mine were forced to watch them go by. In essence, we had been relegated to bridesmaid status. Instead of leading a wing of skillful, motivated professionals into battle, my mission would be to boost the sagging morale of scores of disenchanted fighter pilots dying to get into the fray.

Chapter Twenty

The Peace Dividend

As my Bentwaters tour came to an end in 1992, the free world was watching the demise of Russian domination in Eastern Europe. This was evidenced by destruction of the Berlin Wall in 1990 and Dissolution of the Warsaw Pact as well as the signing of the Strategic Arms Reduction Treaty (START) in 1991. Soviet Union President Mikhail Gorbachev resigned and Russia formally recognized the end of the Soviet Union in December 1991.

Presto! The world was safe for democracy and the US government responded in character by rapidly beginning to dismantle major elements of the US military machine around the world. High on the accountants' hit list were combat units which, by virtue of our triumph over Communism, had become nothing more than a massive drain on the coffers and, as determined by the whiz kids in lofty governmental places, would never be needed again.

The 81st Wing at Bentwaters/Woodbridge was prioritized on the hit list and the wheels began turning to decommission this proud organization early in 1993. As much as I regretted giving up the best job I'd ever had, there were a couple of noteworthy mitigating factors that took much of the sting out of leaving.

Firstly, a new wing commander had been selected to oversee the shutdown of the wing. I'd never met Roger Radcliffe (aka 'Ramjet') so I'll refrain from passing personal judgment. I was literally on my way out when he took over from Roger Carleton, but in the very few brief meetings I had with him I quickly determined that it was my very good fortune not to remain within his regime.

With a lot of help from his two-star benefactor, my deputy, the Seagull, finally achieved his goal of becoming the Deputy Commander of Operations when I disappeared. I mention this only because my feeling of relief at not having to toil under the command of Colonel Ramjet was surpassed only by my pleasure in knowing that the Seagull would be shouldering that burden. The reports I received indicated that his tenure wasn't nearly as enjoyable as mine had been. I can only conclude the two of them deserved each other.

Chapter Twenty-One

Air Warrior: The Last Hurrah

As my tour as DO at Bentwaters drew to a close, I was resigned to the likelihood that my string of good fortune had probably run out and I would finish my Air Force career behind another Big Gray Desk pushing paper back and forth in some godforsaken headquarters. Once again, however, the spirits smiled in my direction and my long-time hero, now Major General Billy G. McCoy stepped in to bail me out. General McCoy had been my boss at 2 ATAF in Rheindahlen's Big House and had moved on to be commander of the US Air Force Tactical Fighter Weapons Center. Apparently, he'd been happy enough with my performance there to keep track of me and reached out to bring me back to 'the Home of the Fighter Pilot'. Believe me, there's no better place than Nellis AFB to close out over a quarter-century of strapping a fighter to one's butt. My final assignment would be as the commander of the 549th Joint Training Division (Air Warrior), a combat flying training organization dedicated to the art and craft of Close Air Support.

After twelve years of flying the Warthog, our premier close air support machine, I was still learning new tricks of the CAS trade when I left the Air Force. I'm now going to demonstrate my audacious nature by attempting to give you an elementary explanation (think *Cliffs Notes*) of this most multifaceted of missions, all in the next few pages. Please bear with me.

Close Air Support is defined, as simply as I can put it, as 'Air action by fixed- and rotary-wing aircraft against hostile targets that are in close proximity to friendly forces and that require detailed integration of each air mission with the fire and movement of those forces.'[1]

Our job at Air Warrior was to give the prime Army players an aviation dimension within which to practice the integration part of that definition. The pieces on the chess board comprised the massed might of battalion-sized armored units conducting their own realistic training.

These deployed Army units faced a dedicated opposing force (OPFOR), the 11th Armored (Blackhorse) Cavalry, elite 'armored aggressors', who employed Soviet formations and tactics against them at the Army's sprawling National Training Center (NTC), Fort Irwin, near Barstow, California, 190 miles south-west of Nellis.

Our visiting fighter units had the unique opportunity to act both as trainers and students simultaneously. Our aircraft served as training aids as we provided Close Air Support to the visiting Army brigades and battalions and our deployed pilots, in turn, soaked up the lessons from the most rigorous, focused and realistic close air support exercise in the world.

This was an excellent opportunity to provide training both to the fighter pilots and the army units. The coordination with these units was delivered by one of the units under my command: a Tactical Air Control Party (TACP) detachment manned by Air Liaison Officers (ALOs). I hand-picked Lieutenant Colonel Jim Nelson to run the show and, because of their unique role and the fact that he lived and worked with the Army at Fort Irwin for three years, he is either most grateful for the opportunity to command or cursing my parentage to this day. I've always been slightly reluctant to ask which.

The ALOs are among those fighter pilots who, through no fault of their own, are hauled out of the cockpit and thrust into an imbedded status with an Army combat unit. Their skill and expertise is crucial as they provide the communications and control linkages (yes, that *integration*) between the Army unit on the ground and the close air support aircraft they rely on to deliver firepower against the enemy. This often occurs in very close proximity to the good guys. A good call by an ALO often results in decimating the bad guys with air power, or at least keeping them at bay. On the other hand, an ALO miscalculation or poor decision can lead swiftly to a 'friendly fire' incident with all the horrors that entails.

Jim's ALOs were there to advise deployed ground commanders on the best use of air power, establish and maintain command and control communications, and provide precision terminal attack guidance of fixed-wing and rotary-wing close air support aircraft, and artillery. The aircraft we sent daily to support the good guys contacted our ALOs inbound to the target area and then, based on their eyes-on command and control and close-in attack guidance, simulated attacks against aggressor armored formations employing virtual bombs, missiles and bullets. This is not as cut and dried as it may sound: these were large-scale tank battles spread over miles of desert terrain and keeping track of friend and foe was not a simple proposition in a fast-moving scenario.

The good news was we had some serious technology to help us out. Air Warrior at this time boasted some of the most advanced learning tools on the planet. Each aircraft and each opposing tank and armored vehicle was fitted with a transmitter which data-linked every movement. In the case of the aircraft, every simulated weapons expenditure was tracked to provide an accurate, real-time panorama of the battle in progress. We could watch this unfold live in our debriefing theater or, more conveniently, record it and replay when the crews (air, ALO and armored) returned from the fray.

The number and quality of lessons learned through this feedback was simply awesome (and virtually impossible to renounce). For example, in every conflict there has ever been, there are examples of blue-on-blue (or friendly-fire) incidents. These are virtually all the result of battlefield confusion: visual target misidentification, imperfect communications, improper clearances and the like. Human nature being what it is, few culprits are quick to accept responsibility for these errors, even in a training environment, and consequently a definitive dialogue was rarely conducted. Our program took much of the guesswork out of evaluating a very complicated ground and air battle scenario.

Consider, if you will, the young fighter pilot who has just completed a demanding and stimulating sortie leading a flight against the OPFOR armored regiment. He's returned safely to Nellis and now, exhausted and sweaty but exhilarated by his performance, he settles back to watch the instant replay on a theater-sized screen in the Air Warrior Ops Building. Jim Nelson's on line to debrief the ALO's-eye view of the proceedings, as are senior armor commanders from the deployed armor battalion and the aggressor OPFOR Regiment.

Playback begins on the big screen in a presentation similar to (but far more detailed than) those you might have seen tracking airliners on an air traffic controller's station. Our protagonist's flight, presented as blue miniature aircraft icons, enters the area. Aircraft, ALO and brigade radio transmissions accompany the video production and each of the participating officers can add commentary as required. The inbound fighter flight coordinates with the ALOs who provide him with an abbreviated checklist, known as a nine-line briefing. This concise storyboard is designed to bring the flight up to speed on the battlefield situation and direct them into weapons delivery parameters against the OPFOR, whose tanks and other vehicles are depicted as moving red icons on the battlefield. The scope of the battle is impressive, with friendly armored forces (depicted as blue icons) maneuvering to counter the red force attack.

As the fighter flight obtains clearance and begins the attack run, something clearly goes wrong. The fighter icons overfly the (red) OPFOR targets and now are pointed directly at friendly (blue) armor. The ALO, having cleared the attack based on the situation as it originally presented, no longer has the aircraft in sight and is unaware that the attack is heading off-piste.

In the front row of the theater, the color drains from the blue flight lead's face as he watches himself press the attack against the friendlies. Simulated weapons releases are made and tracked on the screen and blue armor takes a number of lethal hits as a result of the attack.

What you've just read is a grossly over-simplified narrative of a hypothetical and tremendously complex scenario. Believe it or not, except for the horrible sinking feeling experienced by the flight leader as he watches his simulated ordnance rain down on friendly forces, this outcome is all good news. First and foremost, no one has been killed or injured. There are potentially dozens of reasons for the blue-on-blue (friendly-fire) engagement that has just taken place; miscommunication, misidentification, out-and-out task saturation to name but a few. The essential outcome is the ability to replay the incident, complete with recorded communications and commentary from those involved. This enables the participants and Air Warrior staff to dissect every action and arrive at a logical conclusion as to the contributing factors. As in the aircraft accident investigation discussed previously, the intent here is not to lay blame but rather to learn and apply those lessons in the future. If tactics or procedures are seen to be at fault, these can be modified and promulgated throughout the fighter/ALO communities to mitigate recurrence.

As for the hapless flight lead, he'll temporarily feel very, very dejected and guilty as his blue-on-blue attack was witnessed and noted by many, including his peers, and his self-esteem will take a sizeable hit. Nevertheless, none of these observers will take him to task as they realize on a different day it could very well have been any of them. He's just gone through the most public, direct and brutal debriefing there is, but at the end of the day, he's a fighter pilot, and that's how we learn tough lessons in this business. He'll be back in the saddle – chastened but a lot wiser – very soon and everyone who witnessed the 'incident' will have mentally filed away some most valuable lessons.

Training of this kind has come a long, long way from the days of dusty chalkboards and dependence on the short-term memories of the participants. It was a privilege to have been associated with this level of instruction. (Oh, and as a bonus, I managed to saddle up and fly these missions three or four times a week.) I couldn't have asked for a better swan song.

Champagne to Finish

It finally dawned: that day when one of those two really bad things happened to me and I had to walk out to the airplane knowing it was my last flight in a fighter. I had, to some extent, orchestrated my last hurrah, as I would simultaneously retire from the Air Force and pass the baton as Air Warrior Commander on the same day. A few days earlier I went to have a chat with the wing commander (Brigadier General Jack Welde who was not widely renowned for his compassion). I told him I'd spent all but about forty-five minutes of my career wearing a zippered green bag and thought it would be somewhat hypocritical to tart myself up for a ceremony in a set of Class 'A' Blues that didn't fit very well anyway. (The last time I wore them, Elaine had to staple the inseam together as an emergency repair.) I said I would like to retire in a flight suit in front of my Warthog immediately after my final (aka champagne) flight. To my great surprise, he agreed on both counts.

The day dawned and, because we at Air Warrior hosted guest flying squadrons and didn't possess our own 'Hogs, my good buddies at the Fighter Weapons School were happy to loan me four of their best, as long as they could participate.

I briefed the mission as a low-level ingress to the '70 series tactical gunnery ranges, north-west of Nellis. The aircraft were loaded with two AGM 65 'Maverick' TV-guided missiles, six Mk 82 General Purpose bombs and that awe-inspiring gun, chock full of a sparkling combat mix of armor-piercing and high-explosive incendiary ammunition. I cannot imagine a more lethal configuration. I was leading one of my Air Warrior guys, Major Andy Kleya, and two FWIC IPs (whose names elude me due to age and the passage of time). I won't elaborate on doing what fighter plots do: in a nutshell, we headed out to the gunnery range in tactical formation, and savaged numerous tactical targets with all those marvelous weapons. We then flew a Low Altitude Tactical Navigation route home at 100ft with my wingmen spread in a flexible fighting wing behind me (that's my story and I'm sticking to it). It was during this low-level leg that my mind wandered to something I always wanted to do as a fighter pilot. Unfortunately, there isn't a single bridge in the desert between the '70 Series gunnery ranges and Nellis, so flying under one was out of the question. I had to settle for a maneuver that always sent chills up my spine when I saw it in the movies as a kid. 'Hog flight, continue,' I directed on the radio, ensuring my wingies would not react to my next move.

I pulled the nose up abruptly and completed a smooth, deliberate victory roll over the three or four trailer dwellers residing in that part of the desert. It may not have been as elegant as a Spitfire or Mustang performing the same maneuver, but by God, it was exhilarating. I rolled out in the lead, pretty much where I started, and glanced in the mirrors. The boys hadn't budged and one of them couldn't resist a radio call: '*Gesundheit*,' he said, flippantly pardoning my appalling breach of discipline. 'I'm really gonna miss you guys,' I thought to myself.

I led my four 'Hogs to a VFR overhead pattern. Flying overhead the runway to an initial approach, I broke crisply away to a downwind leg, dropped the gear and flaps and requested a low approach followed by a departure end closed pattern over the Air Warrior building; a final opportunity to salute those who had gathered in a large marquee to witness the end of a flying career.

While my flight members landed, I pulled up over the building in a steep climbing turn, completing the closed pattern, reconfigured the bird for landing on downwind leg and made the obligatory gear check: 'Nellis tower, Warthog 01's base, gear, stop right…for the last time.' The response was crisp, professional and for me very poignant: 'Warthog 01, cleared to land runway 23 right…for the last time. Godspeed, Sir.'

I landed, taxied back, shut down, and kissed my wife (who had been escorted to the aircraft by General Welde). I accepted the flagon of bubbly he proffered; all three of us took a swig from the bottle and we shook hands. Had I simply been moving on to another assignment, I would have been treated to the traditional champagne flight celebration, which involved a thorough drenching by one of the flight line fire appliances. A combination of the retirement scenario and the fact that neither Elaine nor the Wing King would have appreciated the soaking precluded this foolishness and we were forced to maintain a certain level of dignity instead.

We proceeded to the marquee where dozens of friends and colleagues along with my dad and sister had congregated. A retirement, in the context of a fighter pilot, should be a combination of spontaneous sobriety supplemented with a reasonable measure of light-heartedness. This ceremony ticked these boxes very well, thank you. I suggested my guests should chat among themselves while I presented Elaine with another kiss and a flower arrangement. My memories of the details have faded, but the Boss provided a flattering speech about what a wonderful human being I was. I babbled a few words about how great it was to have spent my adult life as a fighter pilot, and I recall trying to recognize those with whom I had served by quoting a legendary philosopher – Tina Turner – whose song title *Simply the Best* seemed like an appropriate tribute to folks who were exactly that (I spared them the melody). Following the verbosity we all went to the bar for a long and enjoyable afternoon. I'm sure there are guys out there who had comparable Champagne Flight experiences, but I'll bet there aren't many of them.

In this book, as in life, there's always room for one more party. I'd flown the last flight and passed the baton to another commander, but there was no way I was going to depart without a celebration. In achieving this, my Air Warriors did me more than proud. Some 35 miles north-west of Las Vegas is Mount Charleston, rising 8,200ft above the desert and boasting a modest ski resort with an antiquated but welcoming hotel. They booked the entire hotel for a weekend and sent retirement invitations to just about everyone I'd ever worked with in the Air Force. We expected a moderate acceptance but the response was beyond any expectations and on the designated party evening, more than 200 guests joined us for drinking, dining and some of that debauchery and uninterrupted hell-raising I missed out on in pilot training. Elaine and I were, beyond a doubt, overwhelmed to greet friends we hadn't seen for years who had come from as far away as South Korea and the UK to help us celebrate.

The festivity included all the elements of camaraderie I will never experience as a private citizen. Swirling around us throughout the evening were mini-reunions of old friends who hadn't seen us or each other for many moons and as the man who was about to disappear, I soaked up vast quantities of flak from those who dredged up historic blunders and gaffes from my past. I loved every minute of it, but at the time didn't realize just how much I was going to miss it all.

Finally, gifts were bestowed. Many were humorous: my bullfighting injury certificate, for example, and the ubiquitous unit plaques, but one stands out to this day. Traditionally, retiring general officers are presented with a replica Sword of Excalibur, recognizing their service over the years. This trophy is normally unit-funded (and not cheap), so I was stunned and more than a little choked up when my Master Sergeant Senior Enlisted Advisor presented me with an Excalibur Sword secretly acquired by my maintenance and admin NCOs and airmen. It now hangs prominently on my wall as a symbol of the bond that exists between commander and those professionals that form the backbone of any successful organization.

I have no intention of becoming melodramatic in closing out these memoirs, but there are a few salient thoughts I want to leave you with. Over the span of nearly thirty years, through no great personal skill or cunning, I repeatedly found myself in the right place at the right time. Despite the ups and downs inherent in any lengthy career, I can think of precious little I would want to alter. I was privileged to serve with a brotherhood of professionals who shared my motivations and passions, my philosophy, my love of country and, not least, my commitment to squeezing as much enjoyment out of life as possible.

Now, more than fifty-two years after walking out to that bug-smashing Cessna T-41 for the first time, I contemplate all I've written in these pages and so much that I haven't and one single incident brings it totally into sharp focus: that was the day Brigadier General Mike Kerby asked me that Napoleonic question: 'Steve, are you lucky?'

To paraphrase my answer to him on that day, I've had the opportunity to lead (and follow) some of the most impressive human beings on the planet. You won't recognize their names; they never achieved fame or fortune but they believed in their profession and wrung every ounce of performance out of the aircraft they flew and the life they led. On the ground, they were flamboyant, irreverent and opinionated, while somehow remaining articulate and congenial. They were always my brothers. I struggle to remember a single day during which I did not learn something or achieve an objective, whether large or small. My life as a fighter pilot was rich, rewarding and devoid of boredom.

I spent almost my entire career in a flying squadron or fighter wing. These units are family: supportive, protective, devoted and fiercely protective of its members. They are also encumbered with typical family flaws: low-order politics, extreme competitiveness, petty jealousies and short bursts of internal aggression. Nevertheless, they are close-knit societies, bestowing friendship, social cohesion and gratification to their members. Having spent a number of years in 'Civvy Street' since leaving the Air Force, no one will ever persuade me there are groups of civilian co-workers that bond as comfortably and absolutely as fighter pilots/ aircrew and their significant others (only cops and firefighters might have a legitimate challenge to this declaration).

I am blessed with a partner who has supported me staunchly for the vast majority of my time in 'The Business'. My wife Elaine has been my best friend, my most dependable advisor and my rock for more than forty-seven years as I write this. She has weathered the storms and basked in the triumphs with me throughout my career and I cannot adequately express how grateful I am for her strength, wisdom and understanding but most of all, for just being my Elaine. After all these years, she still makes me laugh every day. Some weeks before I proposed, on a bench in Madrid's Retiro Park, I did the best I could to properly prepare her for a lifetime with a fighter pilot. 'We'll never be rich,' I told her, 'but you'll never want for anything either.' We aren't and we never have. Who could ask for more?

I'm occasionally asked which of the two fighter aircraft I flew was my favorite. A closer race there could never be, even though they were so very different in so many ways. The Phantom was raw power, noise and blinding speed, and the 'Hog was maneuverability, awesome firepower and perhaps the most challenging and rewarding mission of all. If you held a gun to my head and demanded an answer, I suppose the Phantom would win in a photo finish, but not because of the aircraft itself or anything performance-related. Papa said it best:

> You love a lot of things if you live around them, but there isn't any woman, and there isn't any horse, nor any before nor any after, that is as lovely as a great airplane, and men who love them are faithful to them even though they leave them for others. A man has only one virginity to lose in fighters, and if it is a lovely plane he loses it to, there his heart will ever be. (Ernest Hemingway, August 1944)

Was I lucky, General Kerby? Oh, yes sir, I was. Others may have equaled my long string of good fortune, but as far as I know, no one has surpassed it.

Gathering my thoughts to encapsulate this twenty-eight-year journey has been a splendid adventure, covering the spectrum from humor to tragedy and most everything in between. I could never have done it without my wife, Elaine, whose memory far surpasses my own and even those details we've disagreed on have brightened our lives and for a while, the years have rolled back in reminiscence. It was this sensation that resulted in the following passage jumping out at me, and I don't believe there's a better way to bring the curtain down:

> There is no such thing as an ex-fighter pilot.

> Once a young man straps on a jet aircraft and climbs into the heavens to do battle, it sears his psyche forever.

At some point he will hang up his flight suit – eventually they all do – and in the autumn of his years his eyes may dim and he may be stooped with age. But ask him about his life, and his eyes flash and his back straightens and his hands demonstrate aerial maneuvers and every conversation begins with 'There I was at...' and he is young again.

He remembers the days when he sky-danced through the heavens, when he could press a button and summon the lightning and invoke the thunder, the days when he was a prince of the earth and a lord of the heavens. He remembers his glory days and he is young again.[2]

Epilogue: Ode to the Missing Man ('Throw a Nickel on the Grass')

By Elaine Ladd

As a girlfriend, soon to be a bride, I was invited to go to the memorial service for Lieutenant Colonel Gerry Cashman and Captain Ron Bewley (see page 61).

One of the squadron wives picked me up in Madrid and took me to the base chapel at Torrejón Air Base. She explained that a missing man fly-by would take place and my fiancé Steve would be in the formation. As a total novice to American military ways, this was to be a sad and moving initiation into my future life as an Air Force wife. The sonnet reflects how I saw the missing man fly-by.

The four ship of Phantoms roars across the skies
Your heart skips a beat as onward it flies
Then, without warning, one jet peels away ...
All the way up and beyond without a say
Now the three ship continues the flight
Soaring onwards and upwards until out of sight
Then landing together with stoic concern
Three pilots stride to their squadron with so much to yearn
Now still together as if in formation
They reach in their pockets in sad resignation
Then in deep thought each throws a Nickel on the grass
Reverently meant to save a fighter pilot's ass
Quietly they linger with one man now missing
Knowing that somewhere he's seen them and listening

Photo credit: TSgt Rollan 'Yoke' Yocum

Appendix I

Glossary of Terms

Jargon, acronyms & abbreviations made easy

2ATAF	2nd Allied Tactical Air Force

A

Able Archer	German war-game exercise code name
Acoustiscore	Scoring device which "counts" passing bullets by sensing shock waves
ADIZ	Air Defence Identification Zone
AFB	Air Force Base
AFOQT	Air Force Officer Qualification Test
AFRES or 'Reserve'	Air Force Reserve
AFROTC	Air Force Reserve Officer Training Corps
Aggressors	Units that simulate adversary tactics and/or equipment
AGL	Above ground level
AGM	Air-to-Ground Missile
Ahlhorn	A-10 Forward Operating Location in Northern Germany
Air Warrior	World class close air support exercise at Nellis AFB
Aircraft Commander	Pilot in command
Air to ground gunnery	Dropping bombs and strafing
Ak-47	Semi-automatic weapon used extensively by Viet Cong
Alexanderplatz	Primary shopping area in East Berlin
Allied Powers	US, UK, and France
ALO	Air Liaison Officers
Altitude chamber	Simulator which replicates physiological issues linked to altitude
ANG or 'Guard'	Air National Guard
API	Armor piercing incendiary ammunition
Area 51	Highly classified Test and Evaluation site north of Las Vegas
Article 15	Nonjudicial or administrative punishment
Attached aircrew	Aviators whose primary job is administrative, but fly periodically
ATC	Air Traffic Control
Attitude Indicator	Primary flight instrument displays aircraft flight attitude
Autobahn	German high speed motorway

B

B-61	Designation of thermo–nuclear weapon carried by F-4
Balloon going up	Impending trouble or Initiation of hostilities
BAOR	British Army of the Rhine
Barrel Roll	Air interdiction campaign in northern Laos
Base Exchange	Military department store
Bat hanging	Extracurricular activity performed in the bar
Bears	Nickname for Wild Weasel Weapons Systems Operators
Berlin Wall or 'The Wall'	Built by East Germans to limit east/west access
Bermuda (or Devil's) Triangle	region in the western North Atlantic Ocean where a number of aircraft and ships are said to have disappeared under mysterious circumstances.
BFM	Basic Fighter Maneuvers
BGD	Big Gray Desk—the dreaded staff tour
Bible Belt	American South, known for religious zeal
Big House	Headquarters Building at Rheindahlen
Big Ugly	Nickname for the F-4
Black programs	Sensitive highly classified weapons development and tactics
Blue on Blue	Friendly Fire incidents
Blue sedan	Commander's staff car
Boelcke Wing	German fighter wing at Norvenich
Boom (refueling)	Metal conduit through which fuel passes from tanker to fighter
Brass monkey	Warning transmission to aircraft straying near the ADIZ
Bread van	Closed panel truck
brevet	Selected for promotion but not yet wearing the rank
BUF	Big Ugly Fucker (refers to B-52 heavy bomber)
Bug Smasher	Nickname for Cessna T-41 basic trainer aircraft
Bundespost	German postal system
BZ or CEBZ	Central European Buffer Zone

C

Cabbage Patch Dolls	Popular child's doll in 1980s
CABOOM	Clark Air Base Officers' Open Mess
Cam Ranh Bay	Vietnamese Air base used by USAF for F-4 fighter operations
CAS	Close Air Support
Checkpoints, Alpha, Bravo and Charlie	US entry points to East Germany, Berlin, and East Berlin in order
chocks	Inserted in front of wheels to keep aircraft from rolling
CIA	Central Intelligence Agency
Class 'A' uniform	USAF dress blue uniform
Class VI facility	Military liquor store
Cliff's Notes	Highly condensed book summaries & study guides
Close air support	Airborne weapons support of troops on the ground

Closed pattern	Tight abbreviated visual traffic pattern
coed	Female university student
Cold Duck	Horrible alcoholic drink
Cold War	a period of geopolitical tension between the 'Soviet Bloc', and the United States and its allies after the Second World War (1946-1991)
Command Post	Organization Operations and Communications center
Commissary	Military supermarket
Constant Peg	Structured training program versus exploited Mig aircraft
Cookie	Slang for sealed Top Secret codes used to authenticate launch orders
corridas de toros	bullfight
Court martial	Military Court
Crew chief (cc)	Aircraft maintenance specialist responsible for a specific aircraft
Crew dogs	Primary fighter pilots
Cross Country (XC)	a navigational training flight
Crud	Extracurricular activity performed in the bar
Cyrillic	Russian alphabet

D

DCS	Deputy Chief of Staff
D/M	Abbreviation for Davis Monthan AFB, Arizona
Danang	Vietnamese Air base used by USAF for F-4 fighter operations
Dave Barry	Humor feature writer for Miami *Herald* Newspaper
DD Form 214	Complete, verified record of a service member's time in the military
Dead Bug	Fighter pilot pastime
dependents	Military family members
Desert Storm	Code name for the Gulf War
Detachments (dets)	Supporting units geographically separate from the parent organization
Deutsche Bundespost	German Post Office
Deutschland	Germany
Deutschmarks	German currency – East and West Germany had separate currencies
DIA	Defense Intelligence Agency
DISTAFF	Directing Staff (for exercises or training organizations)
DNIF	Duty Not Involving Flying
Dog tags	Identification tags worn by combatants
Dog Whistle	Nickname for T-37 intermediate jet trainer
Don Muang	Passenger and Cargo Air Base near Saigon, Republic of Vietnam
DO	Director of Operations
DOO	Deputy Director of Operations

DOOT	Operational Training Division
Double Ugly	Nickname for the F-4
Dream sheet	Assignment preference request filed by the individual
Drittes Staffel	German 'third squadron'
Duckbutt	Support aircraft for deployments

E

Eagle	Official name for F-15
ECM	Electronic Countermeasures (
Ejection seat	Rocket-boosted escape seat incorporating parachute
EUCOM	US European Command
EWO	Electronic Warfare Officer

F

FAC	Forward Air Controller
FAIPs	First Assignment Instructor Pilots
Farsi	Modern Persian The language of Iran
fernsehturm	German TV tower
Fighting wing	Flexible tactical maneuvering formation
firewall	Forward limit of throttle travel
Flak	Anti-aircraft fire or slang for criticism
Flesh Peddlers	Slang for Personnel Assignment Officers and NCOs
Fliegerhorst / Flugplatz	German for Air Base
Flight Controls	Ailerons, rudders, elevators, trim tabs
Flight leader	Lead pilot in a multi-ship formation
Flight suit	Zippered jump suit worn by aviators
Flight surgeon	USAF Doctor with special Aerospace Medicine credentials
FM (Fox Mike)radio	Frequency modulated short range radio
FNG	Fucking New Guy
Form 781	Aircraft Discrepancy maintenance form
Forward operating locations (FOL)	Bases designed to support aircraft operations nearer to the enemy
Franco, Francisco	Spanish dictator
Fred	Affectionate American nickname for the Shah of Iran
FRG	Federal Republic of Germany (West Germany)
FUF	Fuckhead Up Front
FWIC, FWS or Fighter Weapons School	Fighter Weapons Instructor Course

G

G Forces	Force of acceleration. Can be positive or negative. 1 "G" is the force of gravity on the earth's surface. Hard maneuvering in a fighter generates 6-8 "G"
G Suit	Inflatable trousers which inhibit blood being forced to lower extremities by positive "G" forces
Ganymed	Popular East Berlin restaurant

Gas passers	Air refueling tanker aircraft
Gasthaus	German Inn or Pub
Gatling gun	Machine gun with rotating barrels
GAU 8	USAF Nomenclature for Gatling gun installed in the A-10
Gendarmes	French policemen
GDR	German Democratic Republic (East Germany)
GI Bill	Government financial assistance for veterans' educational pursuits
GIB	Guy in the Back
Golden BB	A lucky shot
Good stick/good hands	Talented flyer
Grab bag	Quick reaction provisions
greenhorns	Inexperienced pilots; rookies
Ground controlled approach	Radar directed final approach to landing
Guard frequency	Radio frequency reserved for emergency use only
Gun cross	A-10 Gun aiming reference on gunsight
gyros	Gyroscopes used to maintain equilibrium or determine direction.

H

Happy Hour	Friday night fighter pilot tradition
HAS	Hardened Aircraft Shelter
Have Idea	Codename for US testing and evaluation of Soviet Aircraft
Heads' up display	Information projected on windscreen for easy access
Heat signature	Pattern of heat generated by jet engine
HEI	High Explosive Incendiary ammunition
Ho Chi Minh (Uncle Ho)	Political Leader of North Vietnam
Hog	Nickname for the A-10
Hogan, Ben	Legendary professional golfer of 1940s and 50s
HQ	Headquarters

I

ICBM	Intercontinental ballistic missile
IIAF	Imperial Iranian Air Force
IMHO	In My Humble Opinion
Immelmann turn	Half loop with rollout on top; results in 180 degree heading change
Initial Approach	First leg of visual racetrack traffic pattern, flown directly over runway
Inner-German border (IGB)	Cold War border between East and West Germany
INS	Inertial Navigation System
IP	Instructor Pilot
Iron Curtain	Virtual 'barrier' between Western Powers and Soviet Blo

J

J85-5A	General Electric engine for T-38 trainer
Jabogeschwader or JaboG	German designation for Fighter Wing
Jax center	Jacksonville Air Traffic Control Center
JHQ	Joint Headquarters
jock	Slang for pilot
JP4	Standard grade of jet fuel

K

KIA	Killed in action
Knock it off	Standard radio call to immediately cease the current activity
kölsch	Light German lager popular in Cologne and vicinity
Kommodore	German Wing Commander
Korat	Royal Thai Air base used by USAF for F-105 fighter operations
Kumbaya	title of a folk song, sarcastically used in this book to refer to the song's suggestions of spiritual accord and relational harmony.

L

L/T	Verbal abbreviation for 'Lieutenant'
La Guardia Civil	Spanish Civil Police force
LATN	Low Altitude Tactical Navigation
Lead Sled	Nickname for the F 105
Leipheim	A-10 Forward Operating Location in Bavaria
LFA (low flying area)	Designated areas for low level flight training
Lindbergh, Charles	Aviation pioneer
Link Trainer	Aircraft simulator built by Link Corporation
Little Boy	Nickname for atomic bomb detonated over Hiroshima 1945
Luftwaffe	German Air Force

M

m-16	Semi-Automatic weapon used extensively by US Forces
M-61 Vulcan	20 millimeter Gatling Gun (in F-4E)
MAAG	Military Advisory and Assistance Group
MAC	Military Airlift Command
Mach	Measure of speed. Mach one equals the speed of sound
Manual reversion	Manual backup flight control system in A-10.
Many-motor	Aircraft with more than 2 engines: bombers, transports, tankers
Mata hari	Famous Dutch female spy for Germany during World War I
Mayday	Distress radio call
Mercury Astronaut	The first 7 Americans in NASA's space program

MIA	Missing in action
Mickey Mouse	Slang for anything ludicrous or childish
MiG	Russian built fighter aircraft series
MK-82	500 lb general purpose bomb
Mobility exercise	Practice deployment
Moody Patch	Slang for Moody AFB
MPC	Military Personnel Center
MREs	Meals, ready to eat
MUNSS	Munitions Support Squadron
Mutually Assured Destruction (MAD)	Postulated result of nuclear holocaust
Mustang	Nickname for P-51 Second World War fighter

N

Na Zdorovie	Russian toast to a comrade. Literally "to your heart's content"
nacelle	Aircraft engine housing
NASA	National Aeronautic and Space Administration
NATO	North Atlantic Treaty Organization
Navy Top Gun course	Similar Weapon course to Air Force's FWIC
NCOs	Non Commissioned Officers
Negritos	Philippine aboriginals
Nellis Tactical Gunnery Ranges	Massive military training area north of Las Vegas
NGS	Nose gear steering
Nickel on the grass	Verbalized tribute to a fallen fighter pilot
No Lone Zone	Area containing nuclear weapons. Can only be entered by multiple authorized individuals
NORTHAG	British Northern Army Group (Germany)
Nörvenich	A-10 Forward Operating Location in north-central Germany
nuke	Abbreviation of nuclear weapon

O

Oberst	Colonel in German armed forces
Officer Efficiency Report (OER)	Performance report card
Officers' Mess or O' Club	Military social club for Officers
Offiziersheim	German Officers' Club
Oh Dark Thirty	military slang for 'middle of the night'
Operations (Ops) Center	Command and control function
OPFOR	Abbreviation for opposing force

P

PCS	Permanent Change of Station
Pentagon	Department of Defense HQ, Washington D.C. Also known as Fort Fumble, the Five-sided Wind Tunnel, Puzzle Palace, etc.

Pershing missile	Army tactical ballistic missile capable of delivering nuclear weapons
Persia	Former name for Iran
Petting Zoo	Nellis AFB Threat Training Facility
Phantom II	Official name for F-4.
Phi Kappa Sigma	The Author's fraternity at the University of South Carolina
Pickle button	Bomb release button on fighter control stick grip
Piddle pack	Urine collection device used as a urinal substitute on long flights
Pipper	Bomb aiming reference on cockpit heads' up display
pit	Slang for F-4 aircraft back seat
PLF	Parachute landing fall
Pointy end of the spear	The leading force
Poopy suit	Anti-exposure suit worn over cold water flight areas
Pow	Prisoner of War
practice bleeding	A thoroughly unnecessary activity
Precession	Change in orientation of a gyro over time. Causes navigational errors
Preflight inspection	Aircraft inspection prior to start, taxi, and takeoff

Q

Quonset hut	Corrugated metal building with a semi-circular cross section

R

RAF	Royal Air Force
Ramstein	US Airbase in Central Germany. Headquarters of USAF in Europe
Ready Thunder	Training program to upgrade A-10 pilots to mission ready status
Red Eagles	4477th Test and evaluation Squadron. Mig 17 and 21 aggressor force
Reforger	German Exercise code name
REMFS	"Rear Echelon Mother Fuckers" Army term for non-combatants-
retreads	experienced pilots retraining to a new aircraft
Rhino	Yet another nickname for the F-4
RIO	Radar Intercept Officer
ROE	Rules of Engagement
Rotary wing aircraft	Helicopters
Route Packs 1-6	Designated North Vietnam campaign sectors. RP 6(a) and (b) encompassed Hanoi and Haiphong
RPM	Revolutions per minute
RTB	Return to base
RTU	Replacement Training Unit

Rated officers	Aviation qualified officers
Read in	Included in information flow
rookie	inexperienced
Run for the Roses	Euphemism for final attack run
Russian Bear	Symbol of Russia
Rube Goldberg	American cartoonist and inventor famed for his popular cartoons depicting complicated gadgets performing simple tasks in indirect, convoluted ways.
RVN	Republic of Vietnam
S	
SA 2	Russian built SAM used extensively in North Vietnam
SAM	Surface To Air Missile
SAR	Search And Rescue
Savak	Iranian Secret Service during the reign of the Shah
Schnapps	German digestive liquor
Sembach	A-10 Forward Operating Location in south-central Germany
SERE	Survival, Evasion, Resistance, and Escape
Shahrokhi AB	Former Imperial Iranian Air Force base in west-central Iran
Shoe clerk	Much more polite Air Force term for non-combatants
Simulator (or sim)	Aircraft procedural trainer
Sky Cop	Nickname for Security Police
slaved	Connected; tethered
Snake School	Jungle Survival Training Course
Snead, 'Slammin' Sammy	Legendary professional golfer of the 1940s and 50s
Sockey	Extracurricular activity performed in the bar
sortie	Single aircraft missions
SOS	Squadron Officer's School or Shit on a Shingle (creamed beef on toast)
Soviet Bloc	Soviet dominated countries east of Iron Curtain
Soviet Sector (Berlin)	Russian zone of divided Berlin
SP	Abbreviation for Security Police
Spitfire	Iconic British WWII fighter
Staff puke	Derogatory reference to non-flying staff officers
Stag bar	Once the male-only domain of an Officers' club. Now defunct
Stan/Eval	Standardization/Evaluation test and monitoring organization
Stars & Stripes	Military newspaper published for US Forces worldwide
Steel Tiger	Air interdiction campaign in southern Laos
Stick or Control stick	Pilot's primary flight control device
strafe	Air-to-ground gun employment
Switch hit	ambidextrous

T

T-80	Russian built battle tank
TAC	Tactical Air Command
Tac Eval	Tactical Evaluation-test of unit operational capabilities
Tac Fighter Weapons Center (TFWC)	Headquarters for advanced training and test programs at Nellis AFB, Nevada
Tac Fighter Wing (TFW)	Central fighting unit comprising 3 or 4 fighter squadrons
TACAN	Tactical Air Navigation Radio beacon
TACP	Tactical Air Control Party
Tactical Weapons Controller	Ground-to-air radar controller specializing in combat intercepts
Takhli	Royal Thai Air base used by USAF for F-105 fighter operations
Tally Ho	Air interdiction campaign in the Vietnamese demilitarized zone
Talon	Official name of T-38 advanced trainer
TDY	Temporary Duty
TES	Test and Evaluation Squadron
TFS	Tactical Fighter Squadron
The Big House	British headquarters at RAF Rheindahlen
Thor's Hammer	Mythical weapon of the gods
Thud,	Nickname for F-105
Thunderbirds	US Air Force aerial demonstration team
Thunderbolt II	Official name for the A-10
Thunderchief	Official name for F 105
TISEO	Target Identification System Electro-Optical
Titanium bathtub	Protective enclosure for critical flight components (and pilot's posterior)
TLAR	"That Looks About Right" Visual calculation of gunnery parameters
TLC	Tender loving care
TNT	Common explosive compound
Tonopah Test Range	Isolated USAF test facility in northern Nevada.
Tornado	Two-engine fighter bomber flown by RAF, Germans, and Italians
Toro Bravo	Brave bull
Torrejon	Spanish/US joint use Air Base outside Madrid
transponder	Aircraft identification radio beacon
Trash haulers	Slang for cargo aircraft
Tweet	Nickname for T-37 intermediate trainer

U

Ubon Ratchathani	Royal Thai Air base used by USAF for F-4 fighter operations
Udorn	Royal Thai Air base used by USAF for F-4 fighter operations
UHF	Ultra High Frequency radio

Uncle Ho	Nickname for Ho Chi Minh
Uncle Sam	Symbol of USA
UPT	Undergraduate Pilot Training
USAF	United States Air Force
USAF Safety School	Specialist training center for safety investigation and related subjects
USAFE	United States Air Force, Europe-Major Command Headquarters
USAFE salute	Gesture of bewilderment
USC	University of South Carolina
USSR	Union of Soviet Socialist Republics

V

VC	Viet Cong
verboten	German for 'forbidden'
VFR	Visual flight rules. Governed by visibility
Victor alert	Aircraft nuclear weapons alert
VIVA	Voices in Vital America

W

WAGs	Wives and Girlfriends
Warthog	Nickname for the A-10
Weapons and Tactics	Specialty organisation in fighter squadrons/wings
Weapons System Operator	Navigator responsible for weapons delivery systems in a fighter
Weekend Warriors	ANG or AFRES pilots who train and fly military aircraft in addition to their primary professions
Whisper jet	Nickname for relatively quiet A-10
White Rocket	Nickname for T-38 advanced jet trainer
Wild Weasels	F-105 units equipped to hunt and kill SAMs in North Vietnam
Wing King	Nickname for Wing Commander
Wing weenie	Staff-assigned pilot who regularly flies with a squadron
Wingman	Supporting pilot in a multi-ship formation
Wolf Facs	F-4 "Fast Forward Air Controllers" based at Ubon
Wolfpack	Nickname of 8th Tac Fighter Wing, Ubon

X

XC	Abbreviation for Cross Country

Y

Young Turks	Aggressive youth

Z

Zero or Negative 'G'	Sensation generated when accelerating downward (such as over-the-top on a roller coaster. Feeling light in the seat.
Zero	Iconic Second World War Japanese fighter

Glossary of Referenced Aircraft

A-1E Skyraider	Second World War attack aircraft used for Search & Rescue in SEA
A-7 Corsair II	LTV single-engine fighter
A-10 Thunderbolt II	The mighty Warthog, better known simply as the 'Hog
Alpha jet	Light attack fighter aircraft manufactured by Dassault/Dornier
Boeing 747	Civilian wide-body passenger and transport
B-24 Liberator	US Second World War heavy bomber
B-26 Intruder	US Second World War and Korean War medium bomber
B-52 Stratofortress	Four-engine heavy bomber (nicknamed BUF)
C-123 Provider	Fairchild two-engine cargo aircraft
C-130 Hercules	Lockheed four-engine aircraft (transport, AC-130 gunship, EC-130 Intelligence)
C-141 Starlifter	Lockheed four-engine jet cargo aircraft
C-21A	Learjet light cargo and passenger jet
C-7 Caribou	de Havilland two-engine cargo aircraft
F-104 Starfighter	Lockheed single-engine fighter
F-105 Thunderchief	Single-engine fighter built by Republic, also known as Thud, Lead Sled
F-111 Aardvark	General Dynamics two-engine bomber
F-15 Eagle	Two-engine fighter built by McDonnell Douglas
F-16 Falcon	Single-engine fighter built by General Dynamics
F-22 Raptor	Lockheed Martin new-generation two-engine stealth fighter
F-35 Lightning II	Lockheed Martin new-generation single-engine stealth fighter
F-4 Phantom II	Also known as Big Ugly, Double Ugly, the Rhino
F-5 Freedom Fighter	Northrop two-engine fighter, combat version of T-38
Halifax	Second World War British bomber built by my mother-in-law (among others)
Harrier	Hawker Siddely British vertical take-off & landing fighter

Jaguar	Sepecat Anglo–French single seat fighter bomber
KC-135 Stratotanker	Boeing Airborne gas station for thirsty fighters
MiG	Aircraft built by Russian manufacturers Mikoyan & Gurevich
MiG 21 Fishbed	Soviet single-engine fighter
MiG 25 Foxbat	Soviet two-engine fighter
MiG17 Fresco	Soviet single-engine fighter
Mirage	Dassault-built French fighter aircraft
O-2 Skymaster	Cessna two-engine propeller-driven aircraft
OV-10 Bronco	North American Rockwell two-engine propeller-driven aircraft
P-47 Thunderbolt	Republic Iconic American Second World War fighter/attack aircraft
P-51 Mustang	Iconic North American-built Second World War fighter
Sea King	British Helicopter built by Westland
Spitfire	Iconic Supermarine-built British Second World War fighter
Sukhoi-25 Frogfoot	Russian ground-attack aircraft dubbed 'Wartski'. Looks suspiciously like the Northrop YA-9
T-37 'Tweet'	Cessna primary jet trainer, 'Tweet' or the 6,000 Pound Dog Whistle
T-38 Talon or 'White Rocket'	Northrop supersonic advanced jet trainer
T-41	Single-engine basic trainer, military version of Cessna 172
Tornado	Panavia two-engine fighter-bomber flown by the RAF, Germans and Italians
Types 1 & 2	Cover names for exploited MiG 17 & MiG 21, Projects 'Have Idea' and Constant Peg
YA-9	Northrop-built competitor of the A-10 in flight trials
Zero	Japanese Second World War fighter produced by Mitsubishi

Chronology of Assignments

UNIT	Aircraft	Year	Location	Mission/Role
3553rd Pilot Training Squadron 'Gators'	T-41/T-37/T-38	1967/8	Moody AFB, Georgia	UPT student pilot
47th Tac Fighter Squadron 'Blitz Bugs'	F-4E	1968	MacDill AFB, Florida	F-4 RTU student pilot
435th Tac Fighter Squadron 'Eagle Squadron'	F-4D	1969	Ubon RTAFB, Thailand	Combat-ready fighter pilot
353rd Panthers/614th 'Lucky Devils' Tac Fighter Squadrons	F-4E	1970–74	Torrejón AB, Spain	Mission-ready/nuclear alert
*94th Tac Fighter Squadron 'Hat in the Ring' (temporary Duty)	F-4E	1971	MacDill AFB, Florida	F-4 RTU student aircraft commander
307th Tac Fighter Squadron 'Stingers'	F-4E	1974–77	Homestead AFB, Florida	RTU instructor pilot
*414th Fighter Weapons Squadron (temporary duty)	F-4E	1975	Nellis AFB, Nevada	Fighter Weapons School student Class 75 CID
* Military Advisory and Assistance Program Iran (temporary duty)	F-4E	1976	Shahrokhi AB, Iran	Instructor pilot
92nd Tac Fighter Squadron 'Skulls'	F-4D	1977	RAF Bentwaters & Woodbridge, England	Mission-ready pilot
81st Tac Fighter Wing	F-4D/A-10A	1978–80	RAF Bentwaters & Woodbridge, England	Chief, Wing Weapons & Tactics Division
78th Tac Fighter Squadron 'Snakes'	A-10A	1979–80	RAF Bentwaters & Woodbridge, England	Assistant Operations Officer

UNIT	Aircraft	Year	Location	Mission/Role
*354th Fighter Training Squadron (temporary duty) 'Bulldogs'	A-10A	1979	Davis-Monthan AFB, Arizona	A-10 RTU student aircraft commander
Detachment 4, 81st Tac Fighter Wing	A-10/A	1980–83	Nörvenich AB, Germany	Operations Officer
A-10 Division, USAF Fighter Weapons School	A-10/A	1983–85	Nellis AFB, Nevada	Commander
HQ 2nd Allied Tactical Air Forces (2 ATAF)	Big Gray Desk	1985–88	RAF Rheindahlen, Germany	Chief, Fighter Operations Division
HQ United States Air Forces Europe	Big Gray Desk	1989	Ramstein AB, Germany	Deputy Director, Operations and Training
81st Tac Fighter Wing	A-10A	1989–91	RAF Bentwaters & Woodbridge, England	Director of Operations
549th Joint Training Squadron (Air Warrior)	A-10A	1991–94	Nellis AFB, Nevada	Commander

*Temporary Assignments

Appendix IV

Maps

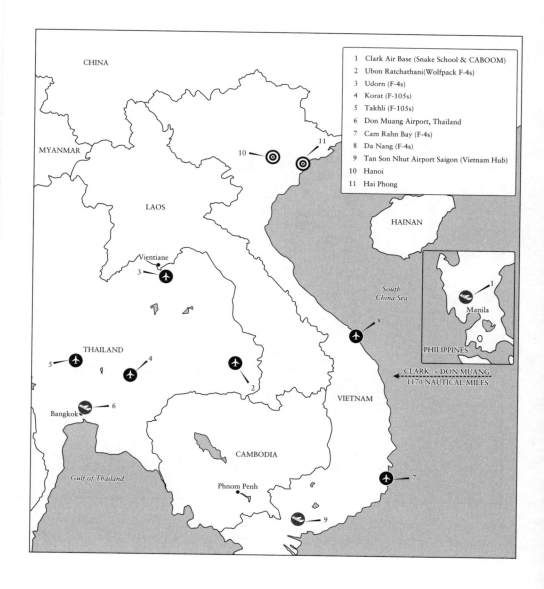

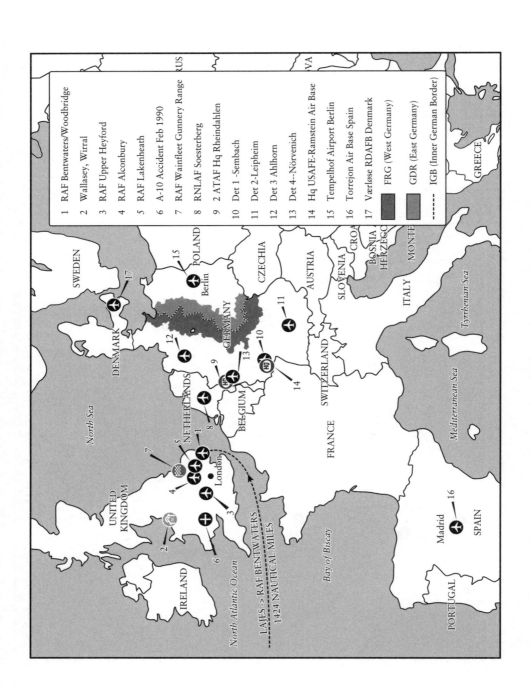

1	RAF Bentwaters/Woodbridge
2	Wallasey, Wirral
3	RAF Upper Heyford
4	RAF Alconbury
5	RAF Lakenheath
6	A-10 Accident Feb 1990
7	RAF Wainfleet Gunnery Range
8	RNLAF Soesterberg
9	2 ATAF Hq Rheindahlen
10	Det 1 –Sembach
11	Det 2–Leipheim
12	Det 3 Ahlhorn
13	Det 4–Nörvenich
14	Hq USAFE–Ramstein Air Base
15	Tempelhof Airport Berlin
16	Torrejon Air Base Spain
17	Værløse RDAFB Denmark

FRG (West Germany)
GDR (East Germany)
- - - IGB (Inner German Border)

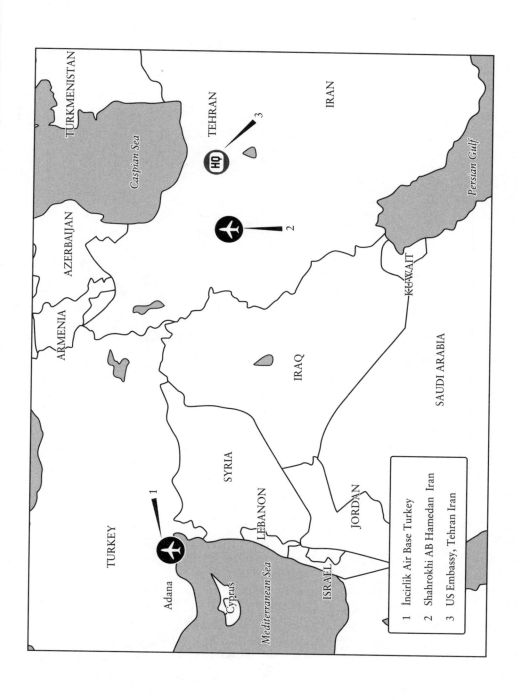

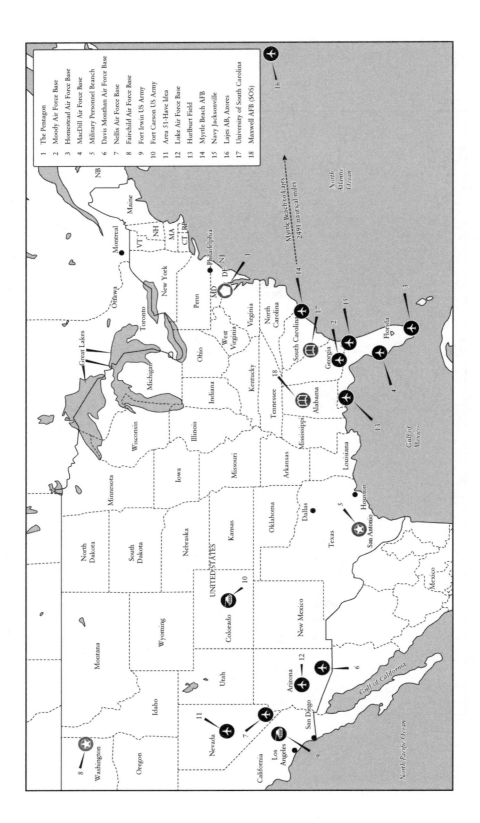

1	The Pentagon
2	Moody Air Force Base
3	Homestead Air Force Base
4	MacDill Air Force Base
5	Military Personnel Branch
6	Davis Monthan Air Force Base
7	Nellis Air Force Base
8	Fairchild Air Force Base
9	Fort Irwin US Army
10	Fort Carson US Army
11	Area 51-Have Idea
12	Luke Air Force Base
13	Hurlburt Field
14	Myrtle Beach AFB
15	Navy Jacksonville
16	Lajes AB, Azores
17	University of South Carolina
18	Maxwell AFB (SOS)

Myrtle Beach to Lajes
2491 nautical miles

Appendix V

Simplified Organizational Chart
(81st Tactical Fighter Wing ca.1991)

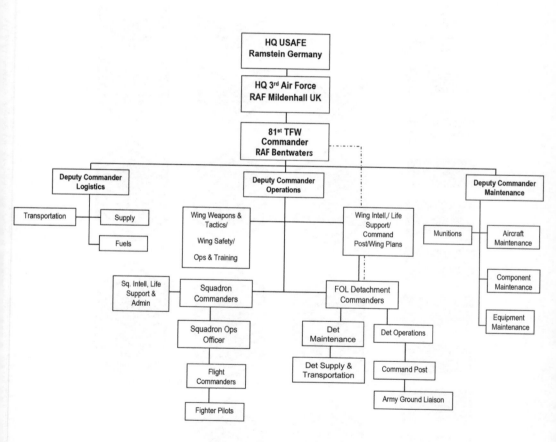

Appendix VI

USAF Rank Structure

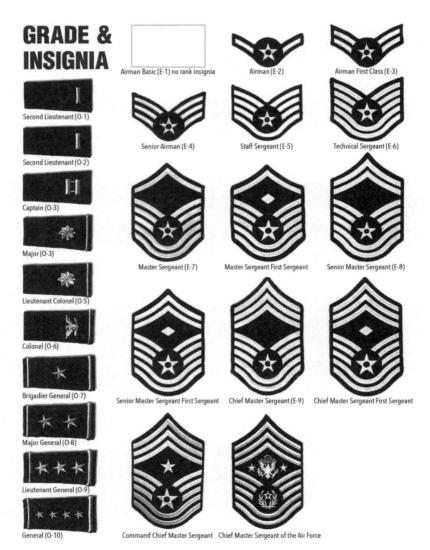

GRADE & INSIGNIA

Airman Basic (E-1) no rank insignia
Airman (E-2)
Airman First Class (E-3)

Second Lieutenant (O-1)
Senior Airman (E-4)
Staff Sergeant (E-5)
Technical Sergeant (E-6)

Second Lieutenant (O-2)
Master Sergeant (E-7)
Master Sergeant First Sergeant
Senior Master Sergeant (E-8)

Captain (O-3)
Senior Master Sergeant First Sergeant
Chief Master Sergeant (E-9)
Chief Master Sergeant First Sergeant

Major (O-3)
Command Chief Master Sergeant
Chief Master Sergeant of the Air Force

Lieutenant Colonel (O-5)

Colonel (O-6)

Brigadier General (O-7)

Major General (O-8)

Lieutenant General (O-9)

General (O-10)

Notes

Prologue
1. Unknown author: appeared in *Grumman Horizons Magazine* (Volume 8, Number 1), entitled *Dogfighters Are In Close! Special Issue: Our race for a better MiG killer* (1968).

Chapter 1
1. Malloy Mason Jr, Herbert, *The New Tigers* (David MacKay & Co., 1967)
2. Personnel Research Division, Human Resources Laboratory, Air Force Systems Command, Lackland AFB, Texas, 1969.

Chapter 7
1. John Barron, *MiG Pilot: The Final Escape of Lieutenant Belenko* (Avon Books, 1983).

Chapter 10
1. Hobson, Chris, *Vietnam Air Losses, USAF, USN, USMC: Fixed-Wing Aircraft Losses in South-East Asia 1961–1973* (North Branch, Minnesota: Specialty Press, 2001).

Chapter 21
1. JCS Joint Publication 3-09.3, Close Air Support.
2. Coram, Robert, *Boyd: The Fighter Pilot Who Changed The Art of War* (Little, Brown and Company, 2002).

Index